The Mechanized Landscape
Statecraft and Environment in the Tennessee Valley

AR+D
Published by Applied Research and Design Publishing, an imprint of ORO Editions.
Gordon Goff: Publisher

www.appliedresearchanddesign.com
info@appliedresearchanddesign.com

Authors: Micah Rutenberg and Avigail Sachs
Project Manager: Jake Anderson

Book Design: Pablo Mandel / CircularStudio
Typeset in URW Geometric and Dala Floda

10 9 8 7 6 5 4 3 2 1 First Edition

ISBN: 978-1-961856-64-6

Prepress and Print work by ORO Editions Inc.
Printed in China

AR+D Publishing makes a continuous effort to minimize the overall carbon footprint of its publications. As part of this goal, AR+D, in association with Global ReLeaf, arranges to plant trees to replace those used in the manufacturing of the paper produced for its books. Global ReLeaf is an international campaign run by American Forests, one of the world's oldest nonprofit conservation organizations. Global ReLeaf is American Forests' education and action program that helps individuals, organizations, agencies, and corporations improve the local and global environment by planting and caring for trees.

Micah Rutenberg and Avigail Sachs

The Mechanized Landscape

Statecraft and Environment in the Tennessee Valley

a.r.+d | APPLIED RESEARCH +DESIGN

Norris Dam

To my mother, Karen.
And to my nieces, Elizabeth and Madeline.

For Adam Alon, his generation of cousins, and mine.

Contents

Introduction

Visitors to Norris Dam, an imposing structure extending across the Clinch River in East Tennessee, first view it from a concrete platform situated in front of a glass-and-steel welcome center. From this overlook, curved staircases descend to a grassy slope that ends in a tangle of power lines, switches, circuit breakers, and steel frames that make up the electric substation below. Just beyond is the powerhouse: a prime example—along with the dam above it—of stoic, well-proportioned Modernist design as applied to utilitarian infrastructure. This orchestrated scene is punctuated with a patinaed bronze plaque, seamlessly integrated into the concrete boundary of the overlook. The plaque positions the visitor and trains their attention toward an iconic view of the dam. The plaque declares that the dam, powerhouse, and landscape—the totality of everything that makes up the scene—were "Built for the People of the United States by the Tennessee Valley Authority under the Direction of the Congress and the President, 1933–1936."

In essence, the plaque conveys the obvious. All infrastructure is, to a large extent, a political act; it delivers the essential resources needed for society to function, while also signifying the presence of the state and its ability to meet the needs of its citizens. Indeed, infrastructure's invisibility—the simple fact that it is present in the landscape and that it operates as planned—is, in itself, the sign of a well-functioning modern government. The prominent location of the plaque in the landscape serves to amplify this message. The words convey the message rhetorically, even as the choreographed scene and its elements add their visual persuasion, while the spatial experience of the environment engages human behavior and emotions. This multilayered messaging was, for the Tennessee Valley Authority (TVA), a form of statecraft—the art of government persuasion and diplomacy.

The plaque spotlighting that iconic view of Norris Dam is but one example of the TVA's messaging efforts. Across the massive structure, another overlook showcases a map of the entire TVA system of multipurpose dams, adding a geographic element to the overt statecraft and giving visitors a sense of the vast spatial scope of the project. And far below, in the river itself, the TVA promotes a popular spot for fishers trying their luck. These two ways of experiencing the river and its tributaries—abstractly, through the language of cartography, and physically, by wading into the water—together serve as a dramatic example of the layered messaging of TVA statecraft.

One mile below the dam, along the Norris Freeway—a scenic road designed and built by the TVA—is an 18th-century grist mill. The TVA

The eastern overlook at Norris Dam

NORRIS DAM
NAMED FOR
GEORGE W. NORRIS
UNITED STATES SENATOR FROM NEBRASKA
IN RECOGNITION OF HIS PUBLIC SERVICE
BUILT FOR THE PEOPLE
OF THE UNITED STATES OF AMERICA
BY THE TENNESSEE VALLEY AUTHORITY
UNDER DIRECTION OF THE CONGRESS
AND THE PRESIDENT
1933 · 1936

relocated the mill from a community named Lost Creek, thus preserving it from being entombed by the rising waters of the reservoir captured by Norris Dam. The mill is a relic of a period in the area's history when it was settled by pioneers of British descent, soon after the Revolutionary War. But much else of the region's history was sacrificed to the dam construction: indigenous sites and artifacts were left to be submerged in the reservoir's depths, and Black Valley residents were altogether forgotten. This selective care for history reveals a symbolic dimension of the TVA's statecraft; it suggests that the construction of large-scale infrastructure, such as dams and powerhouses, takes its place as yet another chapter in the unfolding of America's Manifest Destiny.

Norris, Tennessee, two miles to the south, is a town designed and built by the TVA. If the mill symbolizes and celebrates individualism and pioneer resourcefulness, Norris stands as one of the most comprehensive examples of the communal emphasis of the regional planning ideology of the 1930s. While Norris residents do own their individual plots of land, the environment they live in is shared. There are no fences; the residents enjoy a continuous landscape that alternates between forest and clearing, as well as a network of pedestrian walkways and the central public and commercial buildings.

Behind the dam is the reservoir known as Norris Lake. Here, the environment is explicitly arranged for tourism and recreation—boating, fishing, hiking, and biking—in the sylvan setting of the lake's forested shores. Marinas and resorts offer myriad ways to enjoy the lake; the houses along the shoreline (vacation homes, for the most part) display the entire range of investment, from basic trailers to multi-story rental units. The message embedded in this environment, also created by the TVA, contrasts

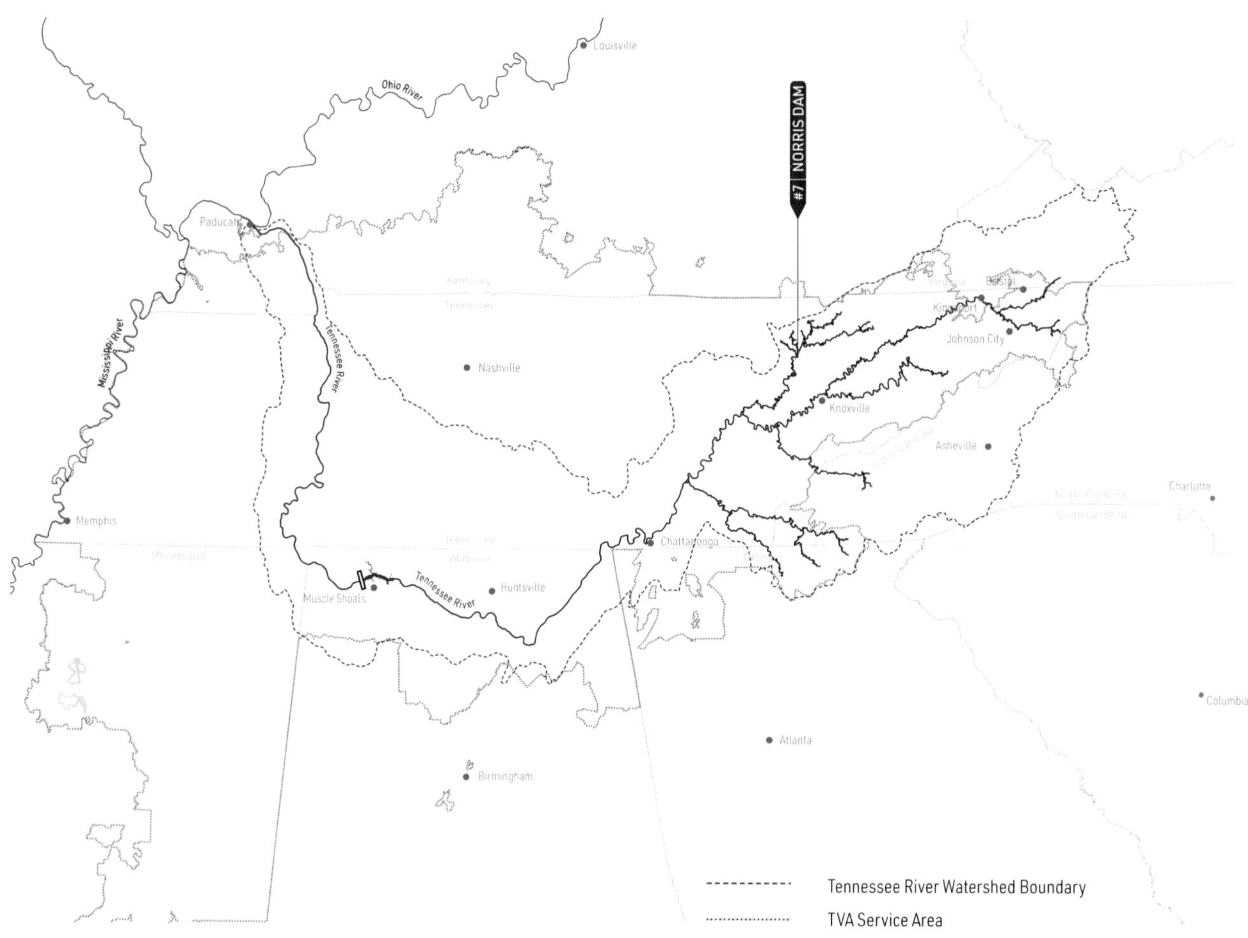

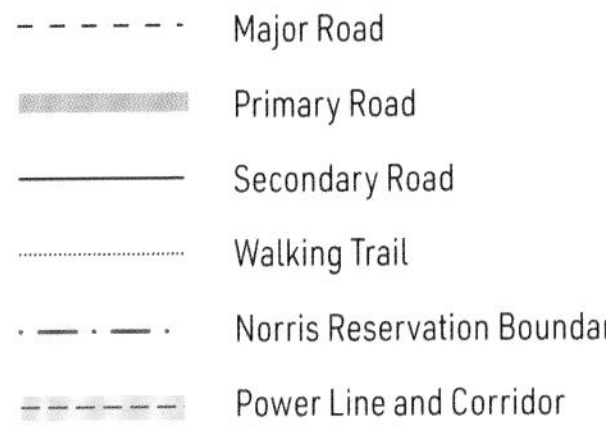

The Mechanized Landscape

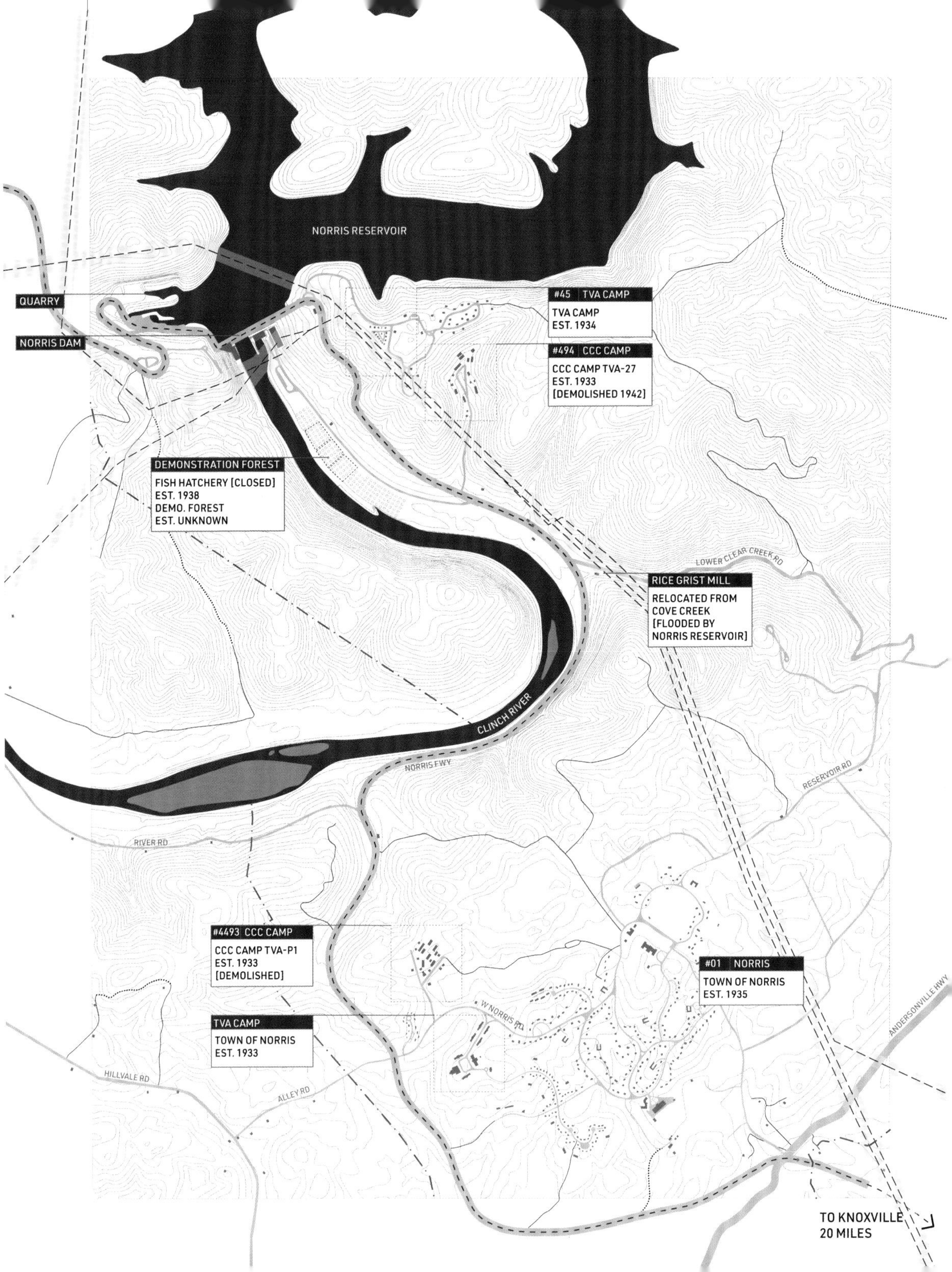

dramatically with the communal emphasis of Norris, Tennessee; it is an overt celebration of a consumer-driven economy.

As architects who are residents of the Tennessee Valley, we have been both fascinated and puzzled by the complex environment of Norris Dam and the Tennessee Valley. Could we reconcile, theoretically, the disparate elements of this territory? This book is a documentation of our joint pursuit of this question. The concept of a mechanized landscape shaped our process from the start, as it captured the extent to which the TVA—a federal agency with jurisdiction over the entire Tennessee Valley—transformed the region, and it conveyed how seamlessly we see geography and infrastructure working together. As we delved further into the TVA's intentions, however, it became clear that the mechanized landscape is also ideological: a physical manifestation of a powerful *statecraft*.

Over the two decades examined here, 1933–1953, the TVA's statecraft was hardly uniform. As a New Deal entity, the TVA was the product of unprecedented experimentation by the United States federal government. The TVA Act, the legal basis for the agency's operation, was written in haste; it drew on multiple (sometimes incompatible) conceptions of American society and democracy. All TVA personnel, however, saw their mission as defined by human needs. Rather than engaging in environmentalism, TVA efforts were firmly rooted in the idea that the environment should and must be shaped for human welfare. What human welfare entailed, and how this might represent the core value of democratic freedom, was, however, a topic of wide-ranging discussion and even disagreement within the agency.

Environment was also a fluid term. Each unit of the TVA focused on a different aspect of the Tennessee Valley, notwithstanding the agency's insistence that its overall goal was regional rather than piecemeal transformation. Some of its interventions were directed at the physical, even the natural, reality of the valley—its water flows, soil, flora, and fauna—while others focused on human settlements, and especially houses.

The intersection between statecraft and environment does not explain every aspect of the Tennessee Valley, but it offers a matrix for exploring the final product—the mechanized landscape. Within this matrix we identified five topics of special interest. The first three can be thought of as *machines* in the environment, and they were clearly authorized in the original legislation creating the TVA. Each of these machines is an amalgam of large-scale projects in resource development. The *river machine* included flood prevention and navigation; the *land machine* addressed forestry and soil conservation; the *power machine* produced power for rural electrification. Two further projects emerged from the operation of these three machines: support for the housing industry, and the creation of a regional tourist economy—here termed the *housing* and *recreation regions*.

It was clear to us from the start that such a multivalent topic would require more than one mode of exploration. We followed three distinct paths that became the elements of this book: mapping, photography, and text. Each medium captures some, but not all, of the aspects of our topic. We were constantly fascinated by the ways these different media complement each other, and by the similarity between our own method and the TVA's approach to both statecraft and environmental transformation. Even though all three media were developed together, our goal was to create a visual document in which the images take center stage. The text is intended to provide context for these images, but it does not attempt to explain them.

As a modernizing force in the Tennessee Valley, the TVA also introduced new types of

Norris Dam from the western overlook

Norris Dam viewed from the Clinch River

documentation to the region, including accurate geospatial mapping and detailed surveys. The vast amount of data recorded by the TVA has been preserved by the federal government as part of the public record; it is available for study. The maps we prepared for this book draw on the depth of this archive, supplemented occasionally with external studies, media reports, and field accounts that offer a perspective from outside the Authority. We took the TVA information at face value; rather than critiquing the agency's decisions, we sought to visualize their consequences. We did not, for example, "correct" the TVA terminology but adopted the words they used, which at times seem outdated or jarring. Nor did we assume that the TVA is an example of either "good" or "bad" government; it rather represents a complex and sustained, yet shifting, effort to enmesh statecraft and the environment.

The maps are geographically accurate and, with some exceptions, drawn to scale. They adhere to the cartographic convention of creating detached, abstract views. Preparing the maps, however, highlighted fundamental differences among the three "machines" and the two regional "efforts." The *river machine*, for example, was tightly controlled and was thus more easily mapped than the *land machine*, which was diffused across the valley on private lands. Understanding the *power machine* required mapping not only the TVA's original projections but also the outcomes of a series of legal challenges brought against the agency in its early years. Mapping individual houses helped us unravel the TVA housing enterprise; focusing on Norris Lake brought the tourist industry into view. This diversity is evident in the maps selected for this book.

Photography, the second mode of exploration, involved extensive travel by car and boat throughout the Tennessee Valley. It required paying close attention to the water levels of Norris and the other TVA lakes, often rearranging the schedule to take advantage of unusual rainfall. Being immersed in the environment meant not only visiting each of the TVA dams, but also staying overnight in lakeside cabins. The TVA allowed us to visit the interiors of some powerhouses (no longer open to the public), and we learned a lot from the operators of the dams. As part documentary, part artistic expression, the photographs are meant to situate the reader within a scene and to contextualize the historical and cartographic data. We hope that the photos can also be appreciated for their aesthetic quality as much as for the mechanized landscape they capture.

The book can of course be read linearly, but this is not necessary. The layout and the combination of media are intended to allow the reader multiple entry points, to pick up and leave off as guided by one's interests. We hope the complexity of the mechanized landscape of the Tennessee Valley will prove as fascinating in print as it is in life.

The electric substation at Norris Dam

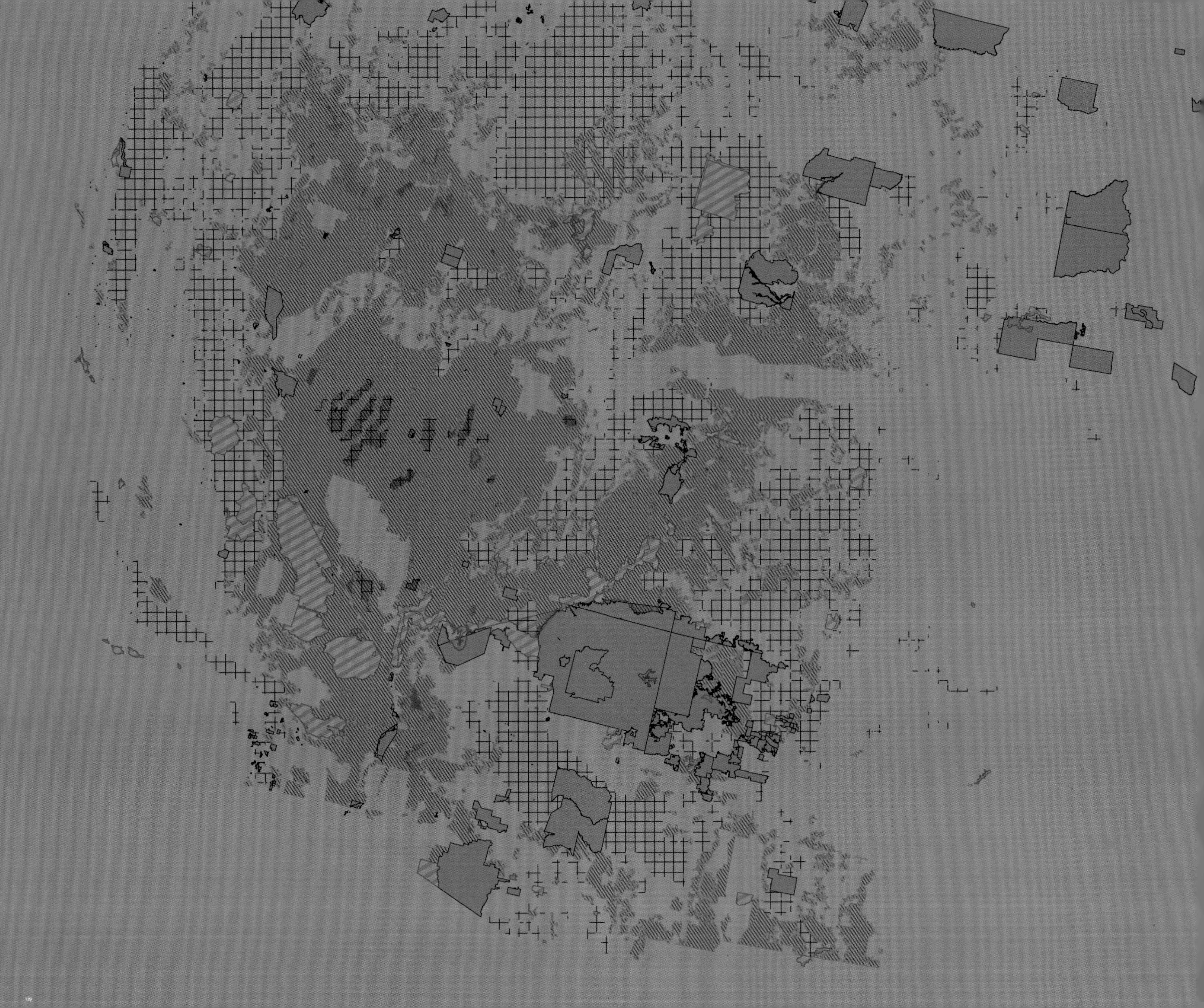

1

Historical and Theoretical Background

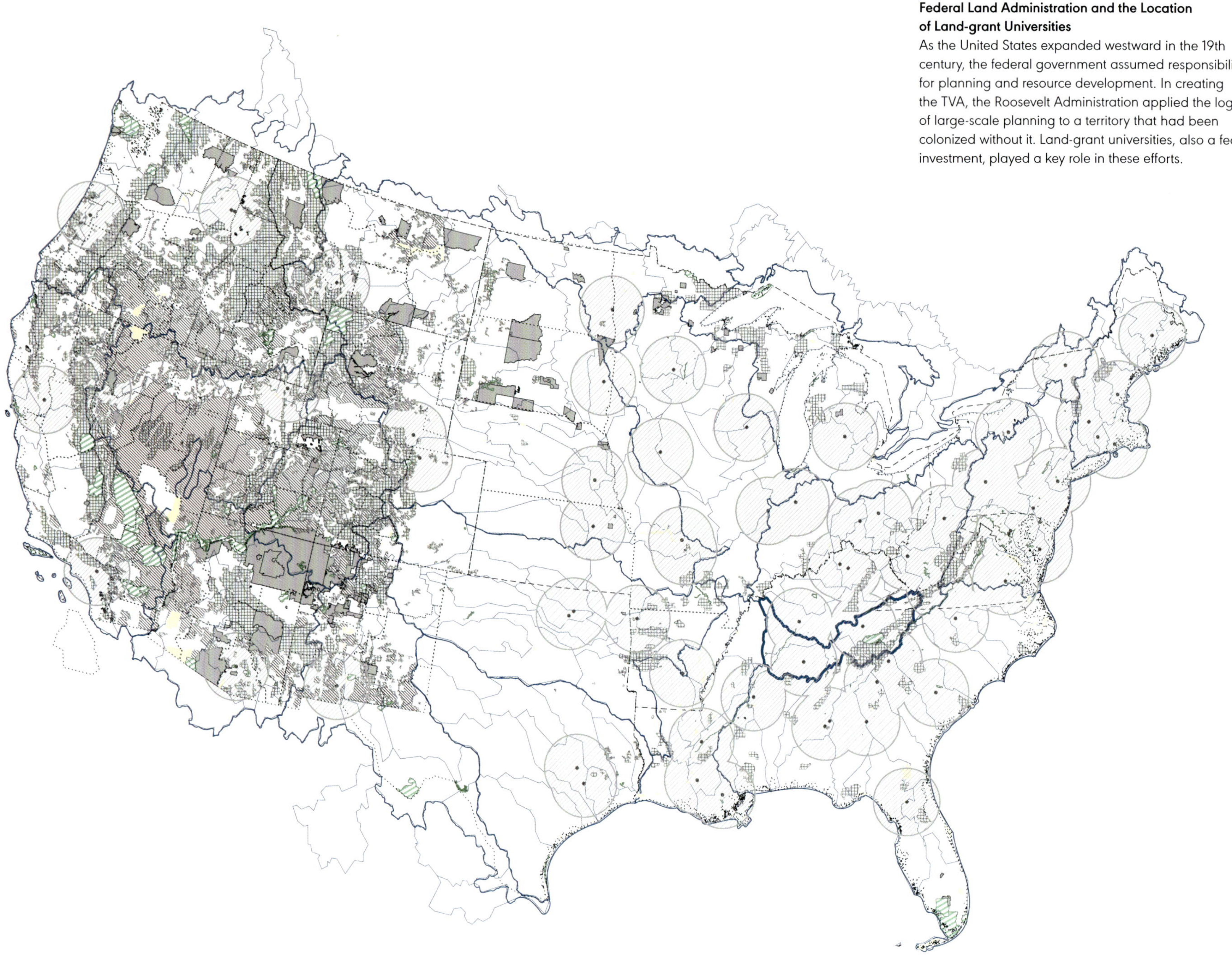

Historical and Theoretical Background

I n 1862, in the midst of the Civil War, the Union government enacted the Homestead Act. Would-be homesteaders—any head of a household, male or female, who was already a citizen or simply declared their intention to become one—could lay claim to 160 acres of "free" land. This was land seized from Indigenous Peoples, through treaty or coercion or both, that had been opened for settlement. To then gain title to those acres, homesteaders had to be industrious, investing their labor to make the land agriculturally productive for five years. The Homestead Act extended the frontier of early British colonialization across the continent, legalizing the passing of land expropriated from Indigenous Peoples into private—mostly white and Protestant—hands. Its social goal was to create a nation of freeholders rather than tenants or serfs, who would rely on their own labor—not that of servants or enslaved people—and who would actively participate in a democratic society.

In the early 19th century Thomas Jefferson had singled out farmers as the "chosen people of God," uniquely endowed with virtue and independence, giving them iconic status in American society[1]. Not all homesteaders became farmers, however; the new settlements also needed artisanal production and small-scale industry. But all these frontiersmen (and to some extent frontierswomen) were accorded special prestige as people of industry, not of leisure. This status was translated into policy in the 1862 Morrill Act, empowering the states to sell public land to individual owners and use the proceeds to support institutions of higher education. These "land-grant colleges" were expected to focus on agriculture and the mechanic arts, to develop and disseminate knowledge about these topics of vital importance to pioneers on the frontier.

The logic of the frontier was rooted in a specific interpretation of the environment. The North American continent was seen as an uncontrolled and terrifying wilderness, to be conquered and subdued by virtuous pioneers[2]. The success of this process, referred to as Manifest Destiny, was reflected in the emergence of a rural ideal of tilled plots and green pastures—not cities—replacing forests and deserts. This was a modern-day interpretation of a classical trope, identified by Leo Marx as the pastoral ideal[3]. This ideal, of a middle landscape untainted by the corruption of civilization, would have been familiar to educated Americans of the day, especially if they had studied Roman rhetoric and poetry. In North America, Marx argues, the seeming abundance of "free" land made the pastoral ideal into a possible reality.

In 1893, historian Fredrick Jackson Turner translated the ideas associated with Manifest Destiny into a national myth, later published as *The Significance of the Frontier in American History*[4]. His account, which celebrated individual efforts and downplayed the importance of federal support, was widely accepted. By this time, the majority of federal land that had been opened to settlement was already in private hands; the resource at the heart of the system—the land—had been consumed. Nevertheless, the celebration of the now-closed frontier reaffirmed the role of its frontiersmen and women—primarily white Protestants—as the "imagined community" for the entire nation[5].

The closing of the frontier, which was recorded by the United States Census Bureau in 1890, was attended by a rising interest in the inhabitants of the Appalachian mountain range, especially of its southern portion. The area had been colonized by Europeans in the late 18th century, but its steep terrain limited agricultural production, so many settlers bypassed it on their way further west. The efforts to remove the Indigenous Peoples from their homeland became legal with the passage of the Indian Removal Act; the forced exodus of the Cherokee in 1838 became famous as the "Trail of Tears." Still, inbound immigration to the mountains remained slow, and the area remained isolated by the terrain and by the lack of federal investment in transportation and industry. The absence of government and the suspicion of central authority that characterized early settlement would persist in the frontier mentality of mountain communities, long after it had dissipated elsewhere.

In 1899, William Goodell Frost, the President of Berea College in Berea, Kentucky, coined the phrase "Appalachian America" to argue that the Southern Mountains were the home of "our contemporary ancestors."[6] He argued further that this "last frontier" had remained isolated and protected for a divine purpose—to offset undesirable foreign elements, referring to the

influx of Catholics and Jews to industrial cities in the Northeast and Midwest. As James C. Klotter explains, the conflation of the myth of the frontier and Appalachian culture allowed other Americans, especially social reformers, to distinguish between the "Black South" and "White Appalachia," a distinction that assuaged some of their deep disappointment about the outcome of the Reconstruction efforts that followed the Civil War.[7]

The Homestead Act, intended to support individualism and free competition, was often abused for capitalist purposes. Speculators saw the public domain as an economic sandbox, as a source of commodities—timber, minerals, agricultural products—rather than as a space to inhabit and cultivate. Many Americans saw "progress," in the sense of scientific, technological, and industrial control over nature, as the true goal of the United States.[8] For many, "freedom" was defined not as the independent life of the freehold farming family, but rather as the freedom of the individual from government interference. It also meant freedom to reap immediate profit with no concern for the depletion of natural resources or for future generations[9]. The emphasis on economic progress found its way into legislation as well: in 1897, for example, the Secretary of the Interior was authorized to permit timber harvesting, mining, and water use on lands that were still in the public domain.

Capitalist enterprises also made their way into Appalachia. At the turn of the 20th century, the mountainous eastern portion of the Tennessee Valley attracted commercial timber companies, which extracted the old-growth forests and left behind denuded landscapes. These companies built roads and other infrastructure through the region, an ongoing intervention that shaped a new reality[10]. This investment, however, had little reference to the wellbeing of the inhabitants of the region and was designed to maximize the profits of these corporate entities based outside the region. Some scholars have referred to this and similar economic projects as representing a colonialist dynamic in modern America, highlighting the extraction of wealth out of the region to entities located in more prosperous parts of the United States.[11]

Capitalist expansion depended on limitless resources, and those who agitated and legislated for opportunities to pursue unbounded progress imagined the resources to be endless. For others—known as "progressives"—new scientific and technological knowledge instead highlighted their finite nature. In 1871 George Perkins Marsh published the book *Man and Nature*, which included a stark warning: the United States would collapse if it depleted its natural resources without planning for the future.[12] Progressives did not seek to undermine economic development, but they worried that unchecked speculation would lead to waste and would deprive future generations of the social and economic opportunities that characterized American society. They argued that the United States must conserve rather than exploit its natural resources, that it must engage in long-term planning.

Progressive calls for resource conservation were motivated by yet another interpretation of freedom—the promotion of the happiness, or the greatest good, of the greatest number of people. This approach was encapsulated in the concept of utility and what Samuel P. Hays calls the "gospel of efficiency."[13] Resource conservation, and progressive ideology more generally, thus introduced a new category of social actors, the technological experts (that is, engineers) who were expected to use scientific knowledge and rational decision-making to chart a way forward for both the government and the would-be pioneer.

Resource conservationists identified existing political entities as opponents of their efforts; politicians, they argued, agitated for their own constituents instead of seeking the greater utility. They argued that the very organization of the nation as a union comprised of independent states, and of states comprised of counties, necessarily undermined the efficient management of the environment. It was only government agencies and their experts that could be trusted to oversee the development of the nation's resources. But if not based on federal, state, and county jurisdiction, how to manage the enormous territory of the United States? What unit should engineers and scientists use?

In 1878, John Wesley Powell prepared "A Report on the Lands of the Arid Region of the United States," describing areas that were then unknown to both the public and the scientific community.[14] Unlike William Goodell Frost, Powell used the term "region" to highlight the classification of land by *geographic* features rather than political boundaries. Five years later he would go a step further, to suggest that administrative boundaries in the United States should be set along natural geographic boundaries, governed especially by the extent of watersheds. Rivers, he explained, were not arbitrary concepts but rather "real things" that could be systematically studied and quantified. They could also be scaled and nested: the logic of the watershed applied to rivers and tributaries alike. In making this argument, Powell prioritized his scientific understanding of rivers over the phenomenological knowledge he gained traveling through them.[15] Such language and its political implications, however, was not widely accepted; Powell's proposals did not meet with enthusiasm in Congress.

Early conservation efforts focused on forestry. European settlement had severely impacted forests across the continent; they had been systematically cleared to create arable land, or

Norris Dam from Observation Point, built by the Civilian Conservation Corps in the 1930s.

had been converted into houses, railroads, and other commodities. Timber companies had further devastated forests, removing fine trees and leaving only second- or third-generation trees of inferior quality. Conservationists sought to scientifically manage forests and assure that the timber was renewed rather than destroyed. The Forest Reserve Act of 1891 authorized keeping land in the public domain rather than making it available for homesteading, as well as creating federally managed forest reserves.

In 1902, Bernhard Fernow, the first chief of the Division of Forestry in the Department of the Interior, published a book on the *Economics of Forestry*.[16] He contended that the individualism developed on the frontier did not meet the standard of utility because it assaulted the rights of the many in favor of those of the few. His successor, Gifford Pinochet, fully launched the American forestry movement. Pinochet argued that forests ought to be managed as if they were a crop—an argument he cemented by moving the division, renamed the Bureau of Forestry/Forest Service, into the Department of Agriculture. Among other activities, the service engaged in large-scale surveys of forestry conditions as the scientific prelude to practical action. In 1901, the areas surveyed included the "Southern Appalachian Region."[17]

The utilitarian approach to forests was supported by a spiritual understanding that saw forests and wilderness not as an evil or an obstacle, to be vanquished by the courageous pioneer, but as a haven for humans' personal restoration. This idea had deep roots in American culture, beginning with Henry David Thoreau's sojourn at Walden Pond as recounted in his 1854 book, *Walden; or, Life in the Woods*.[18] Thoreau's insistence that humans lived their best life in contact with nature, together with his advice for self-reliance, were important elements in the development of the American pastoral ideal.

The urge to preserve land for spiritual recuperation, specifically by encompassing it within the wide category of outdoor recreation, was first transformed into policy (at the federal level) in 1872 with the Yellowstone Park Act, which created the first national park. Recreation would later be extended into the government forest reserves created by the 1891 act. The Forest Service, "dumbfounded" at first, eventually came to see recreation as a legitimate purpose of public forests.[19] Progressive reformers celebrated outdoor activities such as hiking and camping, as well as hunting and fishing, as reviving the challenges of the frontier and providing an opportunity to build American character. As fewer and fewer Americans lived the life of the frontier, outdoor recreation in its many forms gained importance as an antidote to the "soft" life of the cities. One of the first clubs devoted to this effort was the Appalachian Mountain Club, founded in 1876.

The most prominent promoter of resource conservation was Theodore Roosevelt, Jr., President of the United States between 1901 and 1909. In 1908 he launched conservation as a national cause in a speech given to the Conference of Governors, making an idea into a movement. Roosevelt revived many of Powell's ideas, and he supported and signed into law the Reclamation Act of 1902. This act resumed large-scale sales of public land, authorizing funds from such sales to be used to construct and maintain an irrigation system in the western states that would enable agricultural production. The 1902 law thus extended the Homestead Act into areas too arid for agricultural cultivation, while also widening the list of "approved" uses for public land well beyond Jefferson's pastoral ideal. At the same time, it transformed the nature of homesteading: these new farmers would be absolutely dependent on the construction and maintenance of public infrastructure.

Roosevelt and his fellow resource conservationists continued to fight for federal control over waterways in the United States, achieving success in the Water Power Act of 1920. By this time, the construction of dams—that is, large-scale water conservation—was closely linked to the production of hydroelectricity.[20] After World War I the Army Corps of Engineers surveyed all the rivers in the United States. The resulting 1928 report included a proposal for the Tennessee River that identified locations for a multipurpose (navigation and power) system: navigable dams would be built along the river itself, along with water-storage dams on the main tributaries.

The Corps survey was not the first federal effort to focus on the Tennessee River. A wartime project was the federal construction of Wilson Dam in Muscle Shoals, Alabama, creating a reservoir around one of the largest shoals in the river that had been a significant obstacle to navigation. The electric power produced at the dam was intended to be used to produce ammunition in two dedicated factories located just south of it, if they had been completed in time to contribute to the war effort.

Resource conservation was not the only example of progressive politics in the national arena. William J. Novak tracks the development of what he calls a "New Democracy," beginning after the Civil War and continuing into the 20th century. These changes, he contends, belie the notion that the United States remained a weak federation, focused on a laissez-faire market and international statecraft. Instead, he sees the creation of a "new regime of American governance—a modern democratic state."[21] In this process many local and regional traditions of self-government gave way to centralized legislation, regulation, and administration.

The "New Democracy" did not, however, produce a strong centralized state in the European model. Instead, the federal government developed what Michael Mann calls "infrastructural" power—in contrast to what he calls "despotic" power, a state's ability to dictate political decisions. Infrastructural power is the capacity to "penetrate civil society, and to implement logistically political decisions throughout the realm."[22] It is composed of a wide range of government actions, including education, public services, regulation, and the construction of infrastructure.

This federal investment in infrastructural power was rooted in a new understanding of "freedom." Beyond the pastoral notion of freedom to cultivate one's land and one's mind, progressive politics championed the Pragmatic ideal that "people had a right to be protected from the tyranny of circumstance and that a democratic government should be their protector."[23] This ideal, especially in its practical implications, challenged the widely accepted understanding of freedom as the right of the individual to make decisions without government intervention. Progressives thus often found themselves having to persuade the public of the meaning of their intentions.

The progressive reform of the "New Democracy" had an environmental dimension as well. Protection from harm included a safe environment, free from the threats of fire and disease. These concerns were especially acute in large urban centers, where the laissez-faire economic model had produced rows of low-quality tenement housing. The government of New York City was among the first to introduce codes for housing, including standards governing fresh air and fire-escape routes.[24]

The environmental reform efforts went beyond resource conservation; they embodied a moral position on the "proper" use of resources. As

Douglas Dam

defined by social reformers, this concept of propriety typically adhered to middle-class notions of a good life, including an emphasis on the advantages of the nuclear family and the single-family home, with clear gender roles. The good life also included "wholesome" outdoor recreation, such as hiking and camping. The primary model for such an environment was Central Park in New York City, designed by Frederick Law Olmsted and Calvert Vaux in the 1850s. The park's meadows, lakes, wooded areas, and meandering paths, copied from English picturesque landscapes, were expected to function much like the wilderness—become a setting for character formation.

Environmental reform efforts in New York and other cities soon coalesced into a new type of expertise: city planning. Planning took the logic of resource conservation—its reliance on technical and rational knowledge—and applied it to all aspects of human social life. The proposals prepared by these new professionals (many had trained as architects and landscape architects) ranged from small-scale interventions in the urban fabric to visions of a complete overhaul of cities. Many planners were influenced by modernist ideas emanating from Europe, where planners and designers could realistically imagine shaping what Mann calls despotic decisions.

Early planning efforts were directed at cities, but in the 1920s a group calling itself the Regional Planning Association of America (RPAA) expanded this discussion to the rural landscape, the very cornerstone of the pastoral ideal.[25] Drawing on ideas formulated by Patrick Geddes, they advocated for a very specific spatial organization intended to oppose the trend towards sprawling cities and preserve the advantages of the middle landscape.

At the center of the regional planning approach was the "garden city," first described by Ebenezer Howard.[26] A garden city was a planned community whose growth would be restricted by a surrounding greenbelt in which no construction was allowed. These communities were to be spread across a planned region that would comprise small industrial and commercial centers and would also block the spread of urban and suburban sprawl.

Regional planners also believed in the importance of outdoor recreation as a basis for healthy bodies and minds. In 1921, RPAA-member Benton MacKaye published a proposal for an Appalachian Trail, a hiking path along the ridge of the entire mountain range.[27] Hikers along the path, he argued, would experience the "last" frontier, imbibing the lessons of this landscape in the process. They would also support its financial and social regeneration. MacKaye's proposal included four elements , though only one, the hiking trail itself, was actually constructed.

By the late 1920s, many Americans accepted the need for government action to undertake large-scale projects such as flood prevention, river navigation, forestry, and soil conservation. They still balked at the idea of bringing the market and everyday life under similar government control. Unlike resource conservation, regional planning remained a radical idea espoused only by a few. This situation changed dramatically with the stock market crash in 1929. The Great Depression was more than an economic crisis; it severely undermined the basis of American identity and called into question long-held beliefs such as the centrality of land ownership and financial autonomy.

Many Americans blamed the severity of the Great Depression on the closing of the frontier—that is, on the disappearance of resources and personal opportunity.[29] The main culprits in these discussions were business and speculation; critics argued that competition had led to significant waste and could doom American society.

Government, progressive reformers argued, thus had a moral duty to regulate business, to transform it into what they called "industry." This was a government-centered variation on the myth of the frontier: such regulation was needed to promote progress and financial growth for the benefit of the public rather than for corporate profit. Promoting industry would return the market to healthy competition and would thus preserve opportunities for individual entrepreneurship.

In 1933, Franklin D. Roosevelt (a fifth cousin of Theodore Roosevelt) took office as the President of the United States, having promised to use the power of the federal government to ease the impacts of the Great Depression. In his first 100 days in office, he directed a spurt of legislation known as the New Deal. Much of this new legislation was improvised and experimental, but it was a concerted effort to overcome the crisis. The New Deal encompassed, to different degrees, many of the ideas about society and environment already under general discussion: the pastoral ideal, the myth of the frontier, and the superiority of free labor. Key elements of resource conservation also found their way into congressional acts: the ideals of science, utility, and efficiency, as well as specific projects to conserve water, soil, and forests. Even regional planning, once a fringe concern, was now given a place at the table.

The New Deal legislation in practice subsumed varying interpretations of democracy, freedom, and environment, pushing those with opposing views to work together. The idea of America as a nation of white Protestant settlers was never far from legislators' minds, and Appalachia, as a last frontier, figured in federal and public discussions. Above all, however, the New Deal represented a willingness by the federal government to openly and clearly invest in both building infrastructural power and regulating business. In May of 1933, these myriad ideas and policies came together as the basis for the Tennessee Valley Authority (TVA) Act and the creation of an unprecedented institution in American politics. The TVA was to be a federal agency with responsibility for a designated region, defined as the watershed of the Tennessee River, and with the authorization to make plans and execute them with minimal oversight from Washington.

2

The TVA

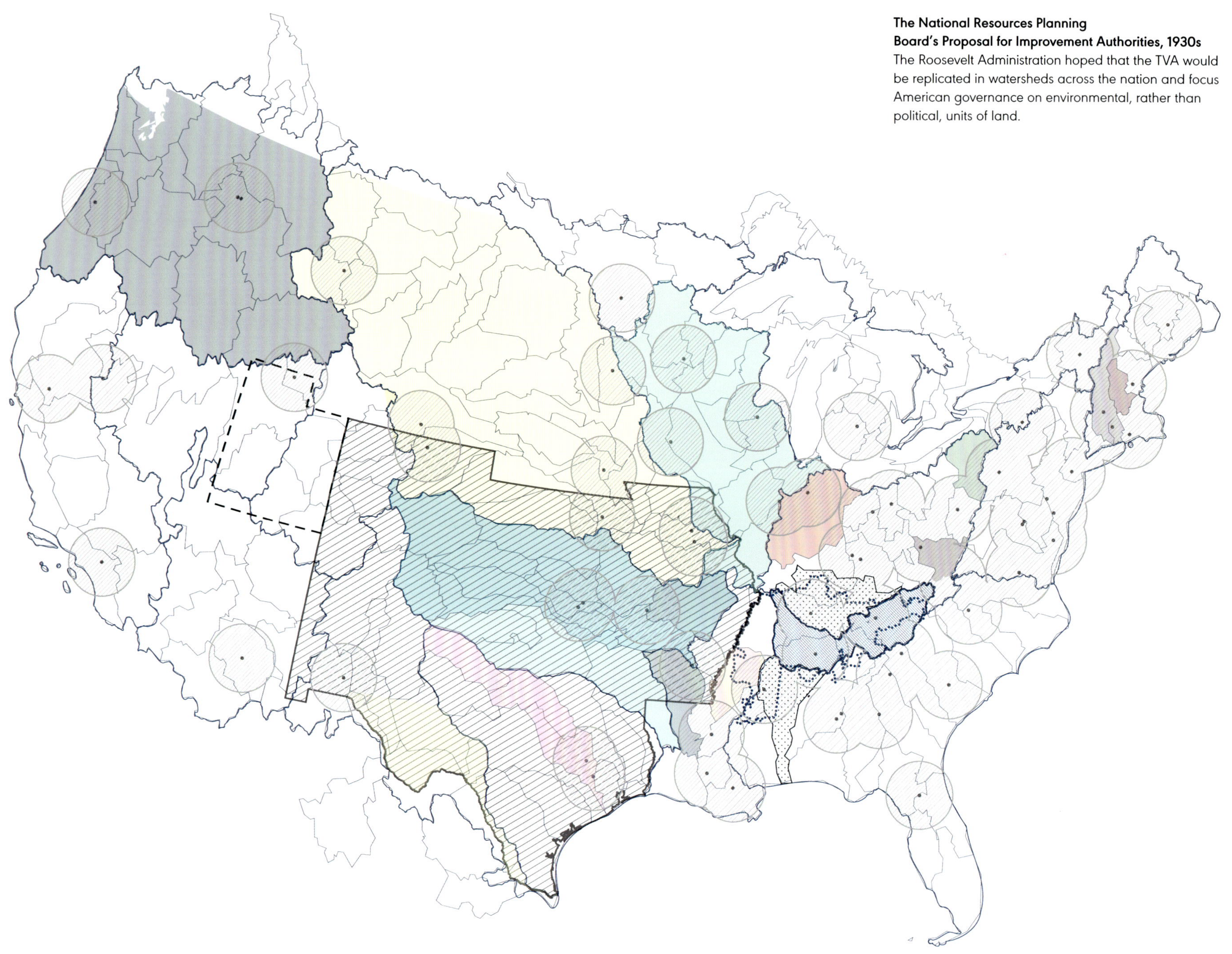

**The National Resources Planning
Board's Proposal for Improvement Authorities, 1930s**
The Roosevelt Administration hoped that the TVA would
be replicated in watersheds across the nation and focus
American governance on environmental, rather than
political, units of land.

The creation of the Tennessee Valley Authority in 1933, as part of the New Deal legislation, reflected a wide range of positions about society, democracy, and land-use. It was nevertheless primarily an essay in resource conservation. Developing resources—water, soil, forests, and electric power—was, by the 1930s, accepted as a legitimate government vehicle for ensuring the economic and social development of families and individuals. The TVA Act, the legal basis for the agency's operation, was explicit in authorizing the president to direct the TVA to undertake plans to achieve six broad objectives, as worded in the legislation:

(1) the maximum amount of flood control;
(2) the maximum development of said Tennessee River for navigation purposes;
(3) the maximum generation of electric power consistent with flood control and navigation;
(4) the proper use of marginal lands;
(5) the proper method of reforestation of all lands in said drainage basin suitable for reforestation;
(6) the economic and social well-being of the people living in said river basin.[30]

To these specific authorizations, the TVA Act added yet another layer: the new agency was to approach these goals as components of a single unified project. To enable this holistic attitude the Authority was assigned responsibility for an entire region, the watershed of the Tennessee River. This was a geographic rather than political demarcation, the first such authorization in American politics.

The designation of the Tennessee River as a region had a basis in environmental conditions: given rain patterns in the valley, efforts to optimize flood control and improve navigation would also maximize power production.[31] It was nevertheless primarily an ideological and political statement. The TVA Act created a symmetry between a natural—more precisely, a topographic—formation and the new administrative unit. The Act essentially allowed the TVA to function as the government of a "meta-state," acting both within and outside the established political system of the United States.

The TVA's regional authorization was unprecedented in federal legislation. Equally radical was the sixth authorization established in the law, as cited above. Congress echoed the language of environmental reform and regional planning when it directed the TVA to work toward "the economic and social well-being of the people living in said river basin."[32] This ambiguous authorization had been inserted into the TVA Act shortly before it was brought to Congress and was approved without extensive debate.[33] TVA planners attributed its inclusion to President

Franklin D. Roosevelt's personal interest in planning and regionalism, though it also reflected the experimental nature of the New Deal itself.[34]

The TVA was unique also in its structure. It was to be directed by a triumvirate of directors rather than a single individual. Roosevelt moved swiftly to appoint Arthur E. Morgan, an engineer with experience in building dams as well as a firm believer in social and environmental reform. He was joined by Harcourt A. Morgan (no relation to Arthur), an agronomer and president of the University of Tennessee, Knoxville, who had been involved in soil conservation in the Tennessee Valley for several decades. David E. Lilienthal, the third member, was a lawyer by training who had engaged in litigation against private electric companies in other parts of the United States. Thus, all the various professional and intellectual interests that had contributed to the establishment of the TVA—and the tensions between them—were positioned in the institution from its inception, beyond the terse instrumental language of its legal authorization.

The TVA engineers soon set about developing the projects authorized in the TVA Act, considering them part of the "Unified Development of the Tennessee River System."[35] In recognition of the comprehensive nature of their approach, we conceptualize their work as an integrated set of three *machines*—three large-scale operations enacted across the environment of the Tennessee Valley. The first, the *river machine*, began with the construction of a system of dams to provide both flood protection and navigation. This project had the largest environmental impact: to build the dams and create their reservoirs, the TVA purchased or expropriated land across the Valley, transforming private lands into public land under federal jurisdiction. To this day, the reservoir lakes and their shorelines remain in the public domain, allowing the TVA

to store and release water in response to seasonal precipitation.

The second system, the *land machine*, responded to the fourth and fifth authorizations: to work toward "proper" reforestation and use of marginal lands—that is, the promotion of forestry and agriculture. Both projects required stemming severe soil erosion in the Tennessee Valley, exacerbated by inefficient farming practices. Rather than buying properties, the TVA developed a program for manufacturing and distributing seedlings and fertilizers and for disseminating the knowledge needed to productively care for forests and crops. The agency's explicit end-to-end control over the *land machine* was limited. Perhaps to compensate, it developed a complex system of infrastructural power that brought the TVA goals to the "people" of the Tennessee Valley.

The third project, which we call the *power machine*, had an environmental imprint even smaller than that of the land machine. The TVA built powerhouses at most of the dams and produced energy efficiently, that is, more cheaply than the market. The challenge of the *power machine* was to make this power available to the rural residents of the Tennessee Valley, who were not then connected to the electric grid. Building such a grid required some innovation, well within the TVA's capabilities. The TVA had to contend, however, with severe opposition from private electric companies in the region, transforming the implementation of an engineering project into a legal challenge. The *power machine* was stalled for several years, but in the late 1930s the Supreme Court decided in favor of the TVA, allowing it to complete its plan for the rural electrification of the Tennessee Valley.

The differences between the three machines, and especially their interactions with Valley residents, produced deep tensions within the organization. Arthur Morgan, who had taken

Approach to the Fontana Dam Visitor Center from the road crossing the dam

The Fontana Dam Powerhouse and Little Tennessee River

charge of the *river machine*, was adamant that the agency should retain control of all aspects of development and should invest in creating the ideal environments outlined by regional planners. He imagined building a region of freehold farmers supported by small industrial centers. Harcourt Morgan, on the other hand, argued that the American democracy explicitly gave citizens the freedom to make decisions about their finances and daily lives, and that Arthur Morgan's approach took government intrusion too far. The *land machine*, for which Harcourt Morgan was responsible, was his ideal model for apportioning the power of decision between government and citizens. Lilienthal supported Harcourt Morgan's point of view, and he made an effort to shape the *power machine*, for which he had taken charge, in a similar fashion.

In the first years of operation, the TVA managed and coordinated three very different projects. This system might have continued if the board of directors had been able to maintain the delicate balance. But in 1938 Arthur Morgan was ousted from his post, to be replaced by Lilienthal as Chairman of the Board. The less muscular ideology of Harcourt Morgan and Lilienthal became dominant; it was maintained and even intensified as the United States prepared for, and then entered, World War II. The war would dramatically affect almost every aspect of American society and government, and the TVA was no exception. The war effort required an immense supply of electricity, and the task of providing this power overtook the TVA's dedicated regional focus, transforming the agency beyond recognition.

Lilienthal was not content with executing policy. A natural politician, he, more than other directors, developed a comprehensive statement about the TVA and its role in the Tennessee Valley and the nation as a whole. He later expanded this argument to the entire globe,

in his book TVA: *Democracy on the March*, first published in 1944.[36] As the title suggests, Lilienthal contextualized his arguments in wider discussions about democracy and freedom. Lilienthal maintained that freedom was the reason for a regional administration, separate from the federal bureaucracy in Washington. Centralization, he argued, "is a threat to the human spirit everywhere, and its control is a concern of all men who love freedom."[37] Like many progressives, Roosevelt included, Lilienthal hoped the success of the TVA would signal a new way of thinking about the United States, as the first of a series of regional authorities. The concept of the region was thus promoted as nothing less than an efficient new vehicle for the perpetuation of American democracy.

Lilienthal's advocacy for regional decentralization was rooted in the idea of grassroots democracy. Development, he argued, "is not only 'for the people' but 'by the people.'"[38] Grassroots democracy combined the ideal of the individualist spirit of the frontier with the more centralized organization needed for resource conservation. The laissez-faire policies that underlaid frontier development assumed that the "people," when operating without restraint in a free market, collectively made the best decisions for overall social and economic good. Resource conservationists and planners, on the other hand, argued that decisions should be made by experts—individuals who possessed the knowledge and education to make rational, well-judged choices.

Lilienthal somewhat radically cast the "people" as the experts. It was their values and preferences, he contended, that should guide the decisions of government entities such as the TVA. At the same time, he expected government to provide the "people" with the knowledge and skills required to elevate their choices and align them with government preferences. The TVA called this work "research," in line with the scientific bent of resource conservation.[39] This rhetoric neatly described the basis of progressive ideas for democracy: government would not impose its choices through direct power but would instead use persuasion—what we are calling statecraft—to build a system of infrastructural power: the physical, social, and legal paths needed to disseminate its guidance and decisions.

Grassroots democracy was powerful as rhetoric, but it had an inherent flaw. The same knowledge that the TVA considered necessary for public expertise could also be used by private businesses with the goal of making immediate profit rather than serving the public good. The most obvious examples were lawsuits brought by electric power companies, who argued that they owned the right to profit from the knowledge of building and maintaining an electric grid. The power companies' position, rooted in longstanding interpretations of freedom and democracy, had the potential to undermine the entire TVA enterprise. Lilienthal and the TVA countered these legal challenges by energetically explaining and promoting the progressive value of industry.

The legal threat from the power companies was compounded by comparisons between the TVA's operations and planning in socialist and communist settings, especially the Soviet Union. If the agency was to be the champion of grassroots *democracy*, it could not mimic socialist planning too closely. Concern over the survival of the agency added a second dimension to TVA statecraft; many of its efforts were geared toward publicly explaining its goals, embedding them in familiar American tropes such as the pastoral ideal and the myth of the frontier. This kind of statecraft was not limited to the TVA, as several of the New Deal agencies worked to make environmental projects widely comprehensible.[40]

The TVA statecraft centered on the notion of "yardsticks": government programs were held up as models for serving the public, aiming to constrain the avarice of private companies and to direct their efforts toward wider public goals. The best-known yardstick was the *power machine*, which was designed as a model for efficient and responsible rural electrification. The idea of the yardstick was also applied to other aspects of the TVA project, and financial regulation became a central element of the TVA project and statecraft.

Two projects included in this study illustrate the TVA's engagement with industry, beyond resource conservation. As the TVA housed the thousands of laborers building the dams, it also developed a complex system for prefabricating single-family homes, and it disseminated this knowledge to the nascent building industry in the Valley. In a second project, the TVA lay the legal, social, and geographic groundwork for a Valley-wide recreation industry which still plays a vital role in the region. It was the TVA, together with other New Deal agencies, that introduced the idea of public outdoor recreation to the Tennessee Valley.[41]

The discussion of research and yardsticks resolved some of the tensions inherent in the grassroots democracy program, but it did not resolve the most unsettling problem: who exactly were the "people"? And, more precisely, how does one identify a potential "expert"? Arthur and Harcourt Morgan, like Thomas Jefferson before them, focused on farmers and other individuals engaged in agriculture. Lilienthal, however, argued that there was no difference "between farm people and industrial workers, businessmen, librarians, ministers, doctors. All who live in the valley are needed in varying degrees, in this task of resource development."[42]

Lilienthal's rhetoric, however, masked deep social biases that shaped the TVA operation from the start. Experts were male and white and held professional positions. (Land-owning farmers were included in this category.) The TVA made room for women and Black citizens, as well as for people engaged in labor, but in subordinate rather than decision-making positions. The TVA statecraft was based on the assumption that all "citizens" strive to fulfill the pastoral ideal, engaging in free labor and enjoying a middle-class lifestyle. This message was promulgated in the TVA's environmental choices, which were presented as modern and progressive models. Single-family homes, designed for a family unit with a single breadwinner rather than an extended family engaged in farming or production, became a central vehicle for this assumption.

The TVA's institutional bias towards people of the middle class was in part a matter of personal predispositions; decisions were made by those who lived such lives. These TVA professionals had professional and academic education; they held creative and managerial roles; and they were paid enough to afford single-family homes and to devote time to leisure activities and travel. Their primary interaction, furthermore, was with those residents in the Tennessee Valley who already had personal or institutional power. In 1949, Philip Selznick conducted a detailed study of the TVA and argued that its work benefited those who already enjoyed some privilege in the Valley.[43]

The middle-class bias was also a sign of the racism at the heart of American society. In the 1930s, Black residents in the Tennessee Valley were still subject to the cruel reality of Jim Crow segregation. TVA personnel, mostly northerners, did not necessarily support this policy, but they did nothing to combat it. The TVA hired African Americans, but only as laborers; it did not offer them the opportunity to become professionals within the organization. The TVA also practiced segregation in its own environments, and the quality of accommodations provided in each section clearly reflected the disparate expectations for each race.[44]

These social, economic, and racial biases made their way into the overt TVA statecraft. The TVA continually referenced Appalachia and its residents as the beneficiaries of its efforts, downplaying the importance of the portion of the Tennessee Valley extending into northern Alabama and southern Tennessee, where many descendants of enslaved people still labored to produce cotton.[45] Suggesting, even obliquely, that the region was defined by both the watershed and Appalachia identified the TVA with a new form of pioneering. The grassroots democracy model took one version of American society and prescribed it for the entire nation, even areas established on a slave-based economy.

The TVA biases were not lost on its critics. The National Association for the Advancement of Colored People, with the help of Dr. J. Max Bond, Sr., an employee of the TVA, threatened to sue the TVA on several occasions. From the opposite, essentially racist position, Donald Davidson saw the TVA as representing colonialism—a federal intervention on behalf of Northern industry and business.[46] Davidson and his fellow Southern Agrarians championed what they saw as distinctly Southern culture and traditions.[47] While we recognize these dimensions of TVA statecraft, our aim is not to evaluate them but rather to examine their workings—how they were disseminated to the public, overtly or tacitly, through the medium of environmental change.

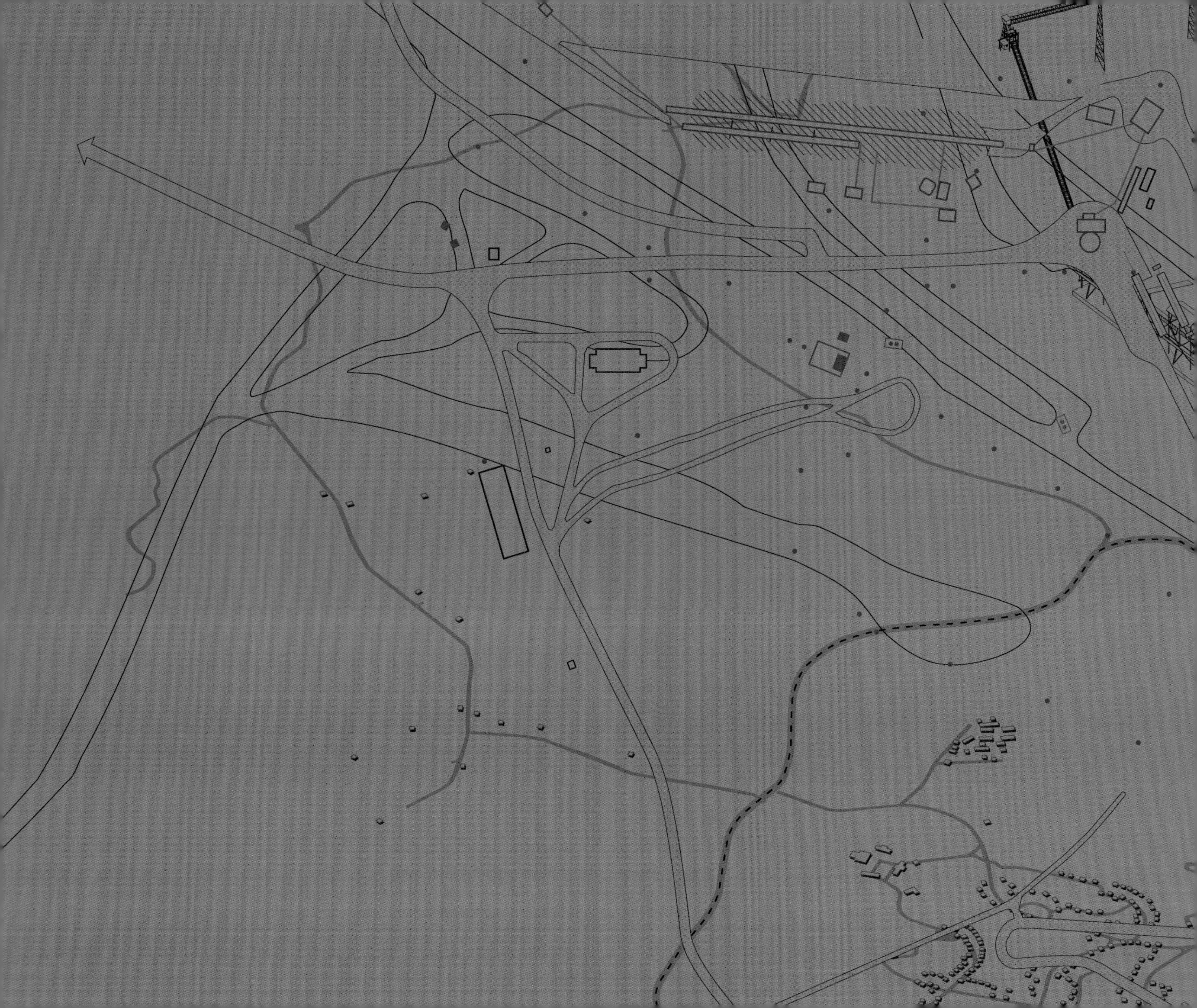

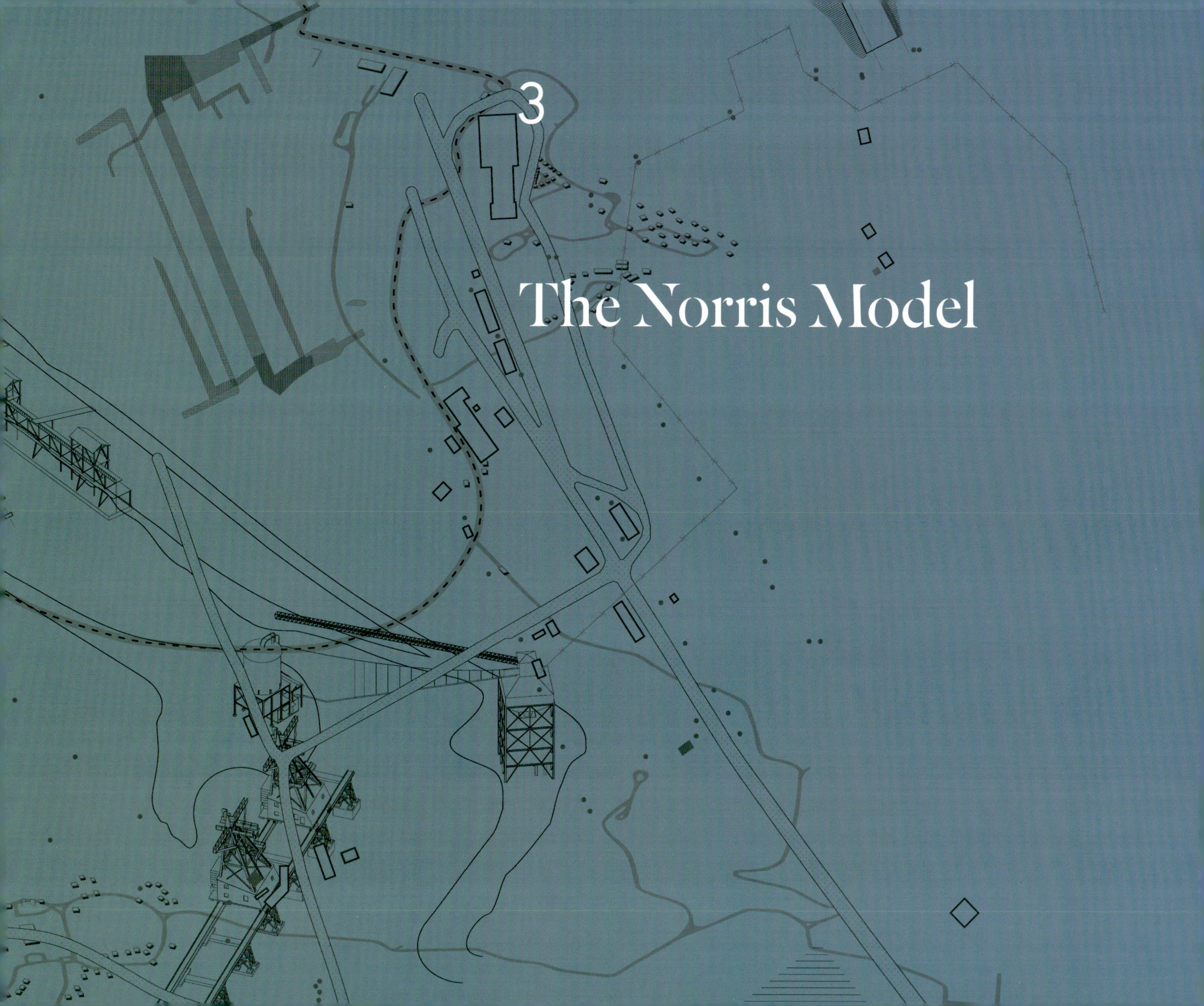

3
The Norris Model

The Norris Model

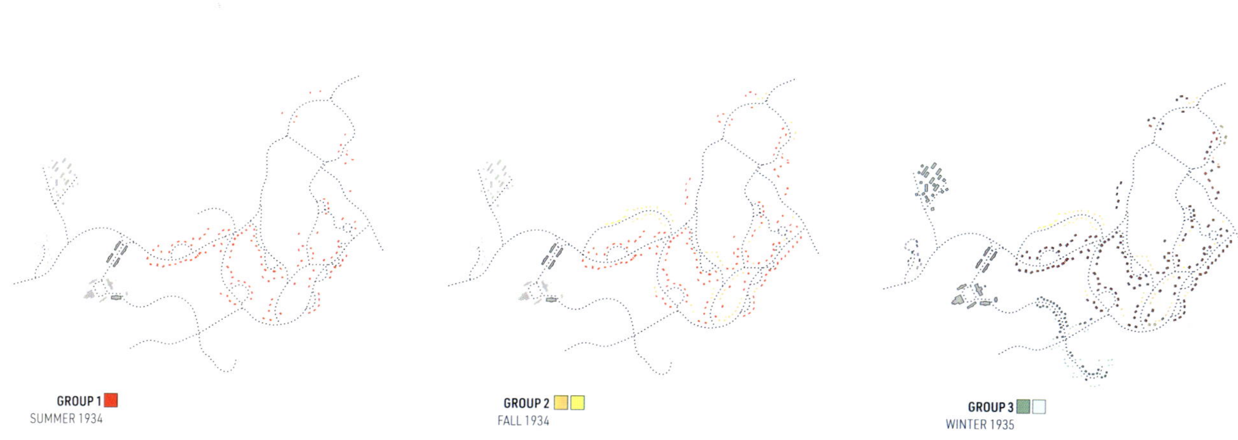

Plan of Norris, Tennessee, 1933-1936
The TVA built the town of Norris, Tennessee, to house employees constructing Norris Dam, but designed it as a permanent model of the Garden City ideal. This was the only model town to be built by the TVA.

The Tennessee Valley Authority (TVA) Act of 1933 authorized the new agency to engage in projects promoting the social and economic welfare of the residents of the Tennessee Valley. TVA Director Arthur E. Morgan interpreted this direction as sanction to engage in comprehensive regional planning, and he authorized the preparation of a plan for a complete reorganization of the territory. Such a plan, he reasoned, would identify the areas in the region suitable for settlement, allowing the TVA to direct residents there and to provide them with the opportunity to thrive socially and economically. The plan would also assure that industry could be properly and efficiently decentralized across the region, while maintaining its mostly rural character.

Recognizing the importance of demonstration, Morgan determined to use the construction of the first TVA installation as a model of his vision for the entire Tennessee Valley. The dam and powerhouse were named for Senator George Norris, the sponsor of the TVA Act; they are located on the Clinch River, a tributary of the Tennessee. The construction of the dam necessitated extensive land acquisition—but Morgan directed the TVA to purchase more land than was strictly needed, to assemble a large contiguous territory that could be refashioned as a spatial and physical model.

Type 21

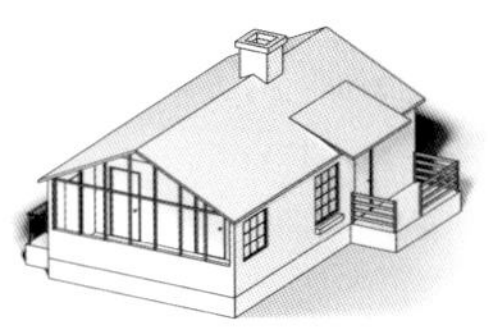

Type 32

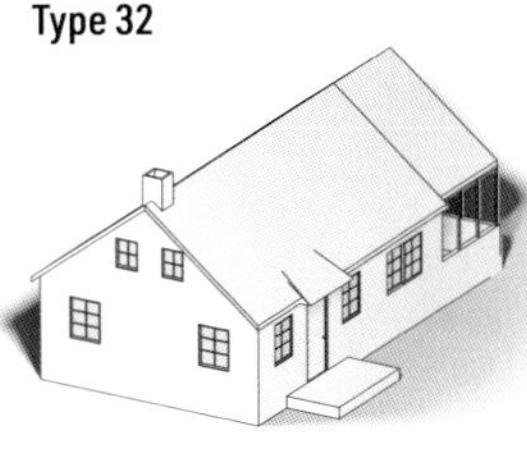

Type 41c

Type 44

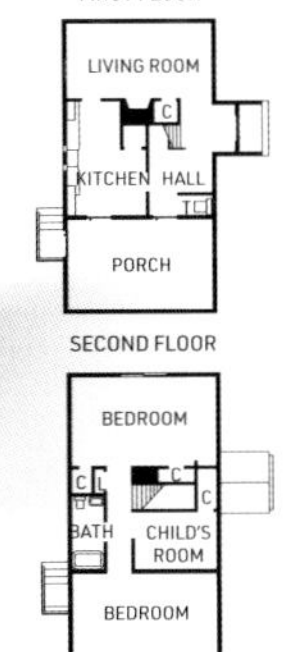

Type D2

Type N2

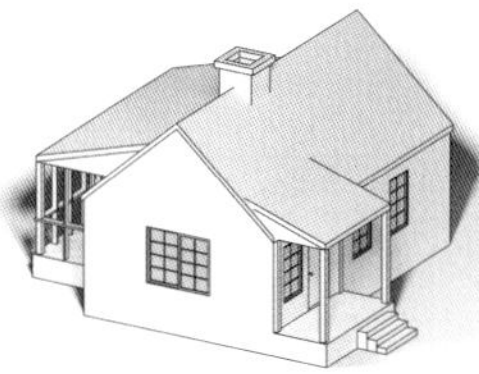

Type A

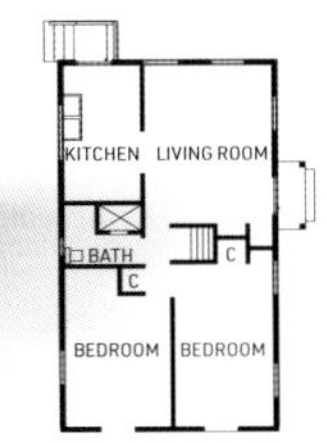

Type B

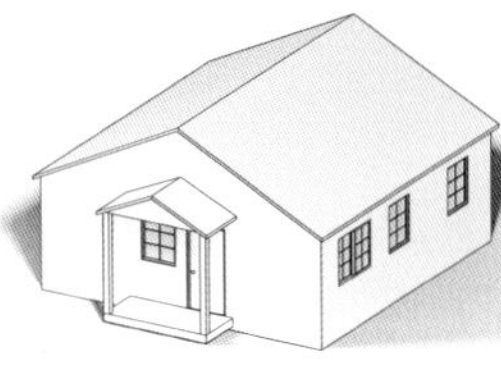

Type C

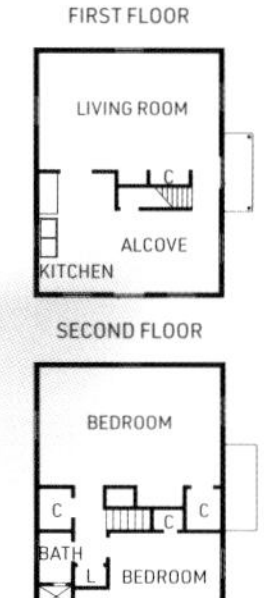

Type D

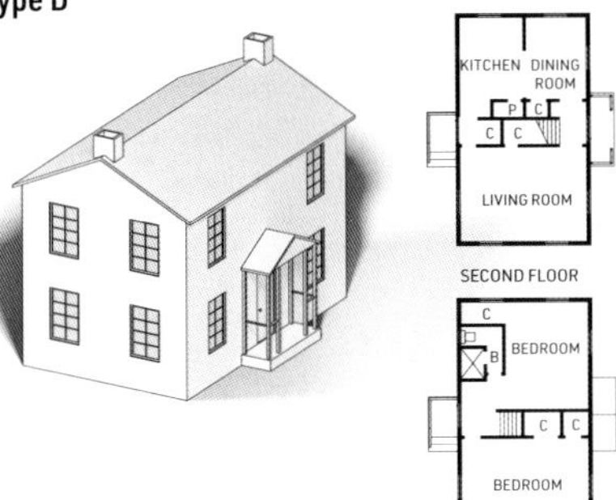

Type KC

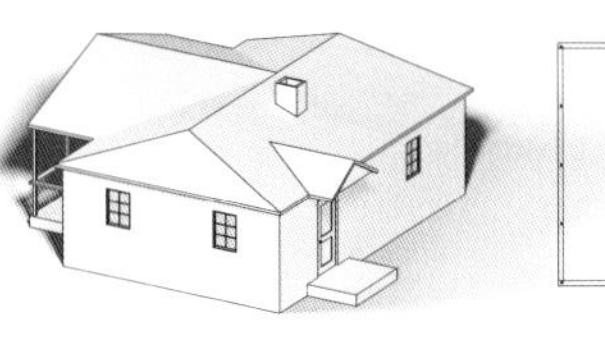

Typical Duplex

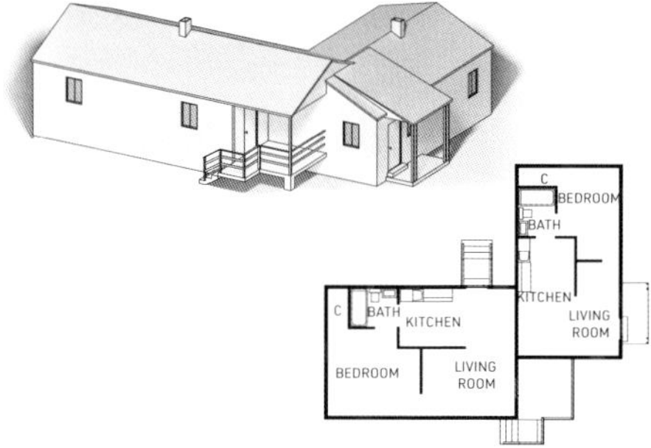

Each house in Norris, Tennessee, was derived from a set of types developed by the TVA architects. These house types represented the TVA's middle-class ideal.

Type 21[1]

Number built: 10
Total cost per unit: $50,391
Cubic feet: 10,300 ft³
Cost per ft²: $6.35

Type 32[1]

Number built: 13
Total cost per unit: $79,158
Cubic feet: 13,700 ft³
Cost per habitable ft²: $6.70

Type 41c[1]

Number built: 20
Total cost per unit: $142,240
Cubic feet: 17,900 ft³
Cost per habitable ft²: $4.72

Type 44[1]

Number built: 11
Total cost per unit: $73,864
Cubic feet: 14,300 FT³
Cost per habitable ft²: $4.30

Type D2[1]

Number built: 15
Total cost per unit: $92,575
Cubic feet: 14,650 ft³
Cost per habitable ft²: $5.26

Type N2[1]

Number built: 9
Total cost per unit: $53,837
Cubic feet: 13,000 ft³
Cost per habitable ft²: $6.89

Low-cost houses

Type A[2]

Number built: 30
Total cost per unit: $2,209
Cubic feet: 8,424 ft³
Cost per habitable ft²: $3.54

Type B[2]

Number built: 10
Total cost per unit: $2,025
Cubic feet: 8,470 ft³
Cost per habitable ft²: $3.34

Type C[2]

Number built: 20
Total cost per unit: $3,090
Cubic feet: 10,500 ft³
Cost per habitable ft²: $3.09

Type D[2]

Number built: 5
Total cost per unit: $3,281
Cubic feet: 10,375ft³
Cost per habitable ft²: $3.28

Type KC[2]

Number built: 32
Total cost per unit: $2506
Cubic feet: 9,600 ft³
Cost per habitable ft²: $3.79

Typical duplex[3]

Number built: 10
Total cost per unit: $1,311

[1] Wood floor construction, electricity for heating, cooking, hot water, and refridgeration, plumbing installed, advanced wall insulation

[2] Attic space for storage, heated by coal or wood stove, flues for heating rooms, precast beam, cinderblock walls, and slab floor construction, fire, termite, and rodent proof

[3] One-story frame, low-cost construction, units arranged for heating and cooking with coal or wood stoves.

Owning the land would eliminate the need for grassroots action and would allow the TVA to focus on embedding its statecraft physically and symbolically in the environment.

At the center of Arthur Morgan's model region is a garden city, also named Norris. Drawing on Ebenezer Howard's blueprint for such towns, Norris is surrounded by a protective greenbelt.[48] As Arthur Morgan hoped that Norris would develop into a hub of small-scale industry, the design for the town included not only service buildings and warehouses but also a lumber storehouse, a dairy barn, a poultry house, and even a ceramic laboratory. A small commercial area, including a space for the display and sale of local agriculture products, was located near the school and commons in the center of the town.

The design of Norris presented a stark contrast to the mining and logging company towns dotting the Appalachian mountains, which prioritized profits over amenities. At Norris, the garden city diagram was carefully adjusted to the site to balance between the utilitarian goal of a compact and efficient layout and a more humane preference for providing residents with privacy and views of forests and mountains. Norris was also planned explicitly to foster community life.[49] Membership in this community, however, was limited: African Americans were completely excluded from Norris. TVA officials argued that creating a "section" for Black families would be an inefficient use of public resources, in a textbook example of cloaking prejudice in the language of utility and efficiency.

The schedule for design and construction of the houses at Norris was short. Construction began in January 1934, and by September of the same year 150 houses were occupied. To meet this tight schedule, the TVA designed several typical houses that could be adjusted to specific sites and the available landscape views.[50] The

Worker Housing for the Construction of Norris Dam

Norris, Tennessee was designed as a permanent village, but it was surrounded by temporary housing for TVA laborers and members of the CCC. This housing was deconstructed or repurposed when it was no longer needed.

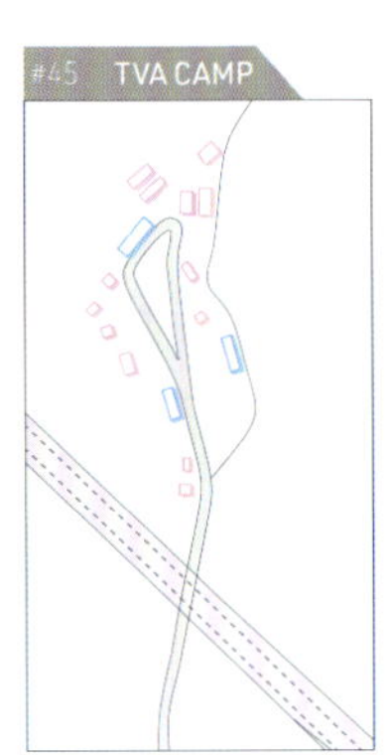

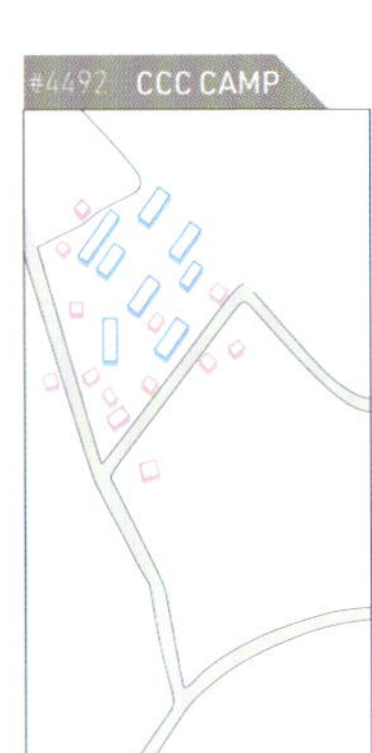

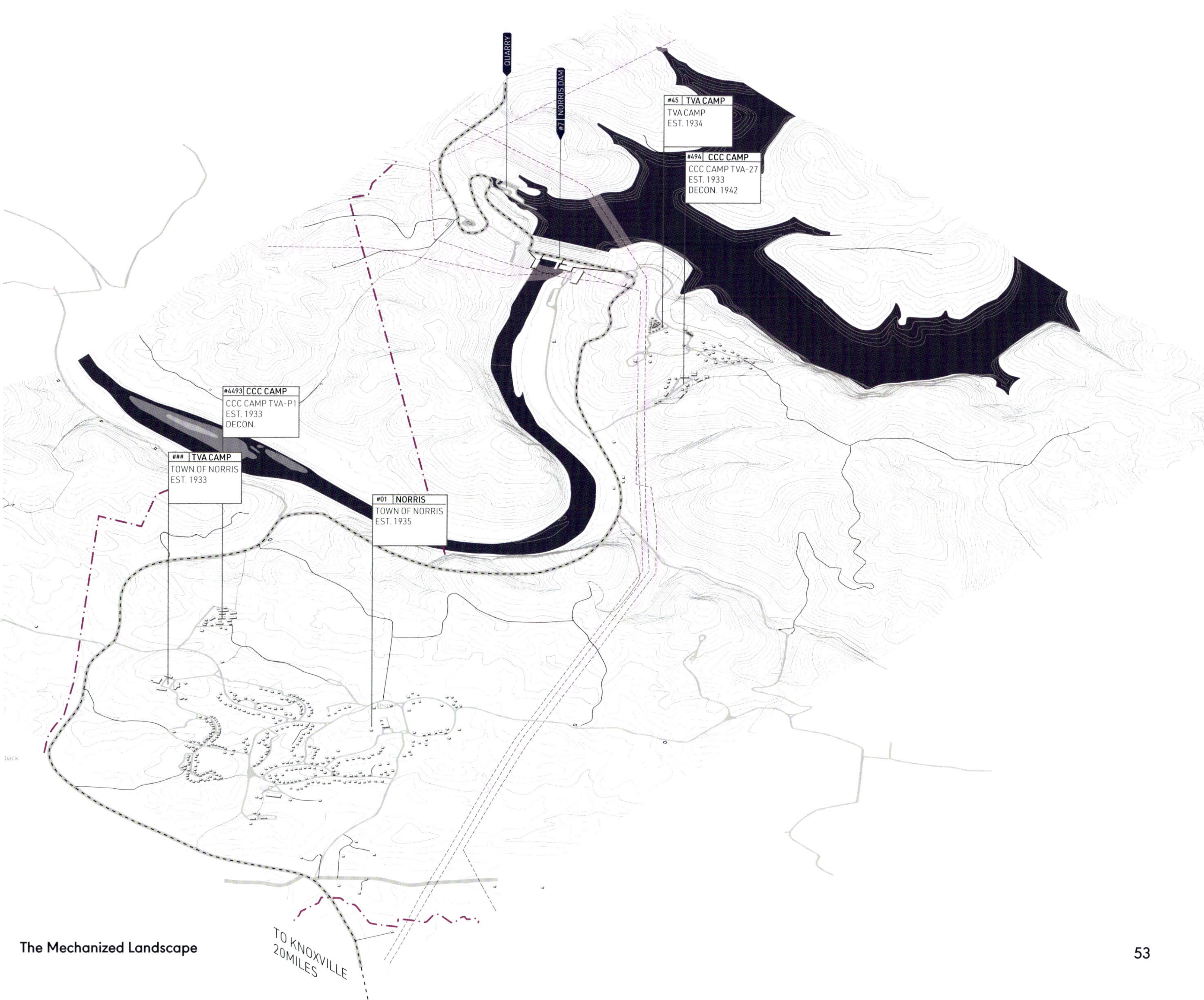

The Mechanized Landscape

Concrete Production at Norris Dam

The layout of the construction site at Norris Dam took advantage of its specific location – The TVA quarried rock nearby and crushed it into aggregate on-site. The concrete produced with this aggregate was delivered directly to the dam builders.

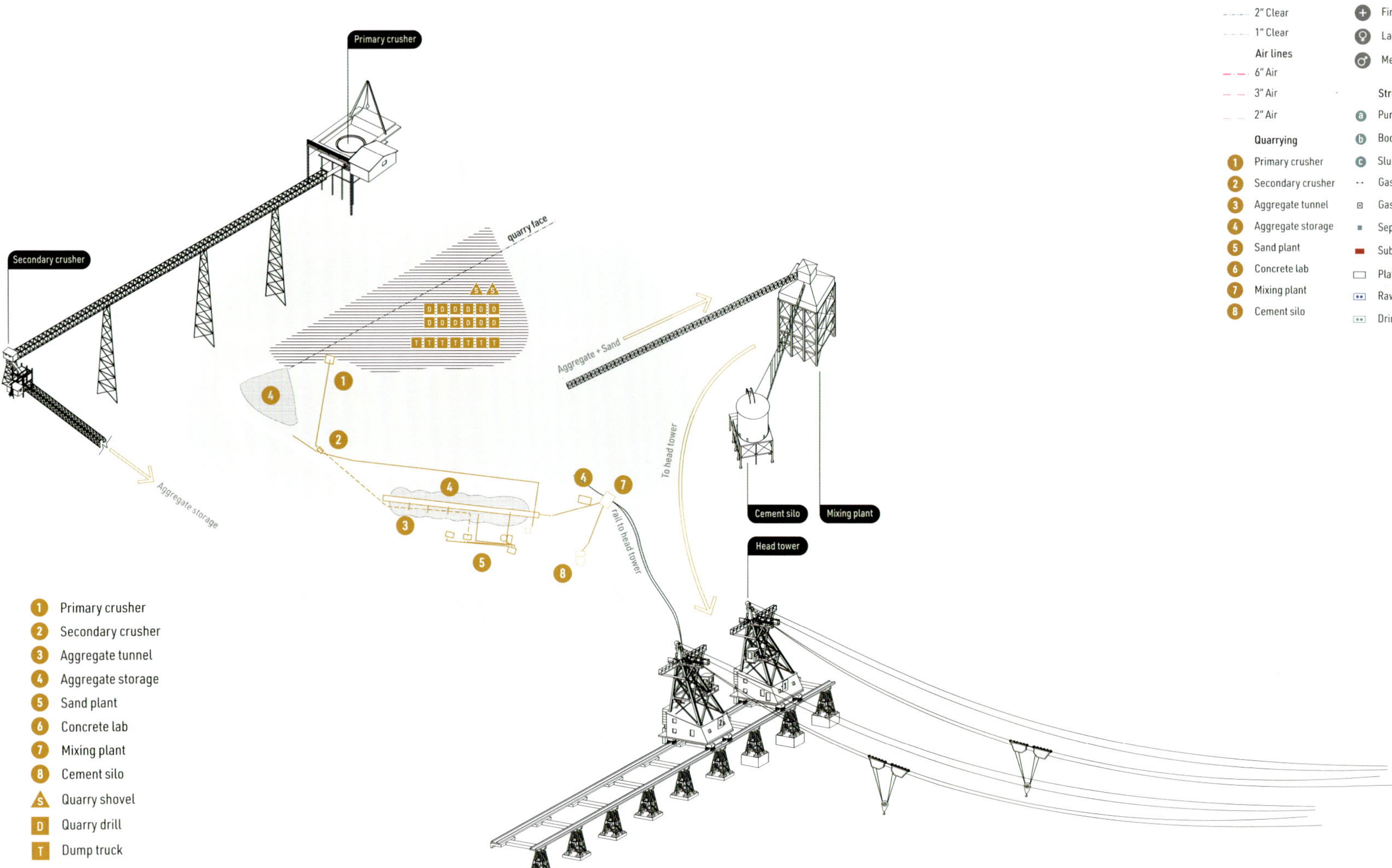

Power Lines
Telephone Lines
Plant Fence

Water lines
12" Raw
8" Raw
6" Raw
4" Raw
2" Raw
4" Clear
3" Clear
2" Clear
1" Clear

Air lines
6" Air
3" Air
2" Air

Quarrying
1 Primary crusher
2 Secondary crusher
3 Aggregate tunnel
4 Aggregate storage
5 Sand plant
6 Concrete lab
7 Mixing plant
8 Cement silo

Utilities
9 Public Toilets
10 Main Warehouse
11 Air Receiver
12 Compressor House
13 Warehouse
14 Exploder Storage + Powder House
15 Wash Rack
16 Oil House
First Aid
Ladies' Restroom
Men's Restroom

Structures
a Pump
b Booster Pump
c Sluicing Pump
Gas Pump
Gas Tank
Septic Tank
Substations
Platforms
Raw Water Tanks
Drinking Water Tanks

1 Primary crusher
2 Secondary crusher
3 Aggregate tunnel
4 Aggregate storage
5 Sand plant
6 Concrete lab
7 Mixing plant
8 Cement silo
S Quarry shovel
D Quarry drill
T Dump truck

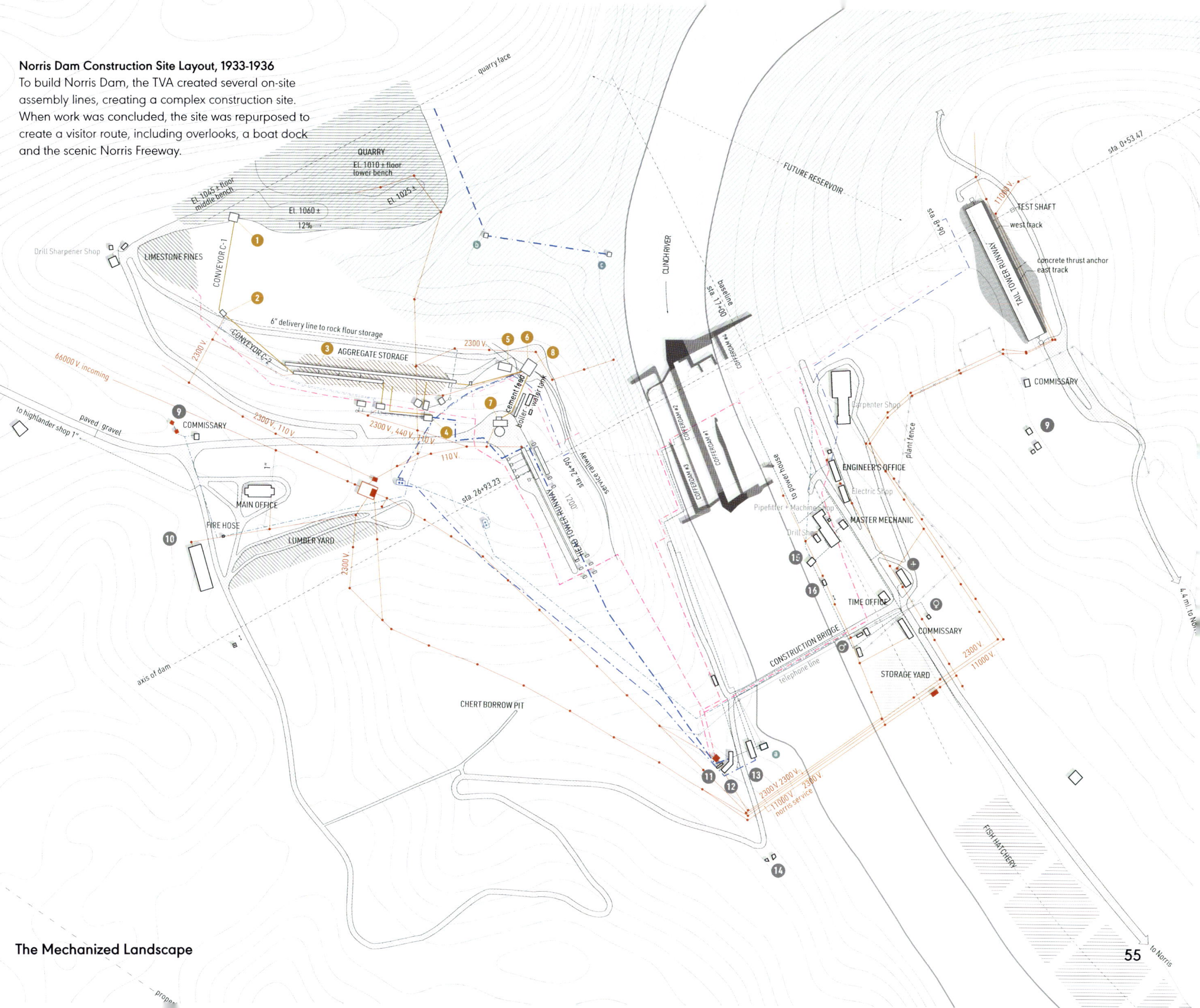

Norris Dam Construction Site Layout, 1933-1936
To build Norris Dam, the TVA created several on-site
assembly lines, creating a complex construction site.
When work was concluded, the site was repurposed to
create a visitor route, including overlooks, a boat dock
and the scenic Norris Freeway.

quarry face
QUARRY
EL. 1010 ± floor
lower bench
EL. 1045 ± floor
middle bench
EL. 1025 ±
EL. 1060 ±
12%
FUTURE RESERVOIR
sta. 0+53.47
11000 V.
TEST SHAFT
west track
concrete thrust anchor
east track
TAIL TOWER RUNWAY
Drill Sharpener Shop
LIMESTONE FINES
CONVEYOR C-1
CLINCH RIVER
baseline
sta. 17+00
sta. 8+90
COFFERDAM #4
COMMISSARY
6" delivery line to rock flour storage
2300 V.
2300 V.
CONVEYOR C-2
AGGREGATE STORAGE
cement feed
boiler
water tank
66000 V. incoming
COFFERDAM #3
COFFERDAM #2
COFFERDAM #1
Carpenter Shop
plant fence
to highlander shop 1"
paved gravel
COMMISSARY
2300 V., 110 V.
2300 V., 440 V., 110 V.
110 V.
service railway
to power house
Pipefitter + Machine Shop
ENGINEER'S OFFICE
Electric Shop
MASTER MECHANIC
1"
MAIN OFFICE
FIRE HOSE
sta. 26+93.23
sta. 24+50.00
HEAD TOWER RUNWAY
1200'
Drill Shop
TIME OFFICE
LUMBER YARD
2300 V.
CONSTRUCTION BRIDGE
telephone line
COMMISSARY
2300 V.
11000 V.
axis of dam
STORAGE YARD
CHERT BORROW PIT
2300 V 2300 V.
11000 V 2300 V
norris service
FISH HATCHERY
4.4 mi. to Nor
to Norris

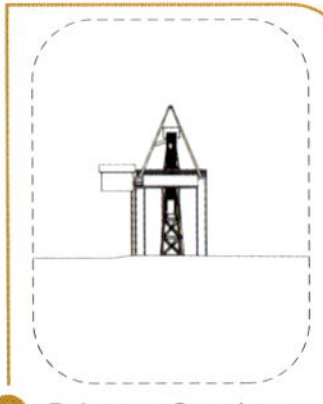

A Primary Crusher

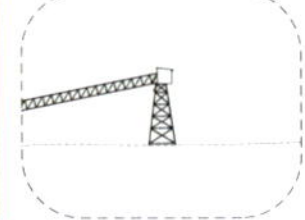

B Secondary Crusher

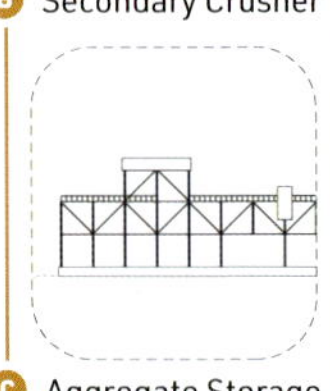

C Aggregate Storage

SHOVEL OPERATIONS

SHOVEL 1
BUCYRUS 75-B
Serial #: 11595
Dipper: 3 cu. yds.
Boom: 29 ft.
Power: 75 hp electric

Date of operation: 06/34 - 10/35

OPERATING TIME
Gross operation: 8337 hrs.
Delays: 1611 hrs.
Out of Service: 2743 hrs.

PRODUCTIVITY
Tons per Load: 14.6
Loads per Hour: 10.8
Total Loads: 72,774
Total Tons: 1,061,040

SHOVEL 2
MARION 4101
Serial #: 6681
Dipper: 3 cu. yds.
Boom: 31 ft.
Power: 75 hp electric

Date of operation: 06/34 - 10/35

OPERATING TIME
Gross operation: 7790 hrs.
Delays: 1550 hrs.
Out of Service: 2930 hrs.

PRODUCTIVITY
Tons per Load: 14.6
Loads per Hour: 10.1
Total Loads: 62,894
Total Tons: 916.998

2 MIXING

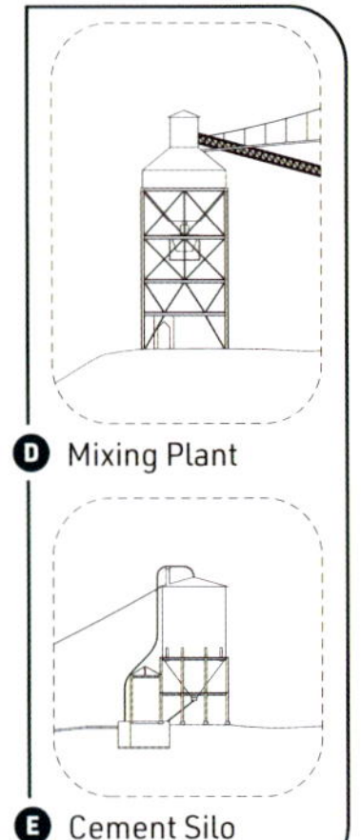

D Mixing Plant

E Cement Silo

MIXING PLANT CAPACITY
Cobble: 210 cu. yds.
Gravel 1: 140 cu. yds.
Gravel 2: 140 cu. yds.
Gravel 3: 210 cu. yds.
Coarse Sand: 210 cu. yds.
Fine Sand: 210 cu. yds.
2 Cement Bins: 410 bbls. ea.

Aggregate capacity: 1,100 cu. yds.
Cement capacity: 940 barrels

CEMENT SILO
Diameter: 30 ft
Capacity: 6,000 barrels

3 POURING

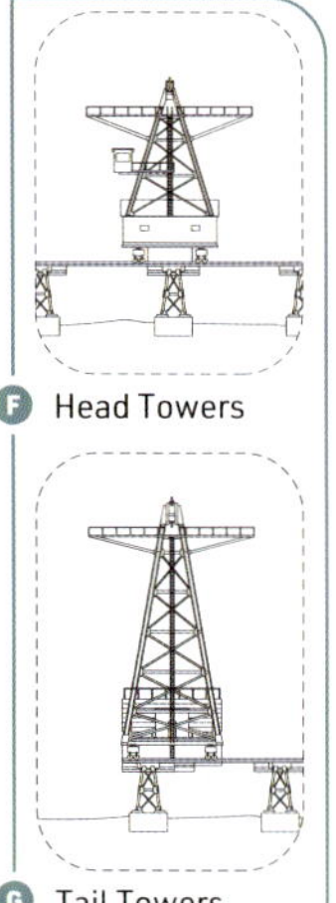

F Head Towers

G Tail Towers

HEAD TOWER
Top Rail Elevation: 1,165 ft.
Suspension Point: 1,240 ft.
Counterweight: 390 tons

TAIL TOWER
Top Rail Elevation: 1,062 ft.
Suspension Point: 1,172 ft.

HORIZONTAL PULLS
Cable Span: 1,925.5 ft.
Track Cable Pull: 362,000 lbs.
Operating Cable Pulls: 31,000 lbs.
Light and Conductor Cable Pulls: 60,000 lbs.
Total without Impact: 453,000 lbs.

PRODUCTIVITY
Full Load: 18 tons
Lowering Speed: 400 ft/min.
Hoisting Speed: 300 ft/min.
Carriage Travel: 1,200 ft/min.
Tower Traversing Speed: 50 ft/min.
Load at Cont. Operation: 16 tons

Axonometric view of Norris Dam under construction, 1935
The layout of the construction site at Norris Dam created an inverse symmetry – the dam rose as the quarry deepened. The void left by the quarry now houses public restrooms, an observation point, and a privately run marina.

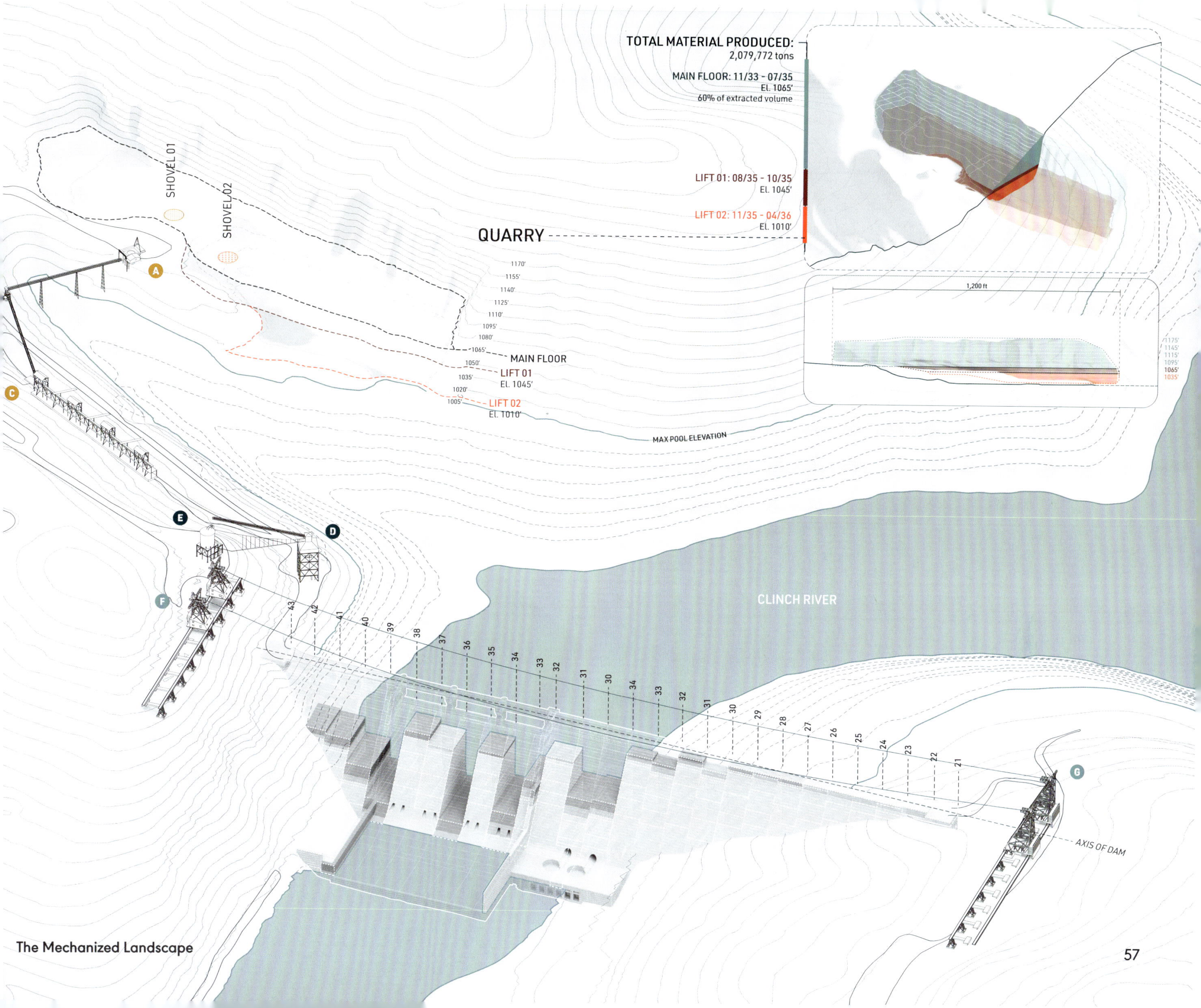

The Mechanized Landscape

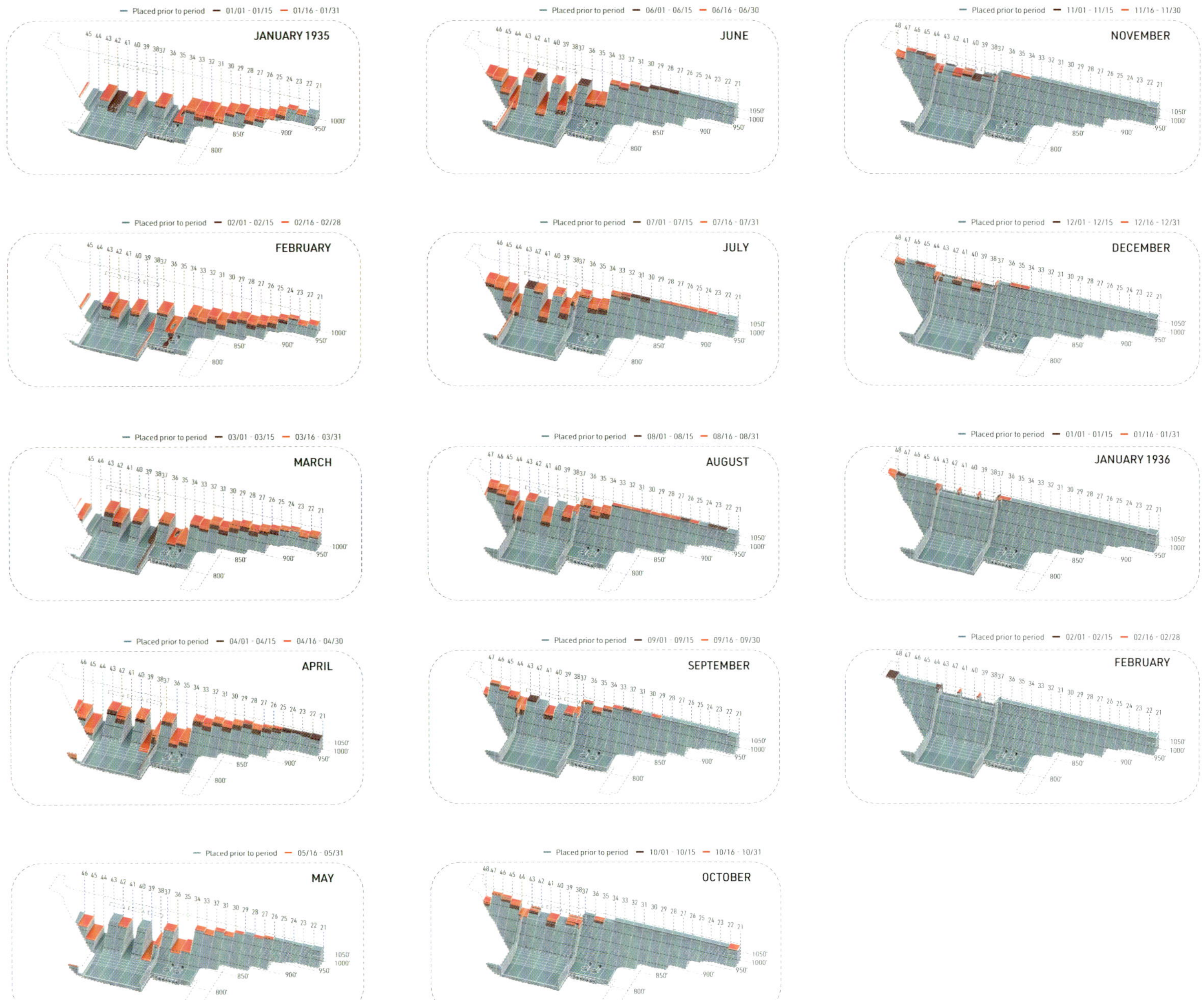
Placed prior to period — 01/01 - 01/15 — 01/16 - 01/31
JANUARY 1935
Placed prior to period — 06/01 - 06/15 — 06/16 - 06/30
JUNE
Placed prior to period — 11/01 - 11/15 — 11/16 - 11/30
NOVEMBER
Placed prior to period — 02/01 - 02/15 — 02/16 - 02/28
FEBRUARY
Placed prior to period — 07/01 - 07/15 — 07/16 - 07/31
JULY
Placed prior to period — 12/01 - 12/15 — 12/16 - 12/31
DECEMBER
Placed prior to period — 03/01 - 03/15 — 03/16 - 03/31
MARCH
Placed prior to period — 08/01 - 08/15 — 08/16 - 08/31
AUGUST
Placed prior to period — 01/01 - 01/15 — 01/16 - 01/31
JANUARY 1936
Placed prior to period — 04/01 - 04/15 — 04/16 - 04/30
APRIL
Placed prior to period — 09/01 - 09/15 — 09/16 - 09/30
SEPTEMBER
Placed prior to period — 02/01 - 02/15 — 02/16 - 02/28
FEBRUARY
Placed prior to period — 05/16 - 05/31
MAY
Placed prior to period — 10/01 - 10/15 — 10/16 - 10/31
OCTOBER

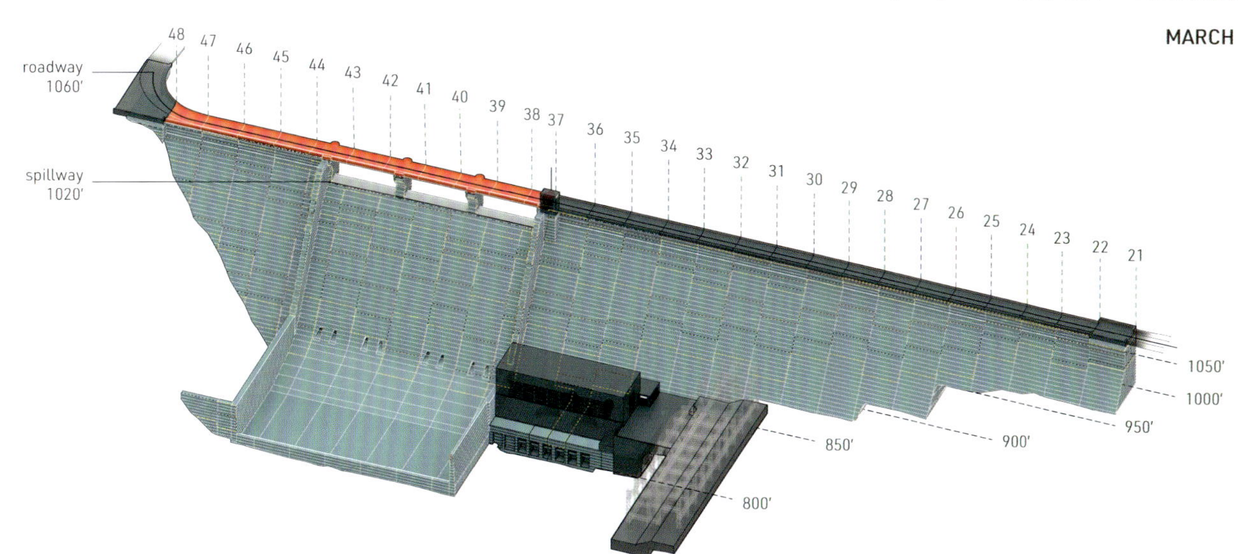

houses were mostly single-family homes, built to high standards (for the region) and equipped with running water and other utilities; most were also connected to the electric grid.

In a physical demonstration of the middle-class bias of TVA statecraft, the layout of the Norris houses follows what Thomas C. Hubka and Judith T. Kenny call the "Progressive Era Plan," which represented progressive reformers' aspirations for American society.[51] The layouts boasted middle-class standards of privacy, efficient kitchens, and ample porches for leisure. Arthur Morgan (and TVA personnel more broadly) expected Norris residents to adhere to accepted gender roles within homes, and the houses reflect this prejudice.[52]

The exterior of the Norris houses, on the other hand, reflected the TVA's regional emphasis; the TVA architects studied vernacular architecture—that is, homes in Appalachia—and then adapted their materials and dimensions to the modern layout. As Walter Creese comments, the product was similar to homes in the region but also distinctly new and modern.[53] The "vernacular" exteriors, moreover, established a symbolic connection between Norris and the "lost frontier" of Appalachia, embedding TVA statecraft in the new man-made environment. The design and construction of the houses conveyed the message that the arrival of new technologies and modes of management was consistent with local ways of life and would modernize rather than destroy them.

The construction of the dam and powerhouse at Norris was an essay in engineering and resource conservation: the goal was not only to build the dam but to do so efficiently, despite environmental challenges. The site for the dam was in the mountainous eastern portion of the watershed, and moving the necessary materials and equipment to the site posed significant

The Norris Model

Tourist cabins at Norris Dam State Park

challenges. The TVA engineers sought to rely on local resources as much as possible.

The quarry that provided aggregate (required for making concrete) was located at the mouth of Cove Creek, near the site for the Norris Dam. The engineers set up an ad hoc production line from the quarry to the dam, transforming the quarried stone into aggregate on site. This practical solution also created a compelling visual symmetry. As the quarry grew deeper, the dam grew higher—a literal transformation of the environment into a mechanized landscape.

The construction of the Norris Dam obeyed the precepts of engineering, but its aspect was designed by architects. Chief-architect Roland A. Wank convinced the TVA board of directors to allow the architectural staff, which had been hired to design the town of Norris, to direct the final look of the dams as well.[54] Wank stripped the concrete structure of all ornamentation and rearranged the elements of the dam, creating a modernist icon. The resulting design seamlessly ties both the *river machine* and the *power machine*—the dam, powerhouse, and electric substation—into the model region. The *land machine* is represented as well, in the area surrounding the dam, fashioned by landscape architects on the model of New York City's Central Park. Technology and the environment thus become designed and controlled, together forming a mechanized landscape.

The TVA also prepared detailed management plans that would develop the area surrounding the dam, including the Norris Forest, as an integrated unit combining watershed protection, timber production, and forest recreation. A tree nursery was located just below the dam, to be used for experiments with different tree species. Its location ensures that visitors will experience the tree nursery—by now, a series of orchards—together with the dam and the powerhouse, tying the entire regional project together.

The vicinity of Norris Dam also provided the model for the TVA's visitor and recreation facilities, demonstrating that individual and public aspirations can be harmonized. Even as construction was underway, the landscape architects reimagined the site as a visitor sequence. The production line for aggregate, for example, included two enormous towers with a cable strung between them. Once the towers were removed, the places where they stood were finished to create overlooks over the dam. The quarry, the source of aggregate for the dam, was blasted down to create a boat dock in what was once Cove Creek. Transforming "sub-marginal" land into locations for recreation gave these tracts new life, turning abandoned property into a public resource.

To the east of the dam, the TVA created the segregated Norris Dam Park. The buildings in the park, built with the labor of several Civilian Conservation Corps camps stationed at Norris, include a lodge, a cabin, and other visitor facilities. These buildings, like the Norris Houses, were finished in "regional" materials, connecting the new environment with Appalachia and its white (not its Indigenous) heritage. The park was transferred to the Tennessee Park Commission in 1953, an entity established with the support of the TVA in a demonstration of the agency's long-term investment in infrastructural power.

The Norris Dam State Park also includes an explicit reference to the "last frontier." A grist mill, salvaged from the rising waters of the reservoir, was relocated alongside a creek below the dam. Here, visitors can temporarily inhabit a heritage landscape—reframed by the promise of a technological future.

Norris Lake with the Norris Dam Marina and quarry in the background

Norris Dam from the western overlook

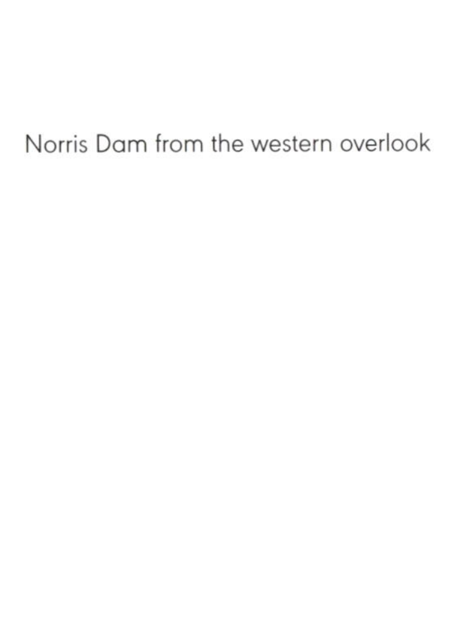

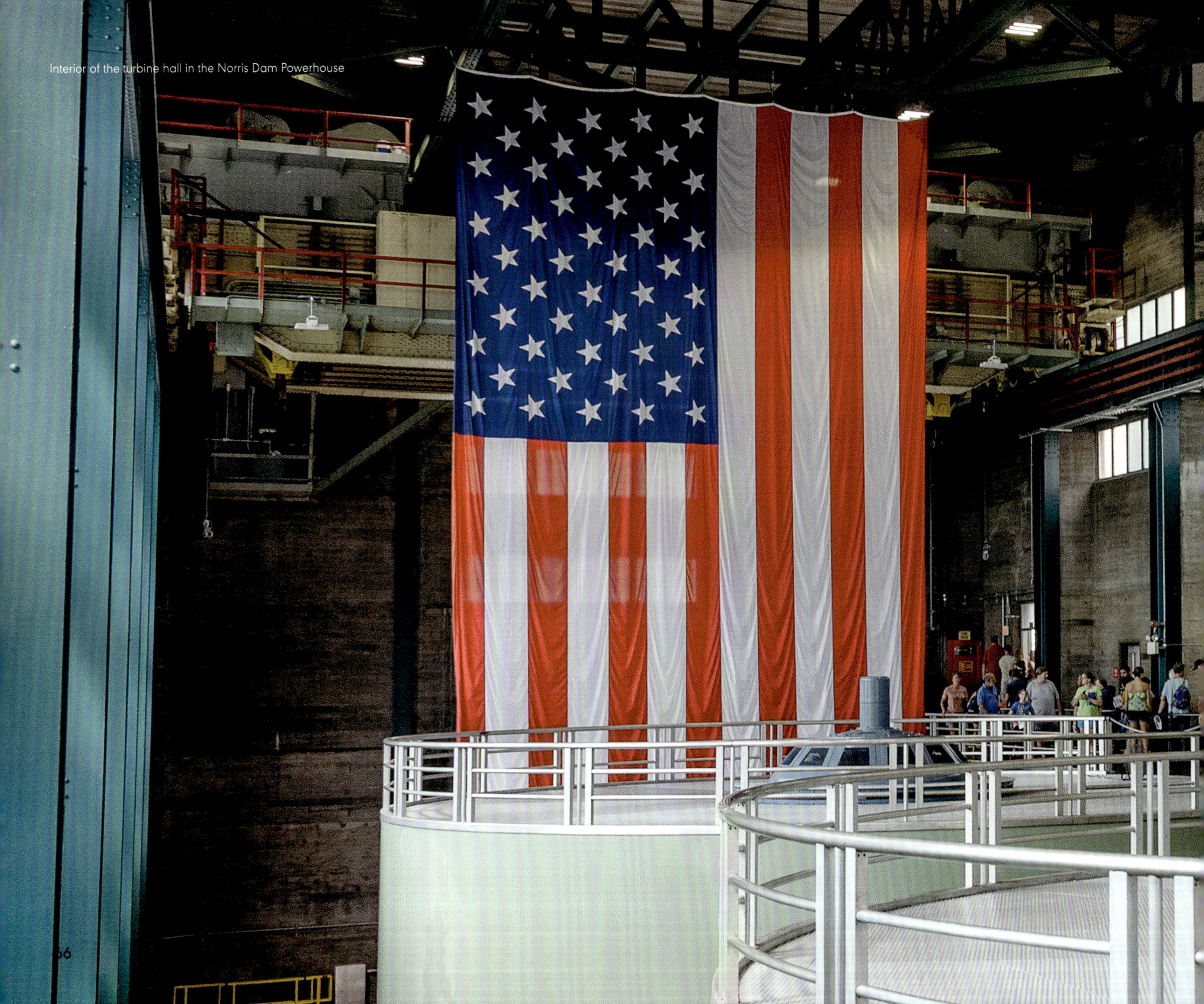

Interior of the turbine hall in the Norris Dam Powerhouse

WORK
THE PROMISE
EACH OTHER
SAFE
Control Room

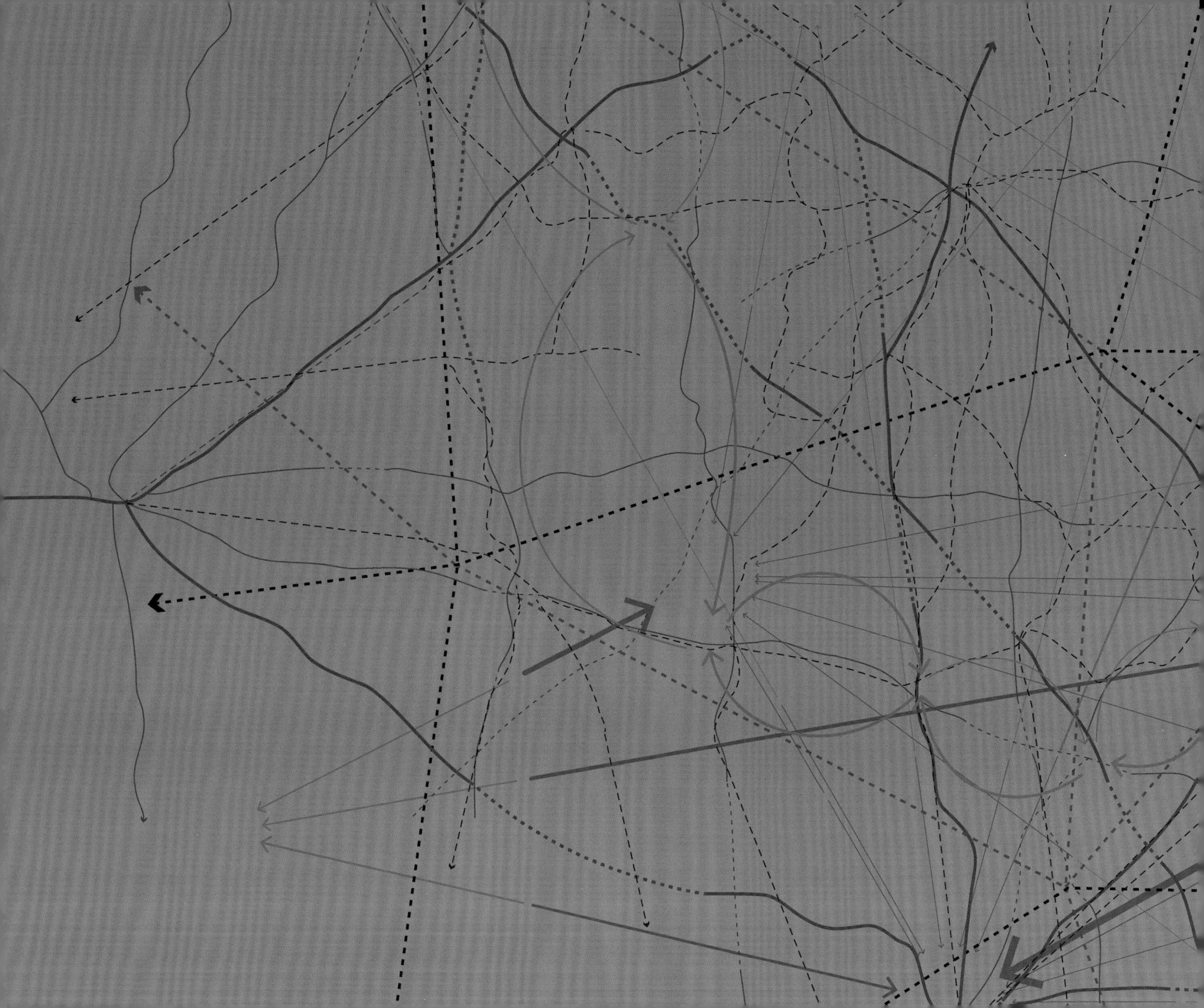

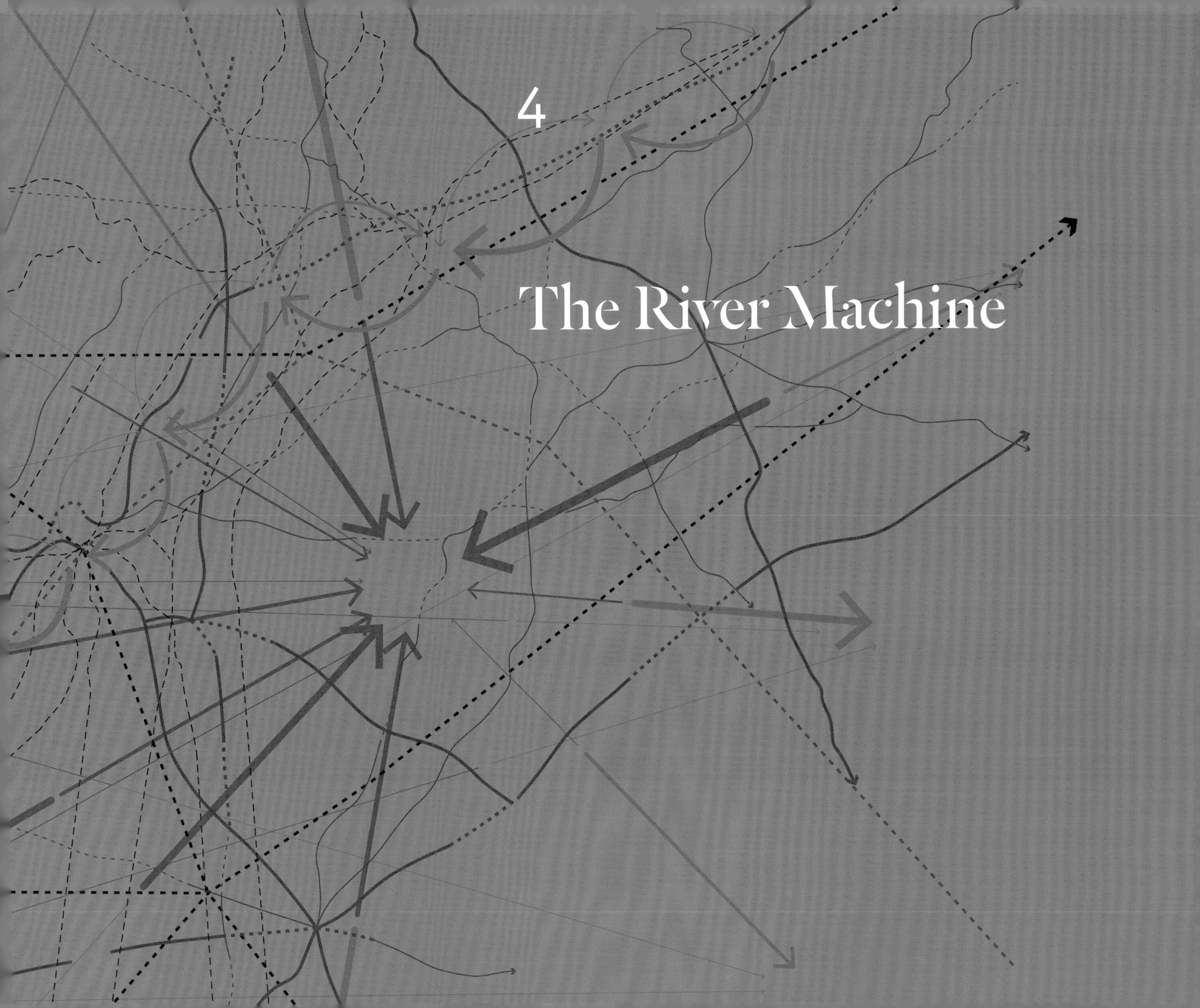

The River Machine

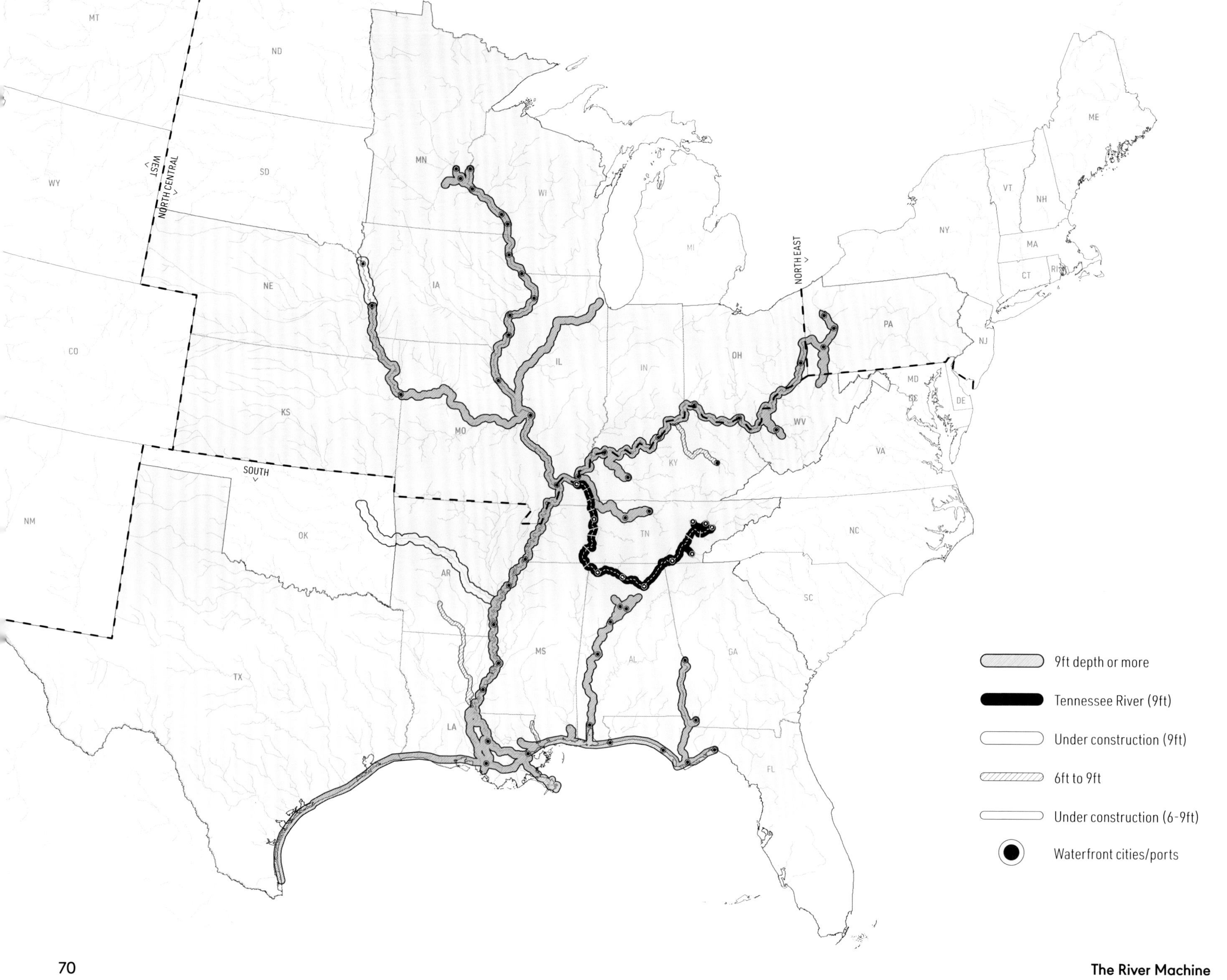

The River Machine

The successful construction of the *river machine* was crucial to the TVA's argument that regional planning was superior to other forms of resource conservation. It was also the easiest machine to justify in public opinion, since the argument for public control of waterways was already widely established by the 1930s. The Tennessee River, moreover, was a prime candidate for projects designed to transform it from a natural phenomenon to a resource for humans. First, the large rainfalls draining from the mountains into the Tennessee caused the river to be erratic, unpredictable, and prone to massive flooding. It carried too much water: specifically, too much *uncontrolled* water. The river regularly caused severe damage in the most populous cities in the valley—Knoxville and Chattanooga. Further, the Tennessee contributed as much as 25 percent to the crest of floods on the lower Ohio, part of the national river navigation route.[55] The TVA estimated that building the river machine could save close to $1,780,000 a year ($33,420,000 in 2024 dollars).[56]

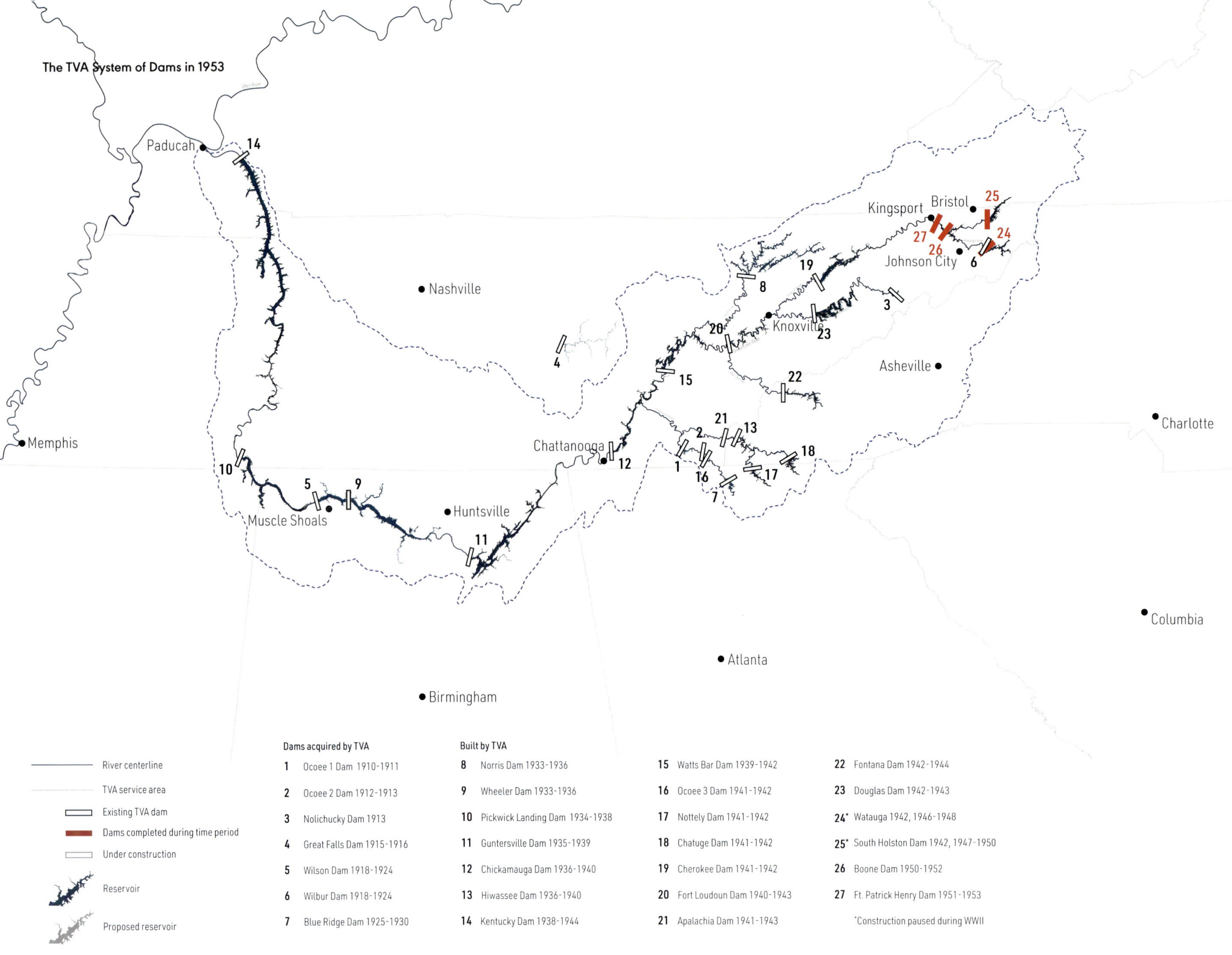

The TVA System of Dams in 1953

Paducah
14
Nashville
Kingsport
Bristol
25
27
26
Johnson City
24
6
19
8
3
Knoxville
20
23
4
Asheville
15
22
Charlotte
21
13
Chattanooga
2
18
12
1
16
17
Memphis
10
7
5
9
Muscle Shoals
Huntsville
11
Columbia
Atlanta
Birmingham

River centerline
TVA service area
Existing TVA dam
Dams completed during time period
Under construction
Reservoir
Proposed reservoir

Dams acquired by TVA
1   Ocoee 1 Dam 1910-1911
2   Ocoee 2 Dam 1912-1913
3   Nolichucky Dam 1913
4   Great Falls Dam 1915-1916
5   Wilson Dam 1918-1924
6   Wilbur Dam 1918-1924
7   Blue Ridge Dam 1925-1930

Built by TVA
8   Norris Dam 1933-1936
9   Wheeler Dam 1933-1936
10 Pickwick Landing Dam 1934-1938
11 Guntersville Dam 1935-1939
12 Chickamauga Dam 1936-1940
13 Hiwassee Dam 1936-1940
14 Kentucky Dam 1938-1944

15 Watts Bar Dam 1939-1942
16 Ocoee 3 Dam 1941-1942
17 Nottely Dam 1941-1942
18 Chatuge Dam 1941-1942
19 Cherokee Dam 1941-1942
20 Fort Loudoun Dam 1940-1943
21 Apalachia Dam 1941-1943

22 Fontana Dam 1942-1944
23 Douglas Dam 1942-1943
24* Watauga 1942, 1946-1948
25* South Holston Dam 1942, 1947-1950
26 Boone Dam 1950-1952
27 Ft. Patrick Henry Dam 1951-1953
*Construction paused during WWII

Boone Dam from the South Fork of the Holston River

Apalachia Dam from the Hiwassee River

Kentucky Dam from the Tennessee River

Chatuge Lake and Chatuge Dam's intake tower

CHATUGE

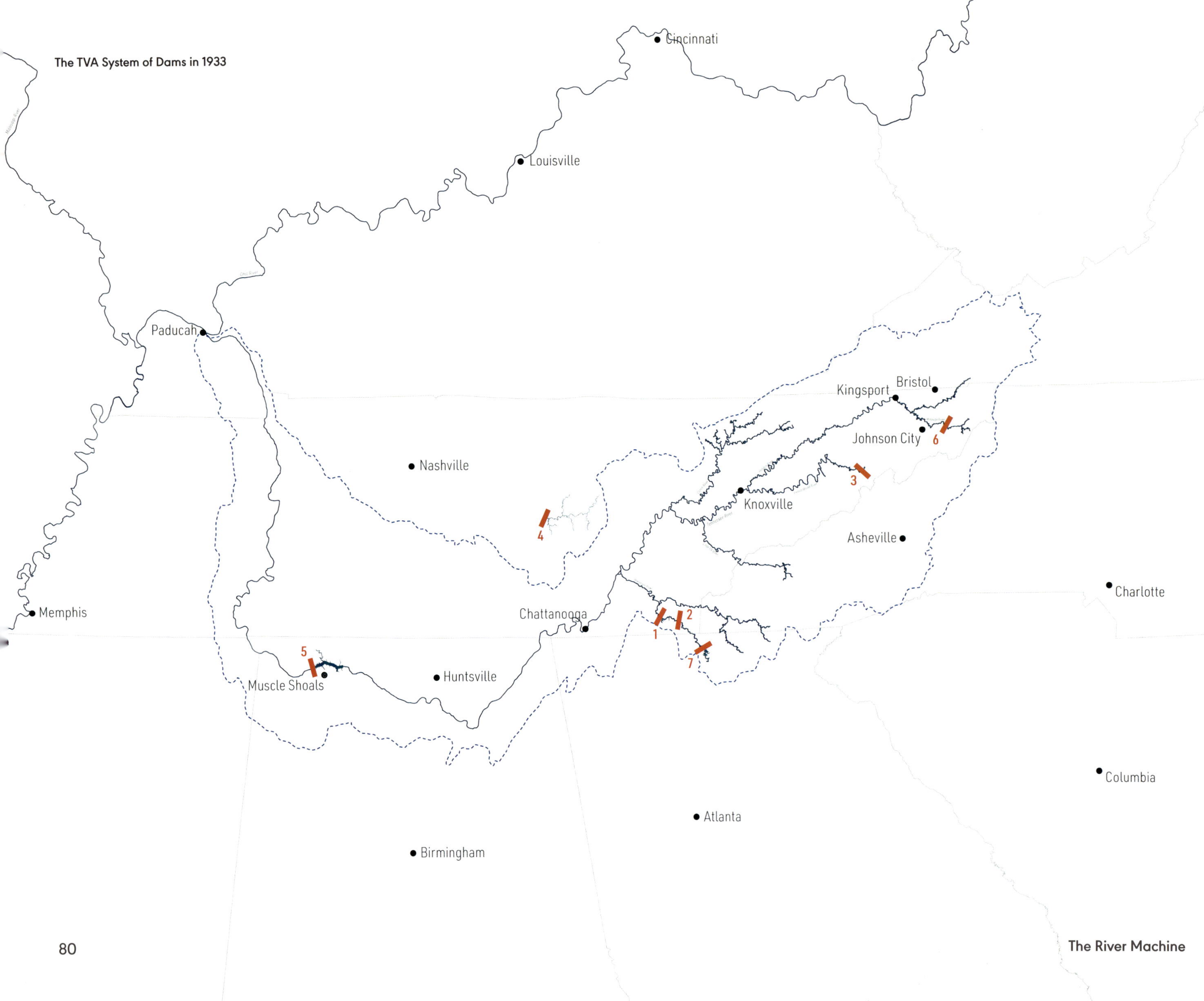

The TVA System of Dams in 1933
Cincinnati
Louisville
Paducah
Bristol
Kingsport
Johnson City
6
Nashville
3
Knoxville
Asheville
4
Charlotte
Memphis
2
Chattanooga
1
7
5
Muscle Shoals
Huntsville
Columbia
Atlanta
Birmingham

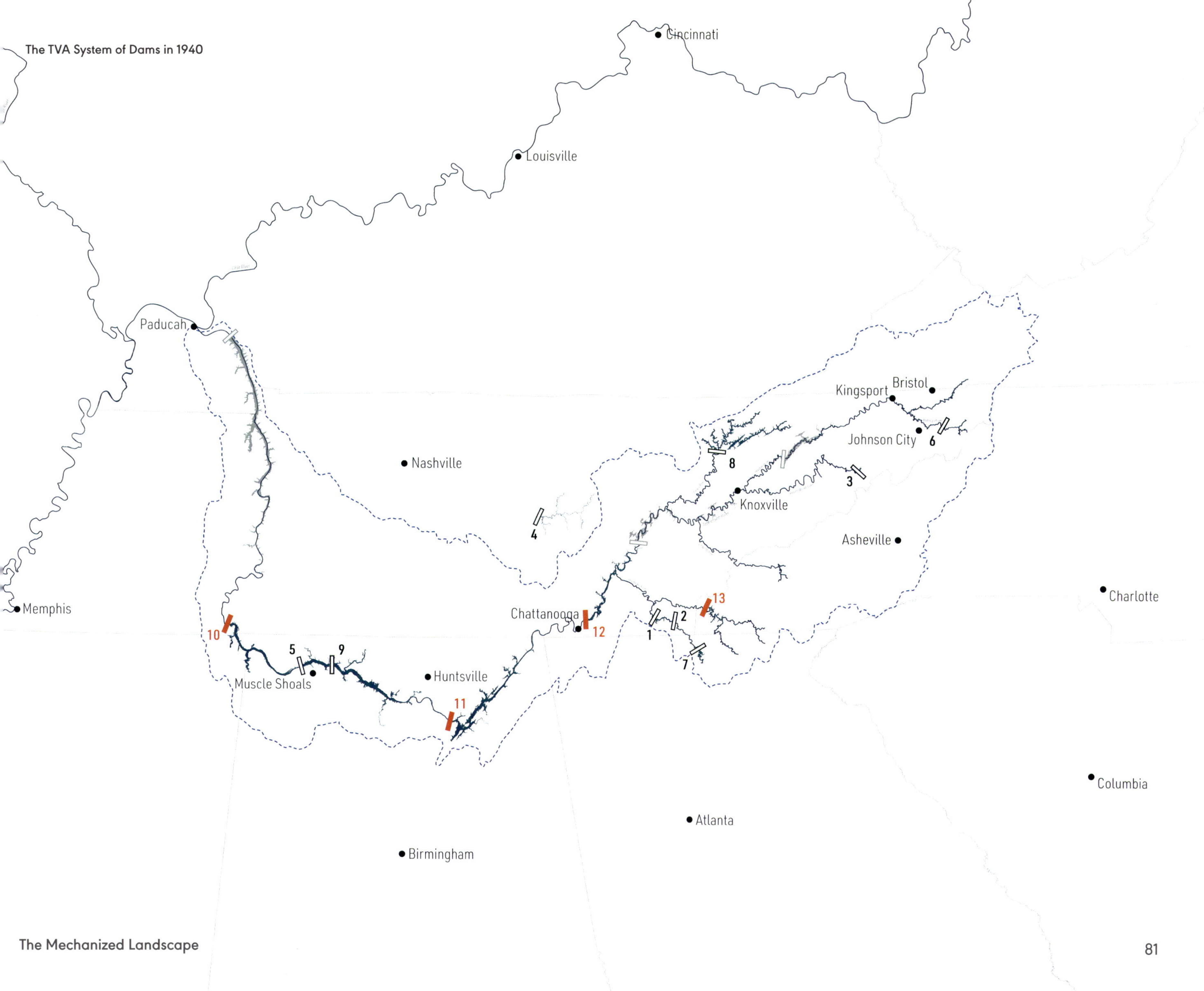
Cincinnati
Louisville
Paducah
Kingsport
Bristol
Johnson City
6
Nashville
8
3
Knoxville
4
Asheville
13
Chattanooga
2
10
1
12
5
9
7
Memphis
Muscle Shoals
Huntsville
11
Charlotte
Columbia
Atlanta
Birmingham

Fontana Lake near Fontana Dam

The untamed Tennessee River was also diffi-
cult to navigate, and different sections required
different types of boats. Thus, trade of commodities was limited in distance along the river, and
local rather than regional.[57] Thomas Jefferson
commented on the most dangerous points, a
seven-mile stretch at Muscle Shoals that could
only be traversed when water levels were high,
and the whirlpool above Chickamauga, which
he describes as a "Sucking-pot, [sic] which takes
in trunks of trees or boats, and throws them out
again half a mile below."[58] Transforming the river
into a reliable navigation channel by assuring
consistent water levels would unlock the potential
of trade and commerce along it. Such a channel
would also connect the Tennessee to the inland
waterway of the United States, which had been
under consideration for comprehensive development from the first decade of the 20th century.[59]

The TVA was not the first to consider taming
the Tennessee River; by 1930, the Army Corps of
Engineers had received approval from Congress
to manage it with dams and locks.[60] The Corps'
plan was limited to navigation and flood control; the TVA added to these goals a regulatory
role, of supporting industry over business. In
his TVA: *Democracy on the March*, Lilienthal
made this objective clear: "What of the river
that flows through the valley—what great things
would happen if its flow could turn the wheels
of new factories?"[61] The TVA plans for the *river
machine* thus deviated dramatically from Arthur
E. Morgan's regional vision of small, scattered
industrial centers.

The TVA committed to creating a nine-foot
channel from Knoxville to the Ohio River in
Paducah, Kentucky, dredging the river when necessary. From there, it is only 60 river miles further
to the Mississippi River, leading down to the Gulf
of Mexico. Work on this channel was slow but
steady, and it was mostly completed by the end
of WWII. The Army Corps of Engineers installed

Industrial port along the French Broad River in Asbury, Tennessee

Cooling towers of a chemical manufacturing plant in Charleston, Tennessee

Industry and Trade on the Tennessee River before 1933
Freight transport on the uncontrolled Tennessee River
was fragmented and costly before the TVA created the
river machine.

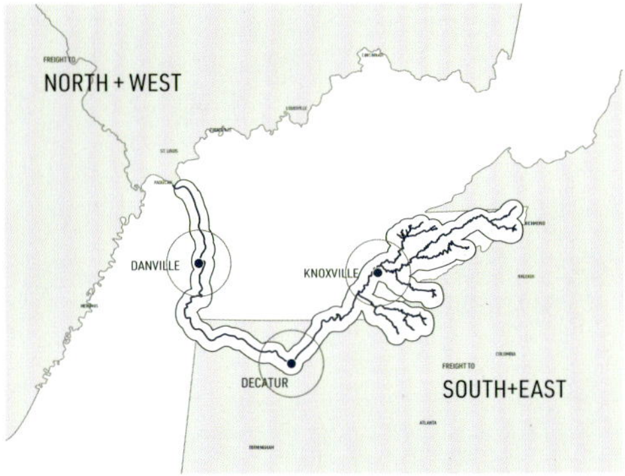

MAJOR PORTS
INBOUND + OUTBOUND RAIL FREIGHT BY REGION [1928]
(thousands of tons)

NORTH + WEST REGION
Cincinnati,Louisville, Evansville, St. Louis, Memphis

SOUTH + EAST REGION
Richmond, Raleigh, Columbia, Atlanta, Birmingham

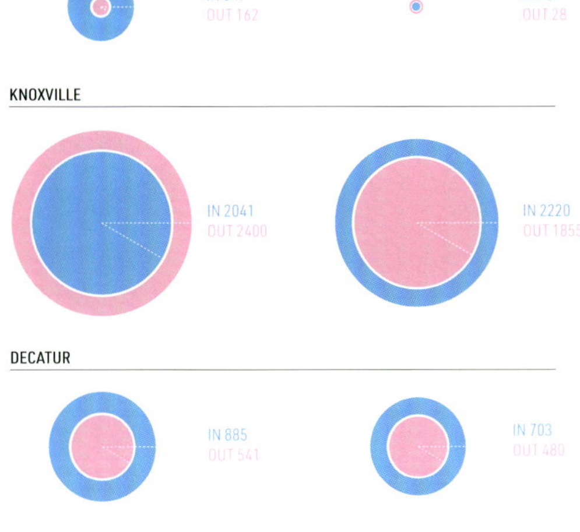

* Flooded by Kentucky Lake

RAIL TONNAGE (thousands of tons)

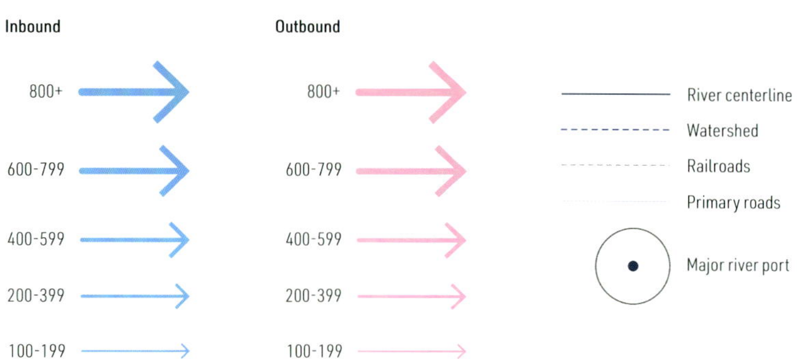

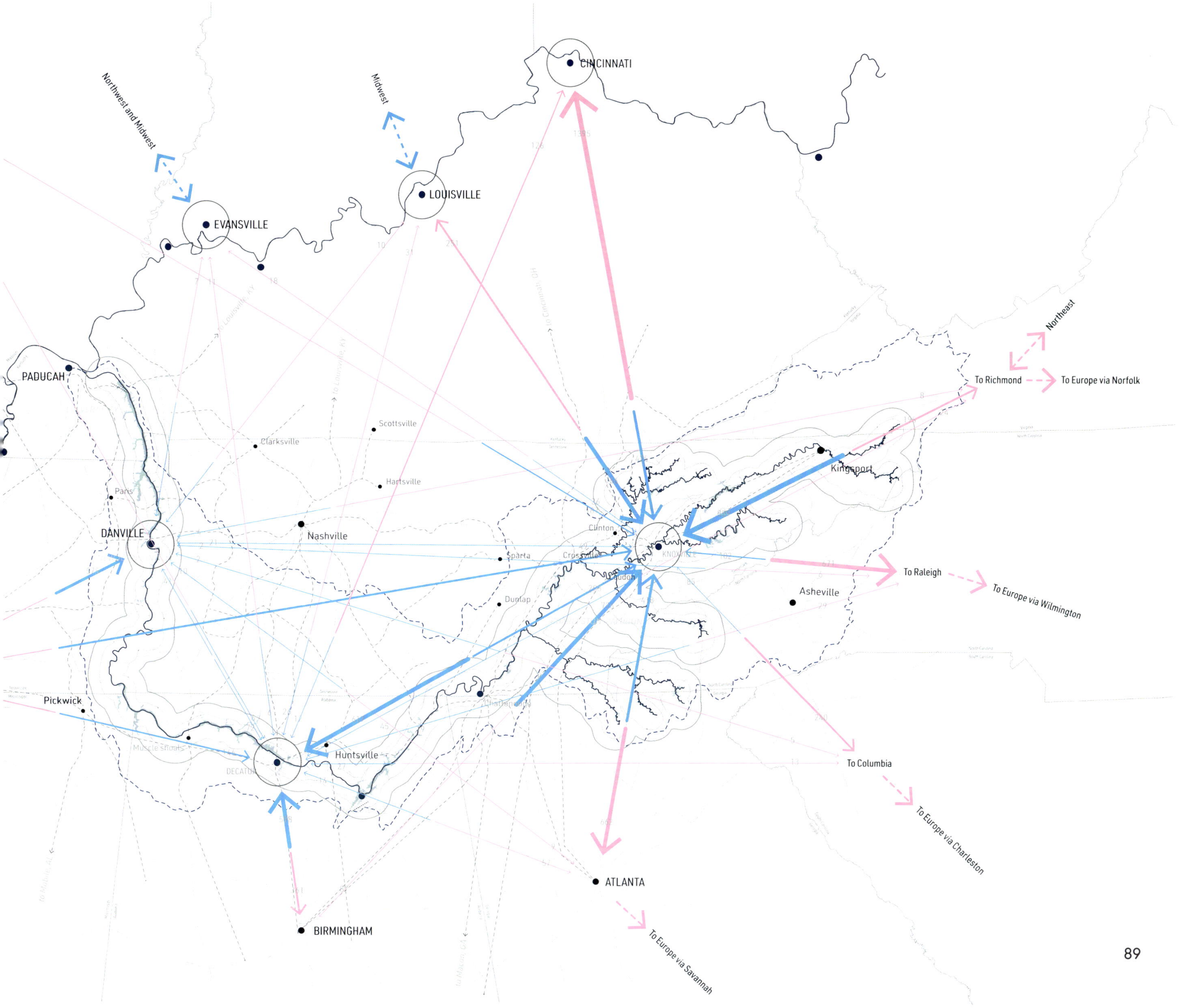

Northwest and Midwest
Midwest
CINCINNATI
LOUISVILLE
EVANSVILLE
Northeast
To Richmond
To Europe via Norfolk
PADUCAH
Scottsville
Clarksville
Hartsville
Kingsport
Paris
DANVILLE
Nashville
Clinton
Sparta
Crossville
Asheville
To Raleigh
To Europe via Wilmington
Dunlap
Loudon
KNOXVILLE
Pickwick
Muscle Shoals
DECATUR
Huntsville
Chattanooga
To Columbia
To Europe via Charleston
BIRMINGHAM
ATLANTA
To Europe via Savannah

Tonnage in 1928 (thousands of tons)

800 +

200-799

50-199

20 -49

1-19

Tonnage in 2021 (thousands of tons)

800 +

200-799

50-199

20 -49

1-19

River centerline

Watershed

Railroad

Primary road

Coal producing areas

Major river port

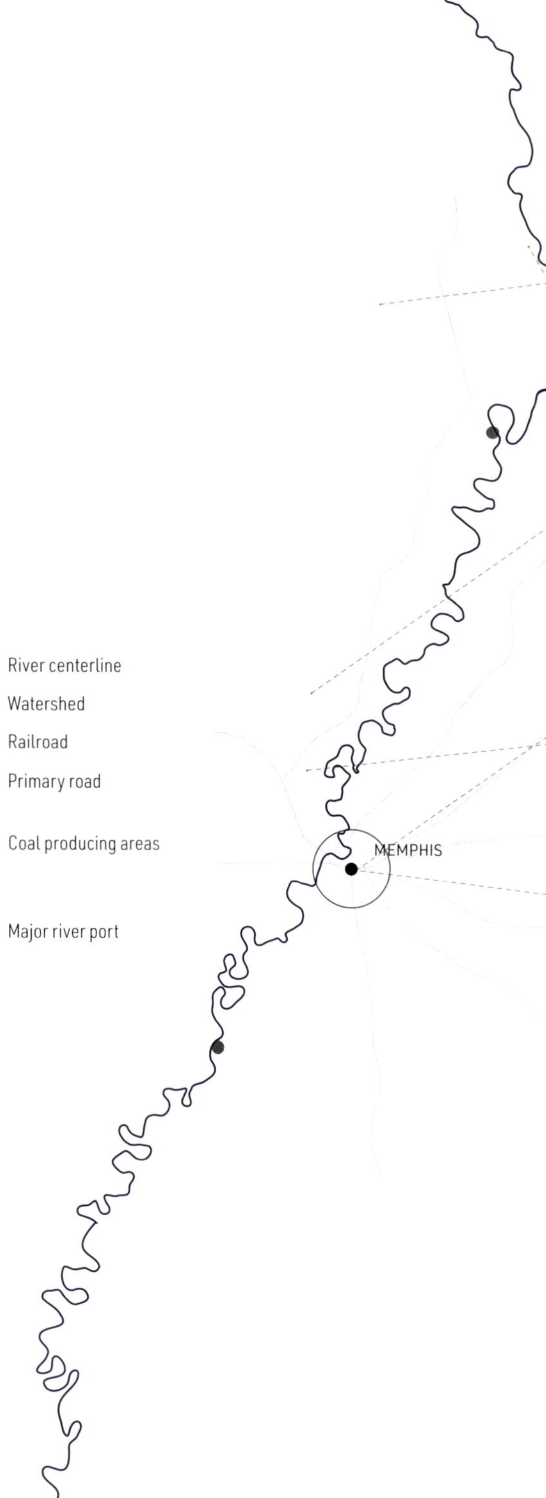

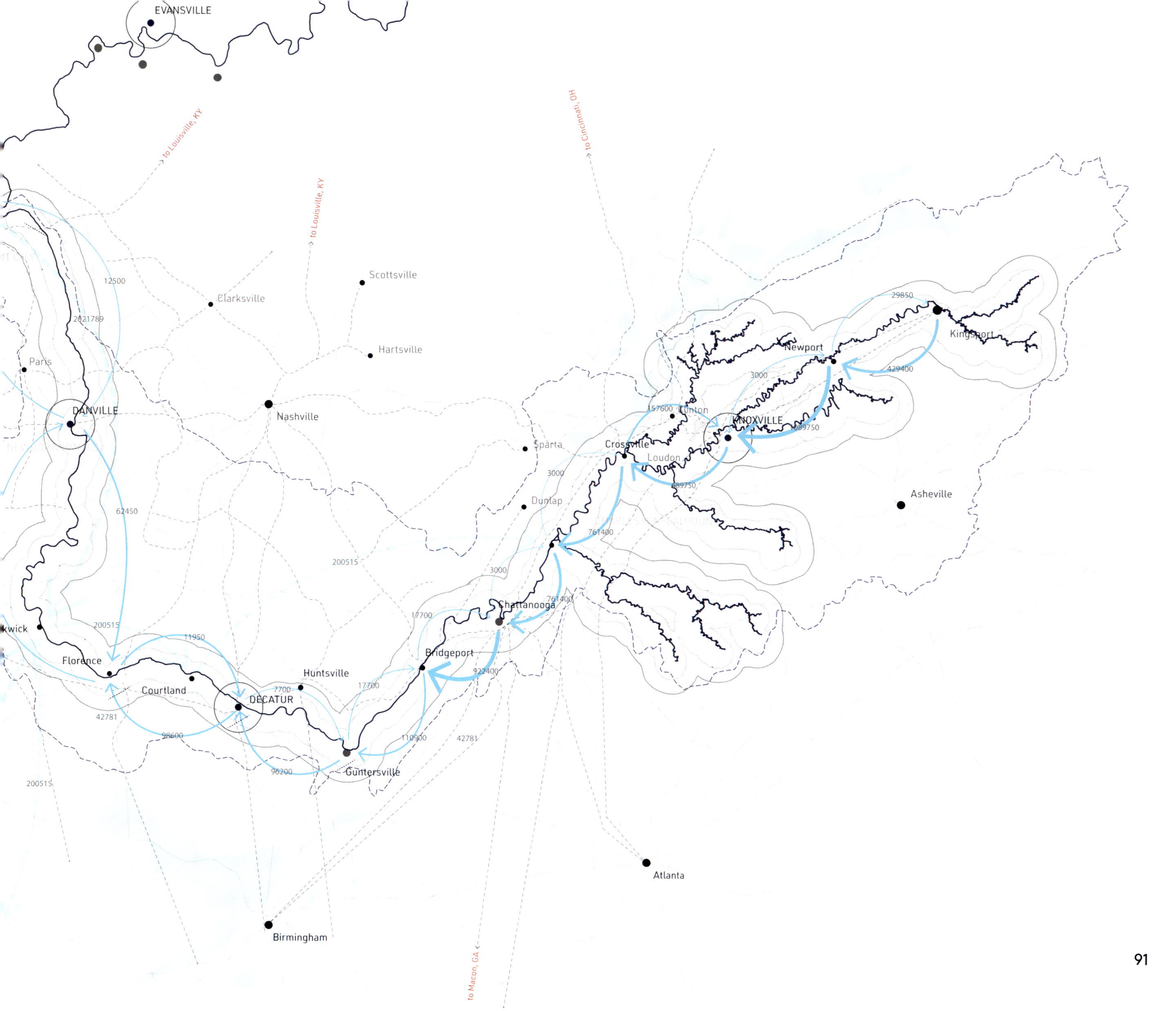

EVANSVILLE
to Louisville, KY
to Louisville, KY
to Cincinnati, OH
Scottsville
12500
Clarksville
2021789
Hartsville
Paris
29850
Kingsport
Newport
DANVILLE
3000
157600 Clinton
Nashville
KNOXVILLE
429400
Sparta
Crossville
Loudon
689750
62450
3000
Asheville
Duntap
689750
761400
200515
3000
Chattanooga
761400
200515
11950
17700
Florence
Bridgeport
922400
Huntsville
Courtland
7700
17700
DECATUR
42781
110900
98600
42781
96200
Guntersville
200515
Atlanta
Birmingham
to Macon, GA

Industrial Freight along the Tennessee River in 1945
The navigation channel created as part of the *river machine* supported trade and industrial development along the Tennessee River and created new transportation hubs.

PRIVATE INVESTMENT IN NEW INDUSTRIAL GROWTH CENTERS

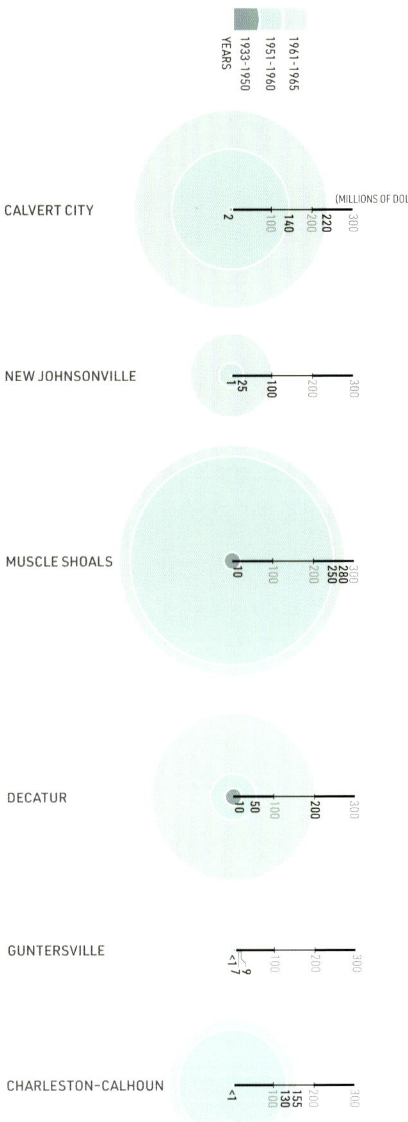

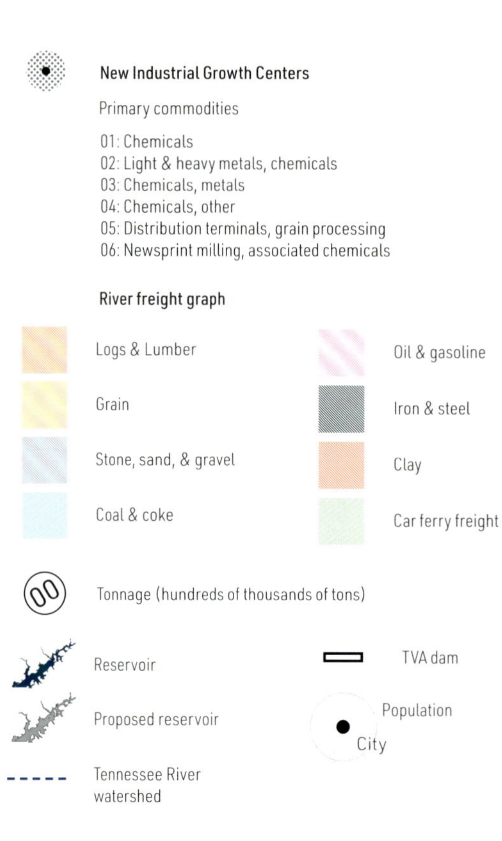

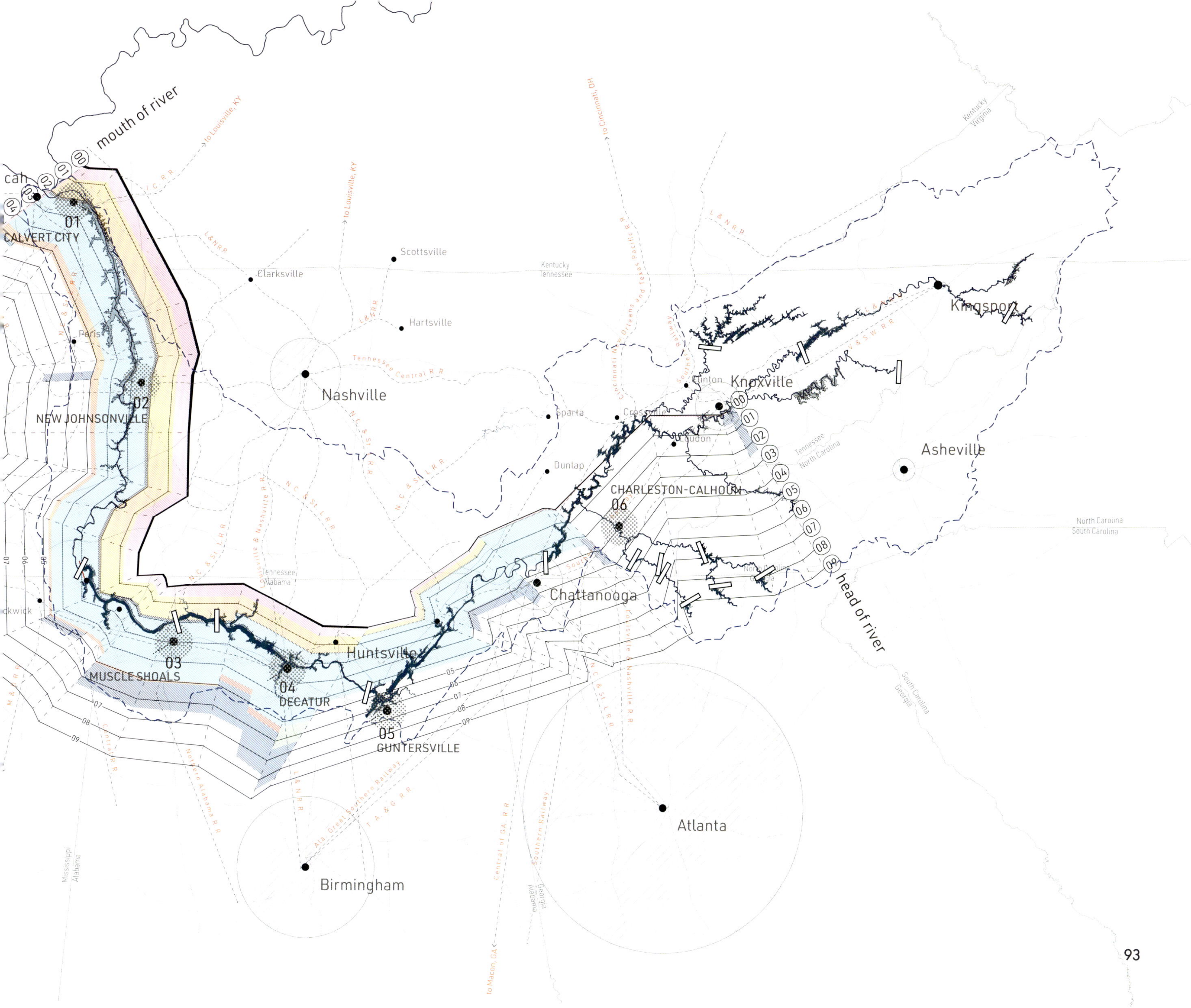

mouth of river
cah
CALVERT CITY
01
Scottsville
Clarksville
Kentucky
Tennessee
Hartsville
Paris
Kingsport
Knoxville
Clinton
Nashville
Sparta
Crossville
Loudon
00
01
02
03
Asheville
Dunlap
04
05
NEW JOHNSONVILLE
02
CHARLESTON-CALHOUN
06
06
07
08
North Carolina
South Carolina
Tennessee
Alabama
Tennessee
North Carolina
09
head of river
Chattanooga
ckwick
Huntsville
05
06
07
03
08
MUSCLE SHOALS
04
09
DECATUR
05
GUNTERSVILLE
Birmingham
Atlanta
Mississippi
Alabama
Georgia
Alabama
Kentucky
Virginia
North Carolina
South Carolina
South Carolina
Georgia
to Louisville, KY
to Louisville, KY
to Cincinnati, OH
to Macon, GA

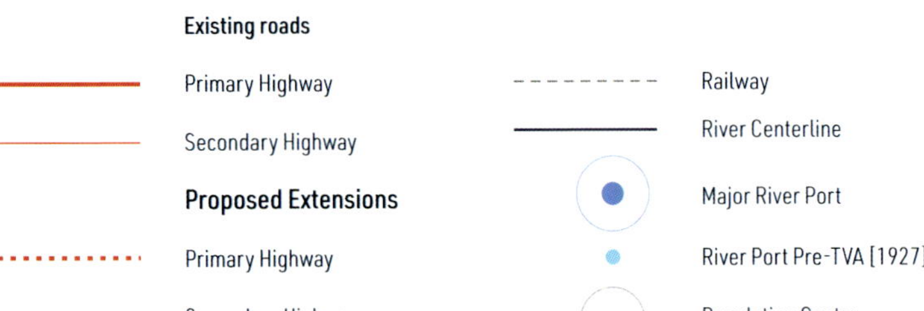

TVA Proposal for a Regional Transportation System in the Tennessee Valley, 1937
The TVA's proposal included adapting the highway network to the existing railroads and the new navigation channel.

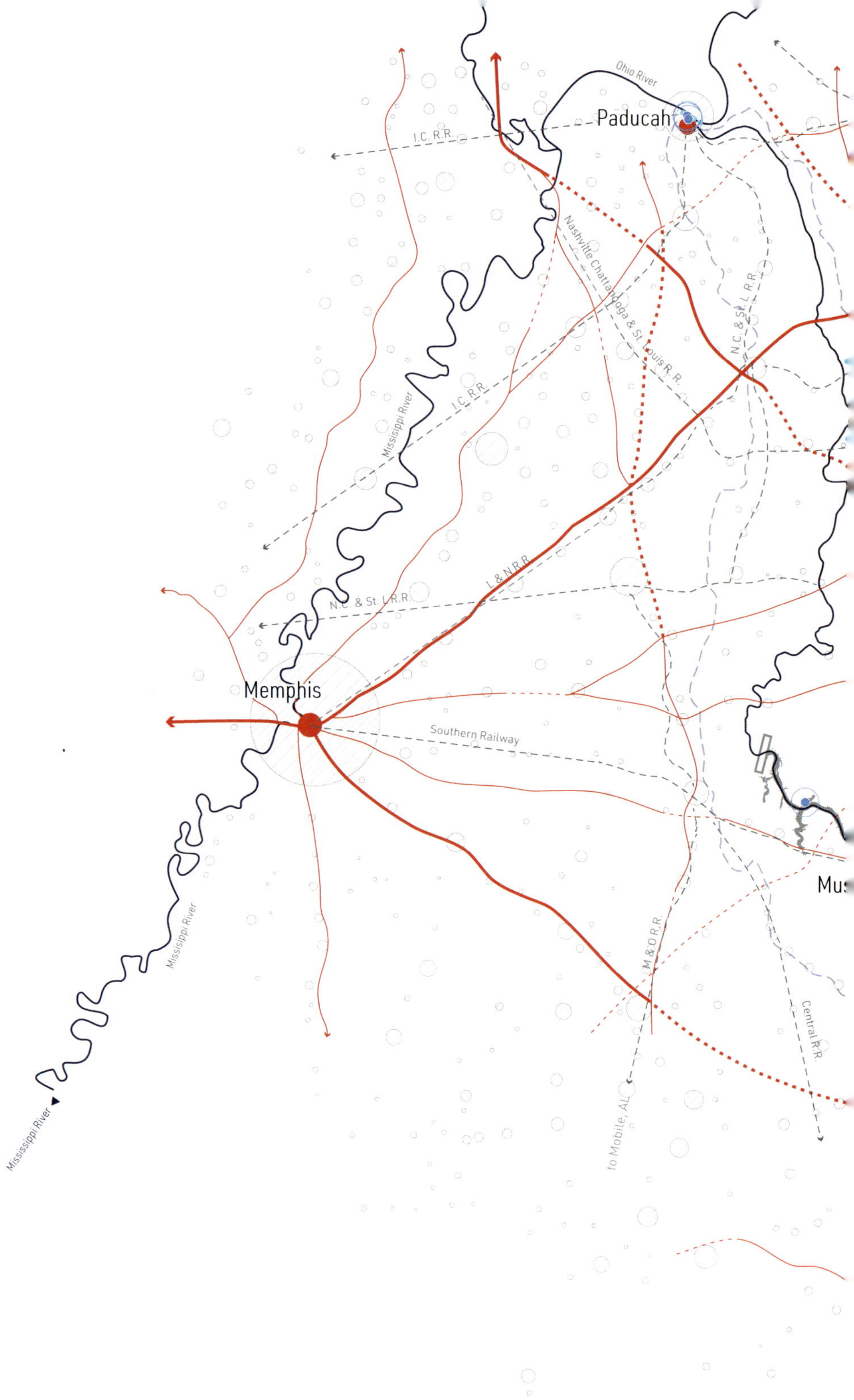

Existing roads

Primary Highway	
Secondary Highway	

Railway

River Centerline

Proposed Extensions

Primary Highway

Secondary Highway

Major River Port

River Port Pre-TVA [1927]

Population Center

to Louisville, KY
to Cincinnati
Scottsville
Clarksville
Kingsport
L & N R.R
L & N R.R
N.C. & St.L.R.R
Hartsville
Nashville
Tennessee Central R.R.
L & N R.R
V & S.W.R.R
Clifty
Knoxville
3
Asheville
N.C. & St.L.R.R.
Pikeville
Cincinnati New Orleans and Texas Pacific R.R.
Tennessee River
Chattanooga
Southern Railway
Southern
Huntsville
N & N R.R.
Louisville & Nashville R.R.
Guntersville
Louisville & Nashville R.R.
L & N R.R
N.C. & St.L.R.R.
Ala. Great Southern Railway
T.A.X G.R.R.
Central of GA R.R
Southern Railway
Atlanta
Birmingham
to Macon, GA

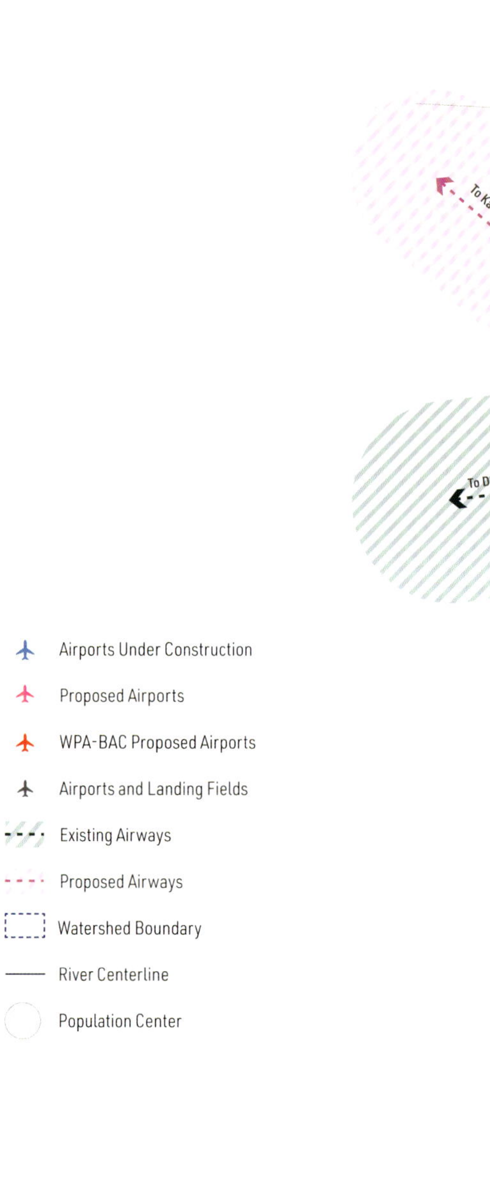

Airports Under Construction

Proposed Airports

WPA-BAC Proposed Airports

Airports and Landing Fields

Existing Airways

Proposed Airways

Watershed Boundary

River Centerline

Population Center

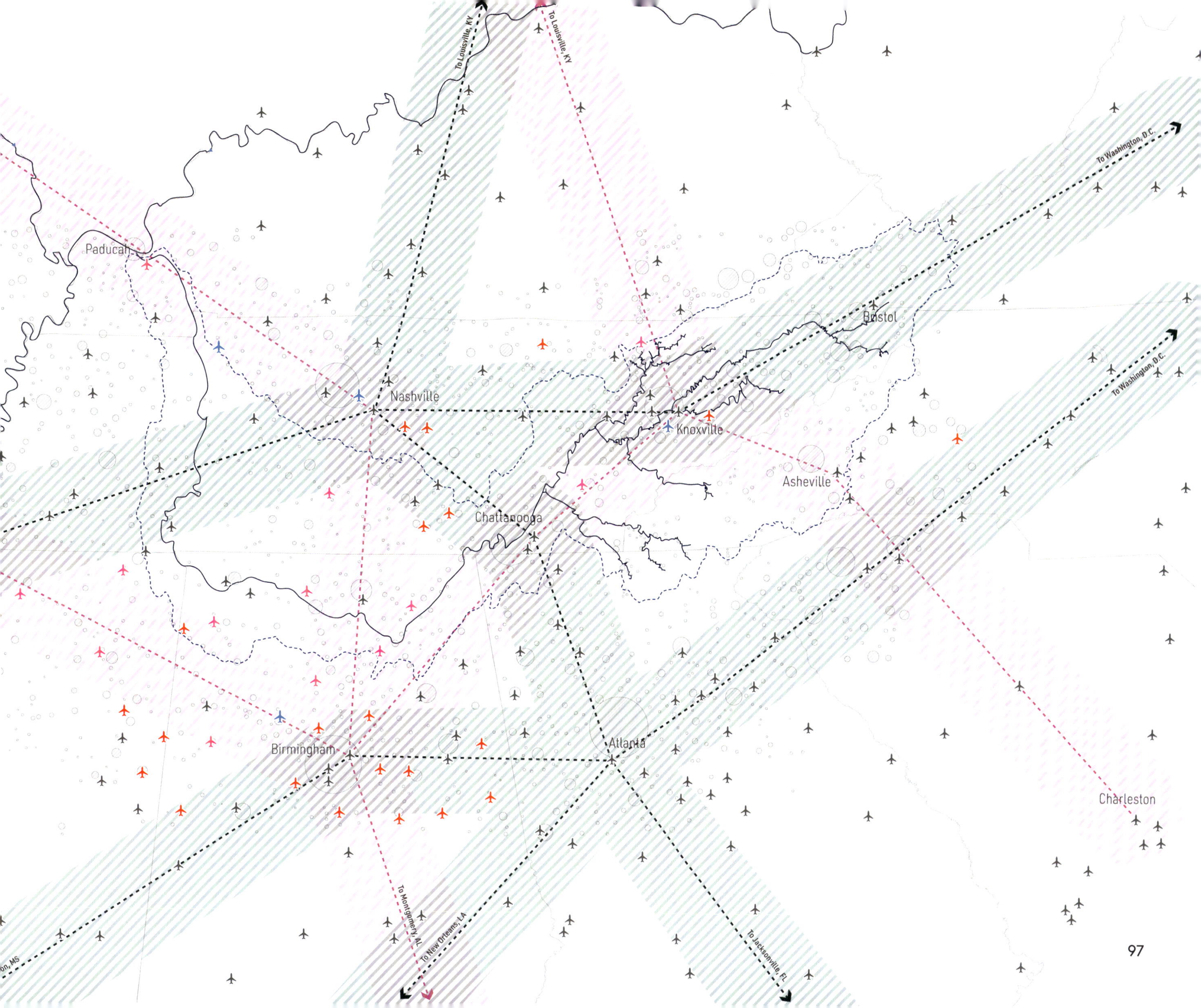

To Louisville, KY
To Louisville, KY
To Washington, D.C.
To Washington, D.C.
Paducah
Bristol
Nashville
Knoxville
Asheville
Chattanooga
Charleston
Birmingham
Atlanta
To Montgomery, AL
To New Orleans, LA
To Jacksonville, FL
on, MS

Upstream view of the lock at Pickwick Dam on the Tennessee River.

Upstream view of the lock at Watts Bar Dam on the Tennessee River.

locks in all the river dams and still operates them today. The TVA also invested in public-use barge terminals at four urban centers along the river—Knoxville and Chattanooga in Tennessee, and Guntersville and Decatur in Alabama. Freight travel along the channel—really, a chain of reservoirs—expanded exponentially after 1945 and supported a wide range of industries, including mills for flour, timber, and paper as well as factories producing chemicals, plastics, fertilizers, refrigeration machinery, and parts for shipbuilding and repairs.

The TVA's actions dramatically altered the economy and landscape of the cities through which the river flowed. The scale of transportation on the river benefited large corporations, and several industries relocated to the Tennessee Valley because of these new conditions. The mechanized river also fostered the development of new industrial centers and nodes in what had been rural locations. At a more personal level, the mobility of goods often led to the mobility of people as well, taking farmers away from their land and small communities and creating the opportunity to pursue middle-class lives in more urban, or at least urbanized, surroundings.

In proposing the navigation channel along the Tennessee River, the TVA revived John Wesley Powell's suggestion to think of the nation as a series of watershed regions. This concept, however, was not widely understood, making the construction of the river machine an intellectual as much as an engineering challenge. For most people, the river was a collection of disconnected features—unstable banks, floods and unpredictable rain, shoals, and depths and shallows. It is unlikely that the people of the western stretch of the Valley would have thought much about the impact of rainfall in Appalachia, let alone about navigation on the Mississippi River. The public needed information in order to conceptualize the river as an integrated whole. As a

unit, the river would appear as "natural" entity, and its transformation into a continuously navigable channel would appear as an equally natural act of enhancing its status.

Thinking of the river as a single unit had the added advantage of bolstering the TVA's claim to managerial responsibility, as Lilienthal explained: "If, however, one admits that a river must be seen as a unit . . . then those who are responsible for developing it must also be a *managerial unit*, with unified responsibility for all parts of the integrated whole undertaking, ranging from the location of the site to considerations of public health."[62]

The TVA began the process of naturalizing the river as a comprehensive unit by representing it as a watershed, in maps and drawings. This process continued after the dams were built. Based on the model of Norris Dam, the TVA architects developed a "language" for the dams that visually articulated the river and its watershed as an interdependent, unified system. They also continued creating public spaces in conjunction with the dams, allowing residents and visitors to enjoy the dams on their own terms. The effect, as Brian Black comments, was to knit the system into its environment, to naturalize the engineering project and to symbolize a mechanized landscape rather than an efficient technical operation.[63]

The River Machine

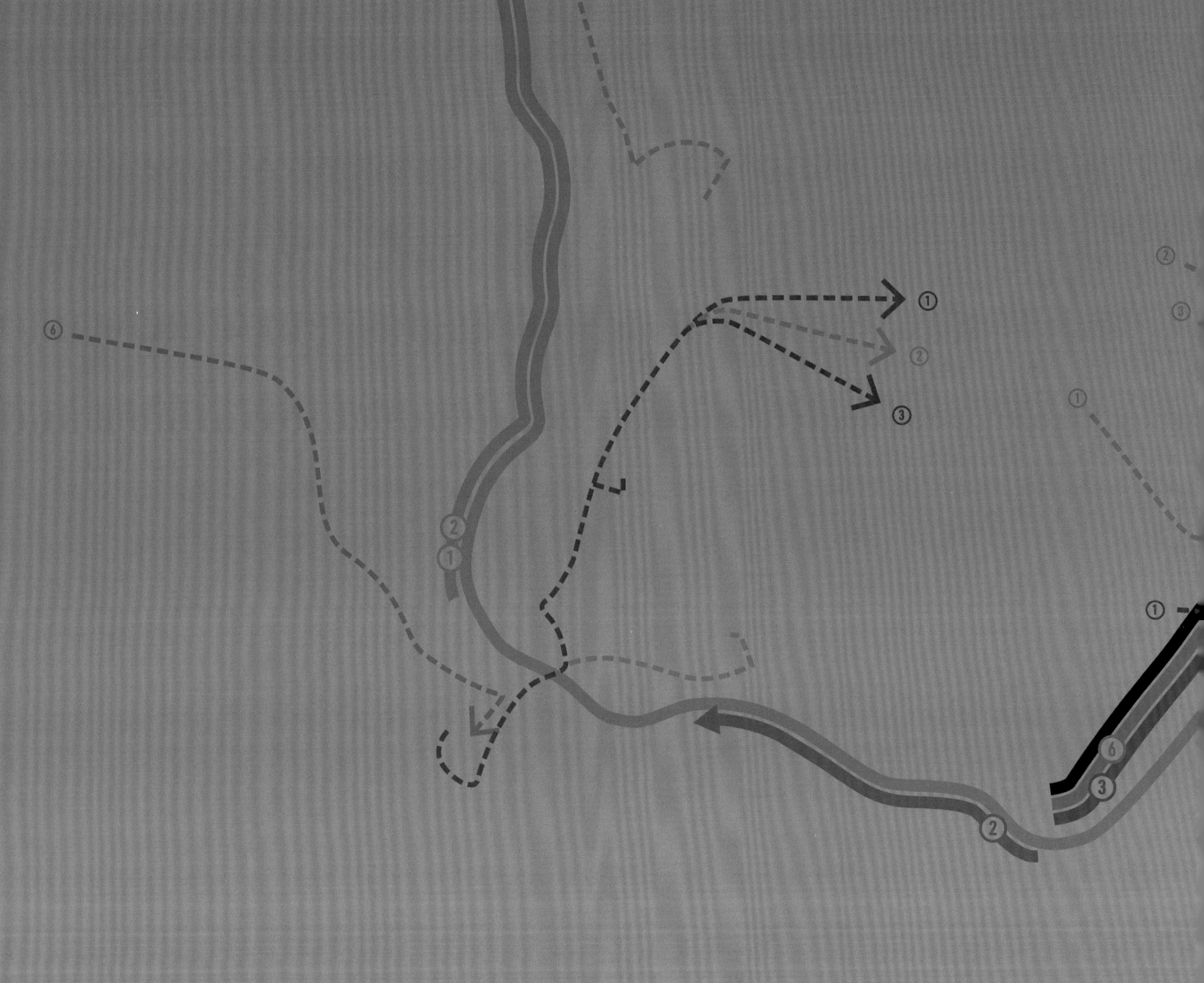

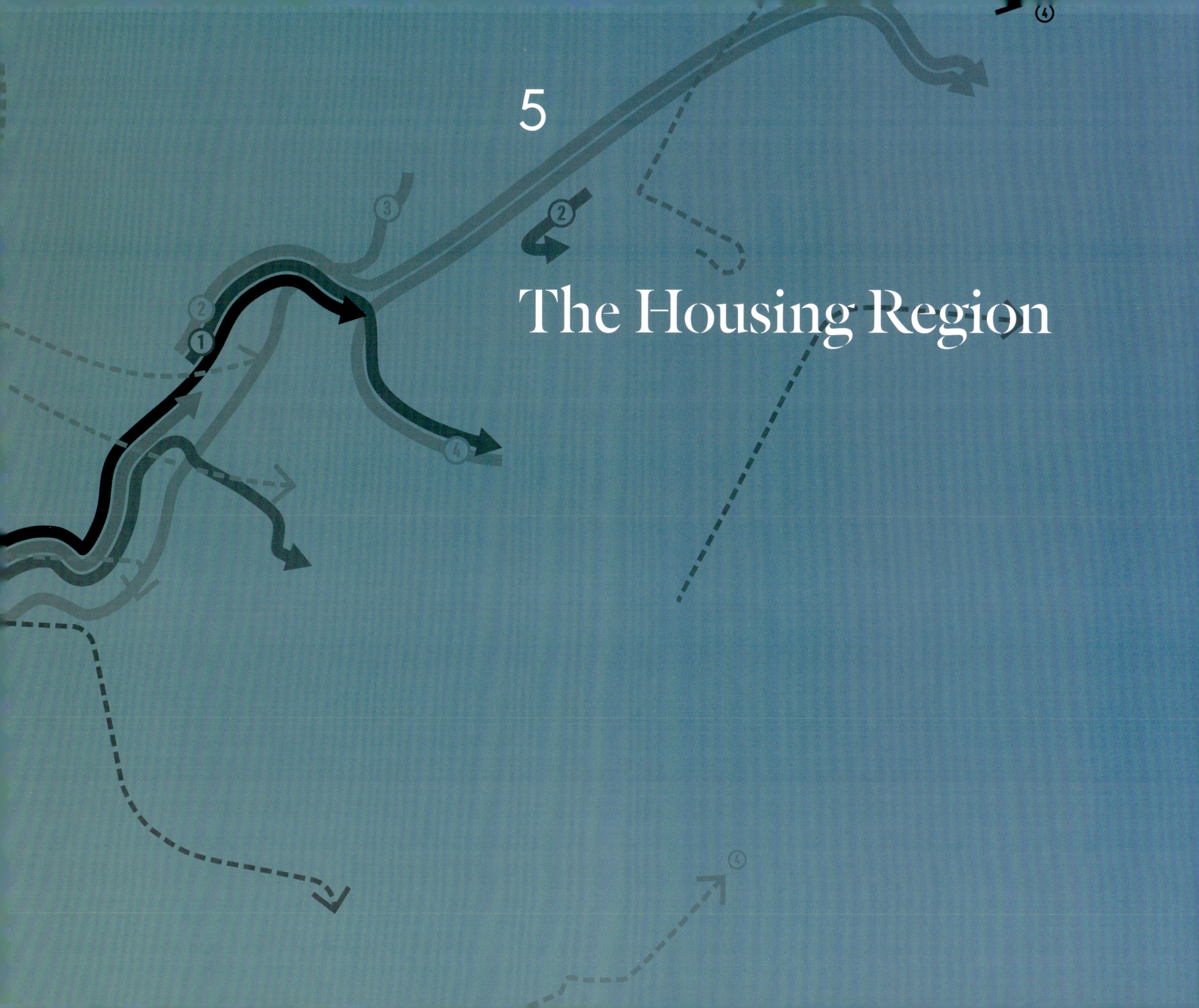

5

The Housing Region

House in Norris, Tennessee

The TVA recycled materials – lumber, sheathing and even nails – used to build employee housing at its construction sites. With time, it also developed a system to reuse buildings without dismantling them; structures were transferred, whole, from one construction site to the next.

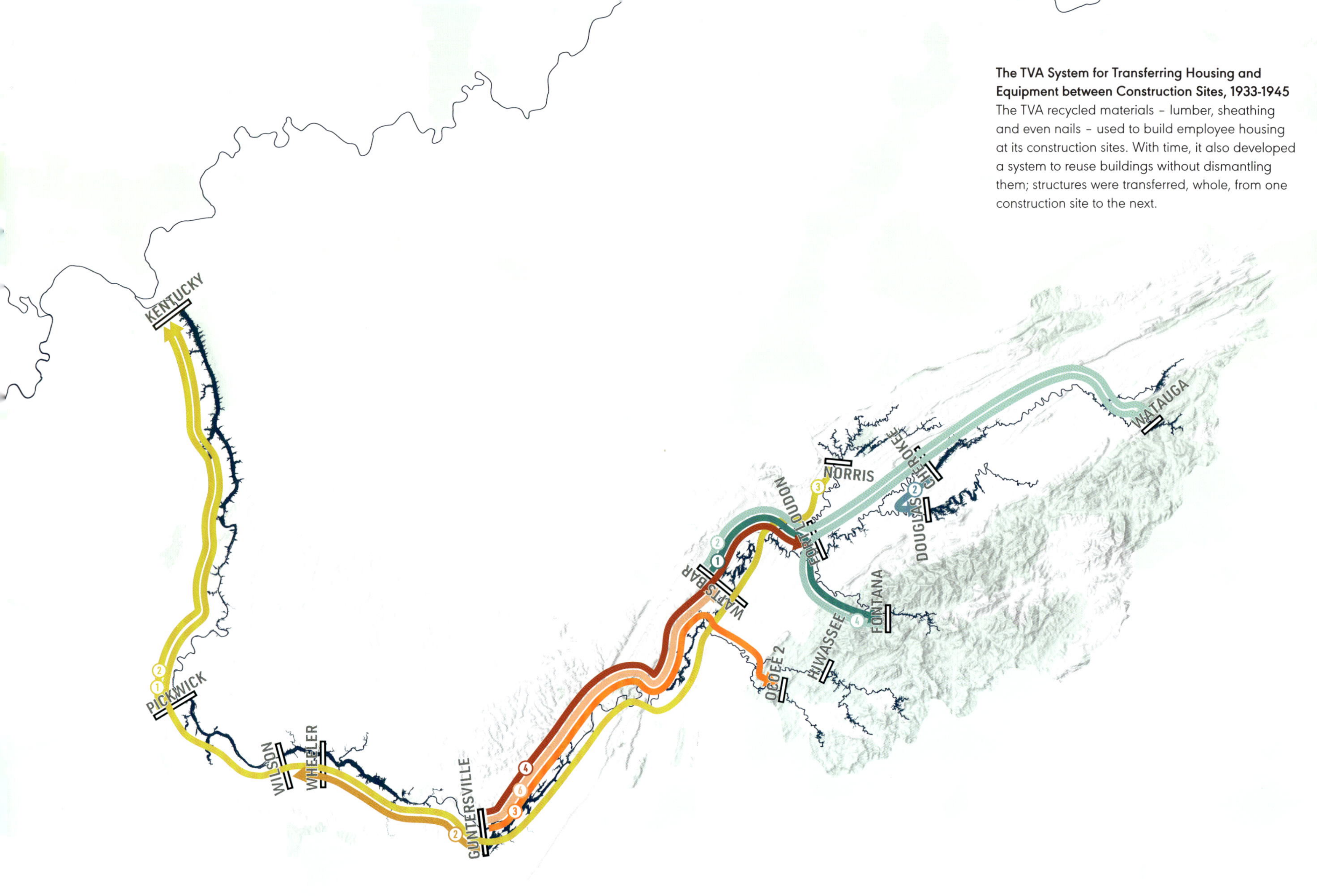

Fontana Dam

The TVA Board of Directors directly hired workers to construct the *river machines* and then assumed the responsibility of providing them with housing. This decision was, in part, a social statement; the Board explained that not providing housing was tantamount to a reduction in pay. The directors explained further that the housing would increase the efficiency of its human resources and would stave off speculation by commercial housing companies in the region.

The TVA built housing camps as part of their effort to create a system of total environments throughout the Valley, modeled after the garden city of Norris, Tennessee. These camps included buildings for the public, open spaces, schools, and recreational facilities. The agency hoped that visitors would see the camps as examples of responsible public planning, but the temporary nature of these sites limited their impact.

The TVA camps offered a range of accommodation, including beds in bunkhouses, single rooms in dormitories, and a variety of single-family house types and duplexes. Special attention, however, was given to the needs of married professionals who, the TVA assumed, would expect the privacy of a single-family home. These houses were intended primarily for engineers, social scientists, and administrators, but cheaper versions were also offered, when possible, to

Norris Dam

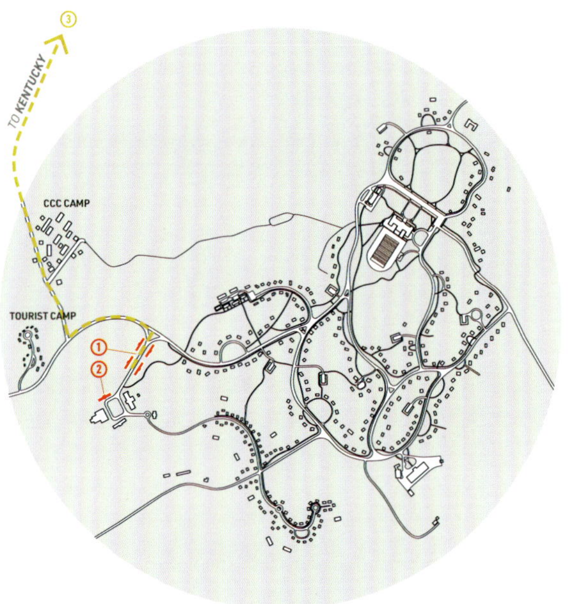

① Group of 4 Male dorms salvaged for materials.

② **1936** Staff dorm destroyed by fire.

③ Central heating plant moved to Kentucky Dam.

Wheeler Dam

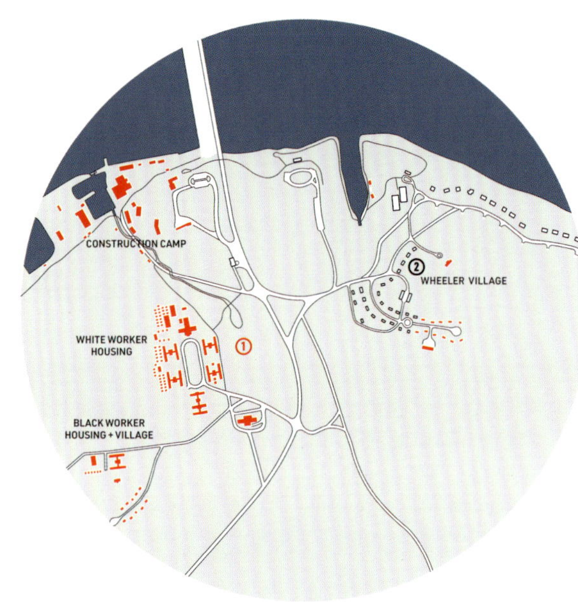

① Dismantled and materials salvaged.

② **1949** Wheeler village leased to state of Alabama. All permanent and semi-permanent houses remain.

Pickwick Dam

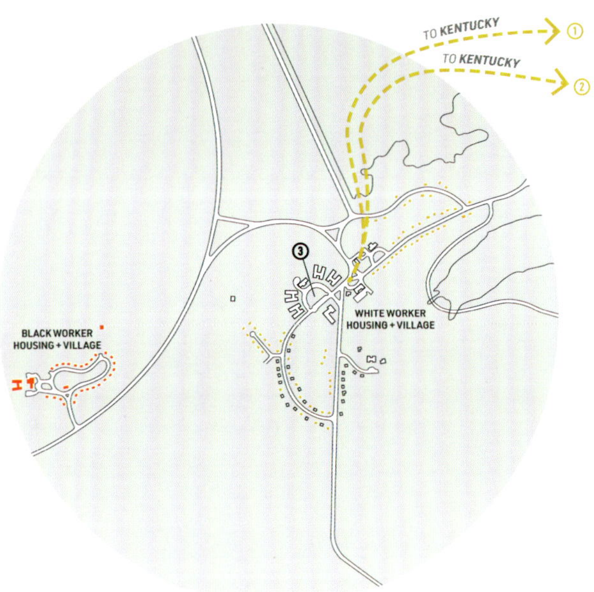

① **1938** 60 temporary houses delivered to Kentucky Dam by barge.

② **1939** 12 temporary houses delivered to Kentucky Dam by barge.

③ **1940** 4 dormitories, community building, and cafeteria leased to National Youth Administration.

Guntersville Dam

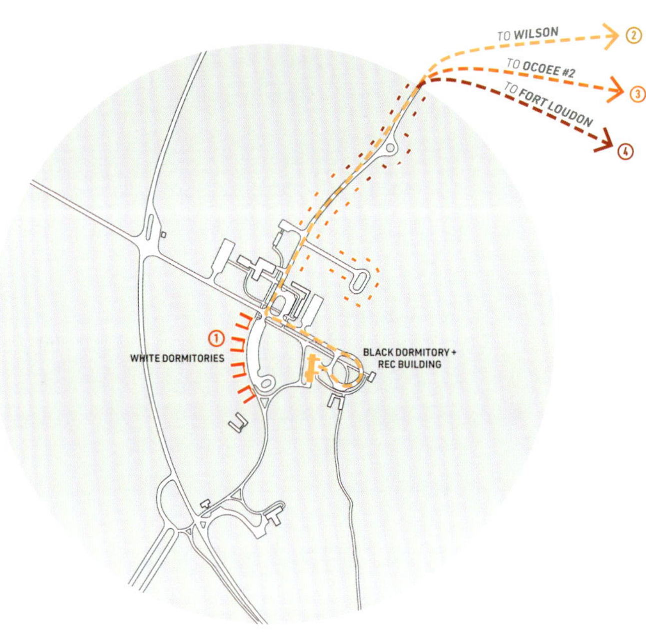

① **1940** 2 dorms demolished.

1941 2 additional dorms demolished.

② **1940** Cafeteria moved to Wilson Dam.

③ **1943** Houses moved to Ocoee #2.

④ **1943** Houses moved to Fort Loudon Dam.

Hiwassee Dam*

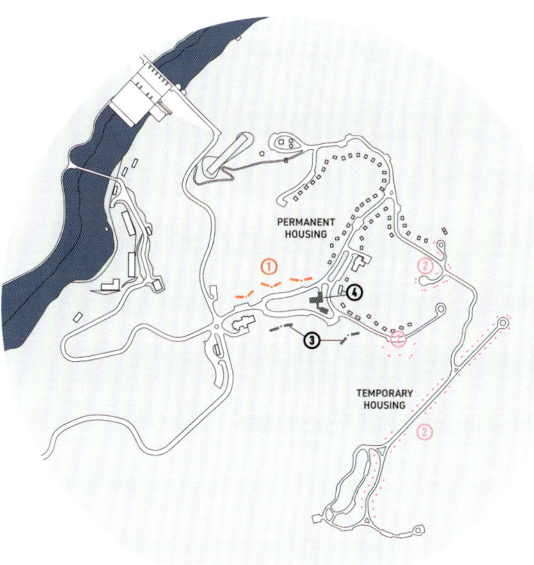

* Hiwassee was occupied twice: First, for the construction of the Dam itself, and later for the construction of the Upper Hiwassee Dams (Apalachia, Chatuge, Nottely, Blue Ridge).

① **1940**
Plumbing, electrical, windows and doors salvaged for use at other TVA sites.

② **1940**
71 of 93 temporary homasote houses sold and sent to other sites.

③ **1940**
Remaining worker dormitory and staff dormitory leased to the Cherokee County board.

④ **1940**
School and community building leased to County Board of Education.

Cherokee Dam

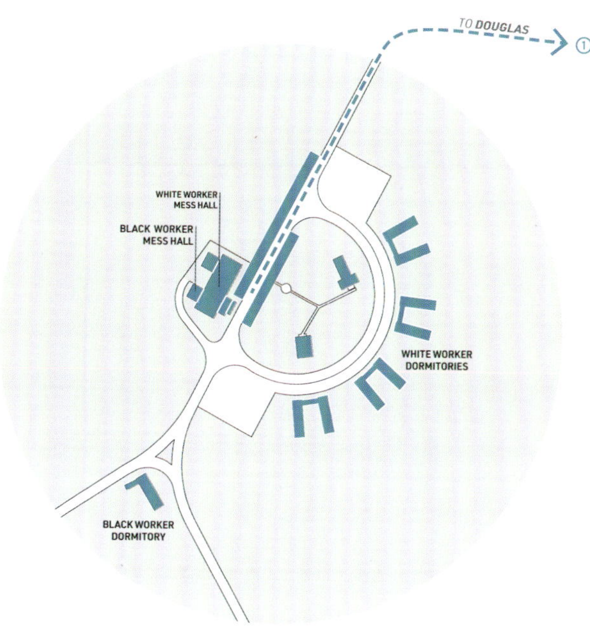

① **1941**
All structures dismantled and reassembled at Douglas Dam.

Watts Bar Dam

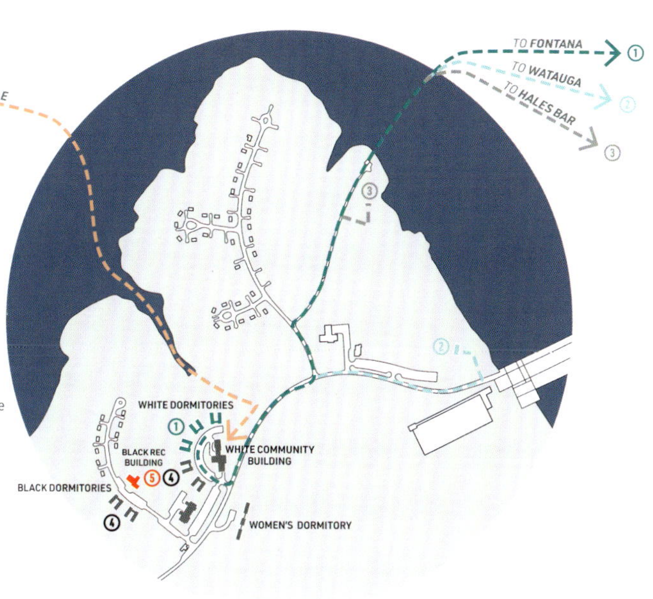

① **1941**
3 prefabricated dormitories moved to Fontana.

② **1941**
Administration building moved to Watauga.

③ **1941**
Filtration plant moved to Hales Bar.

④ **1941**
2 white dormitories, 2 black dormitories, women's dormitory, white community building, hospital, and cafeteria sold at auction.

⑤ **1940**
Black worker recreation building building destroyed by fire.

⑥ **1940**
Equipment from Guntersville used in the construction of the white community building.

Kentucky Dam

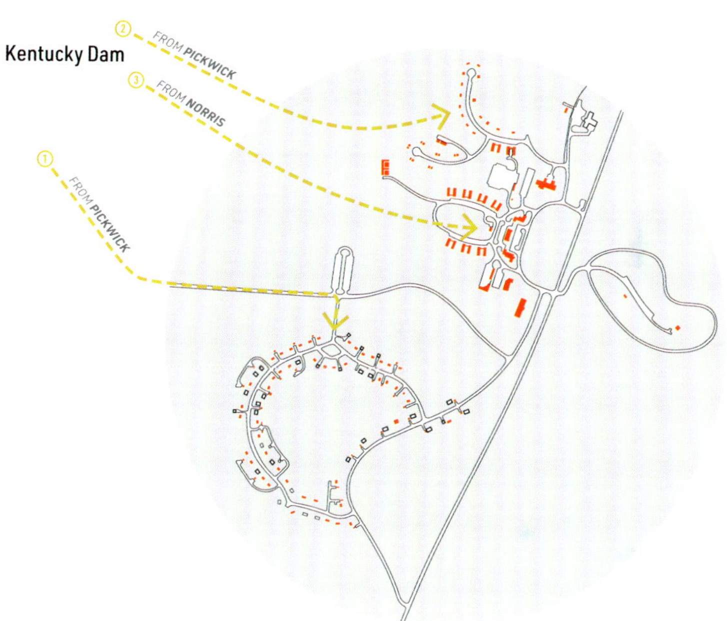

NORRIS (1933-1936)

Type 21

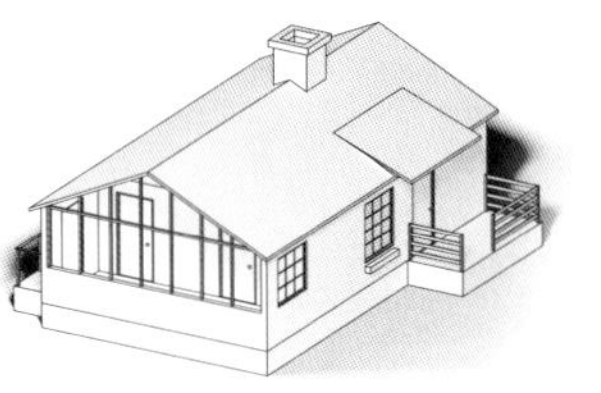

Type 41c

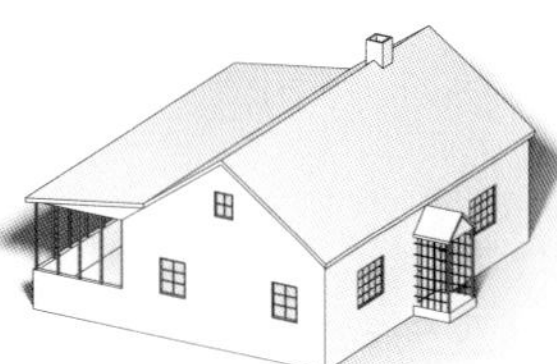

KENTUCKY (1938-1944)

Type 63

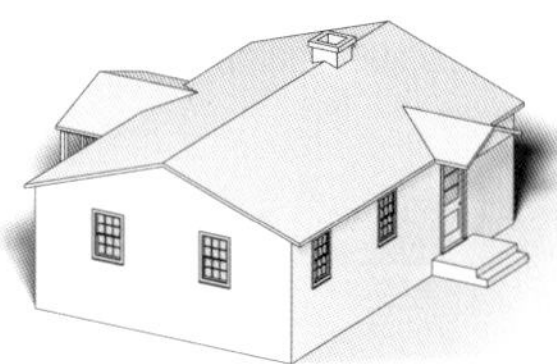

Type A

Type C

Tempoary Duplex

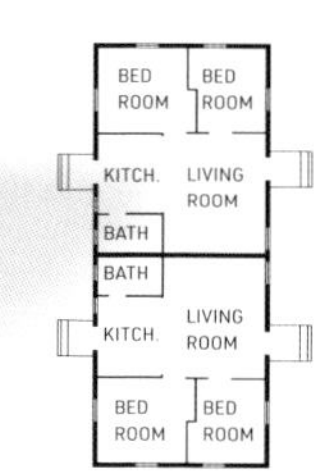

Muscle Shoals

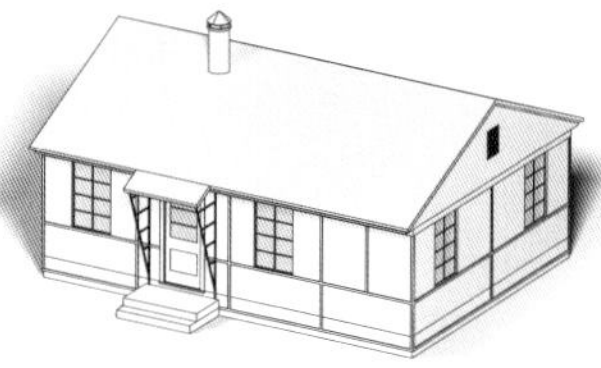

Designs for Houses at TVA Construction Sites, 1933-1945
The TVA architects used several of the house types developed at Norris, Tennessee as the basis for a system of prefabricated houses, including trailer homes.

FONTANA (1942-1944)

Type C

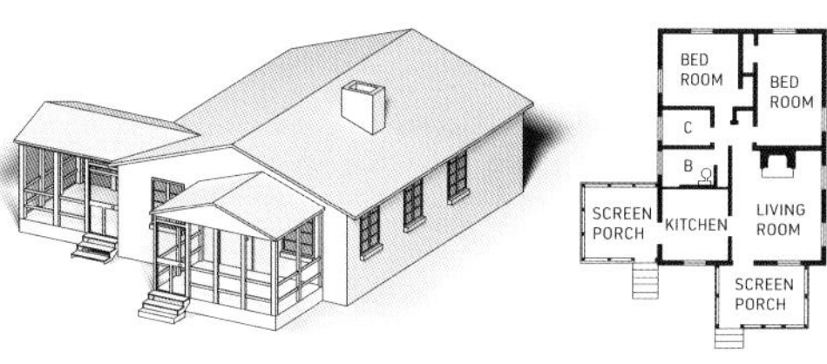

Type D

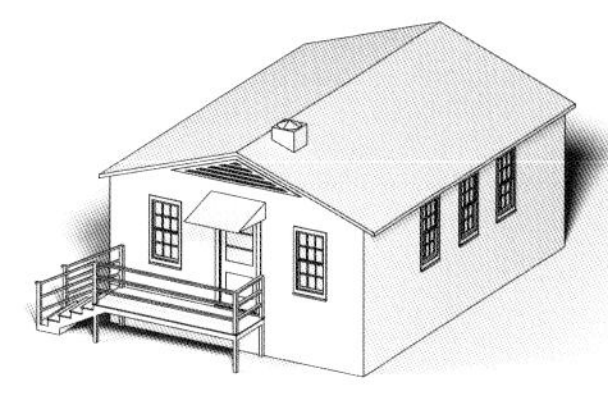
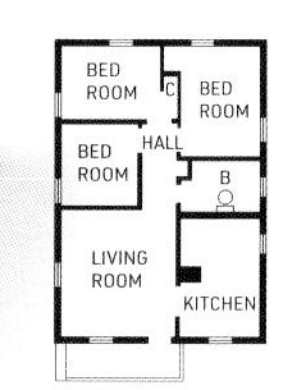

* The Kentucky Type C design
was also used at Fontana.

* Additional low-cost houses were
moved from Pickwick to Kentucky.

Low-Cost Houses

Type K

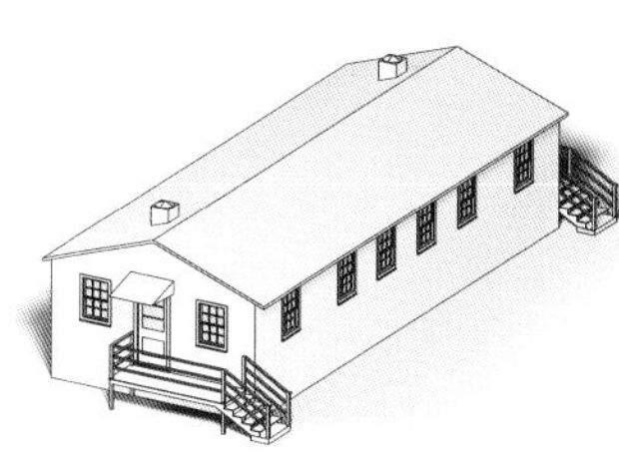
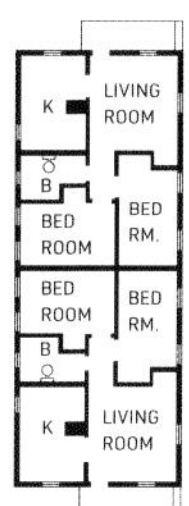

Type L

Movable Houses

Four Cell

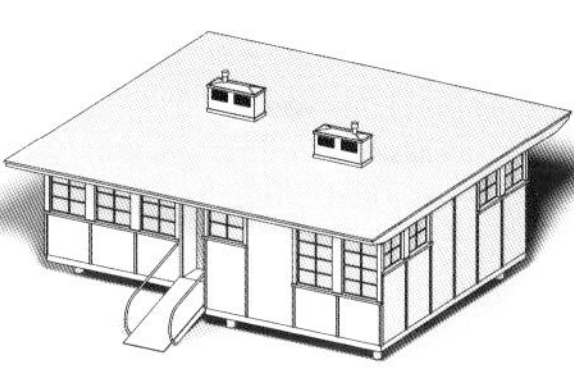
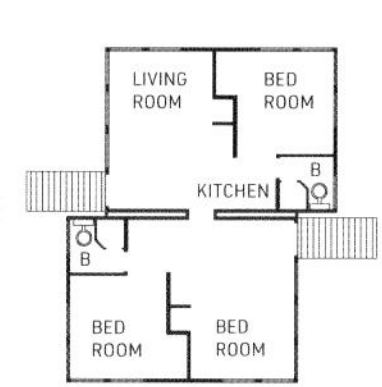

A2

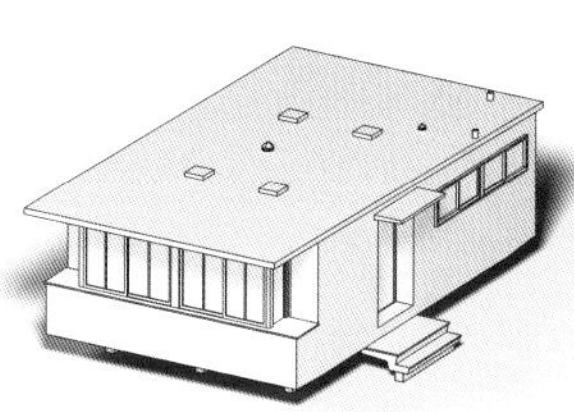
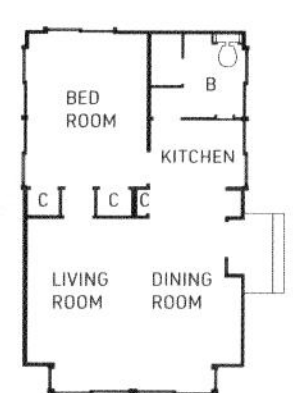

married laborers. These houses were grouped together in "villages," segregated (as were the public buildings) by race. At Norris, the village was also the model garden city; in subsequent camps, the houses and their environment were intended to be temporary.[64]

The single-family homes also played an important role in TVA statecraft. If, as the TVA hoped, Tennessee Valley residents were to model their lives on middle-class professionals, they had to be familiar with "proper" houses. Life in a house embodying middle-class notions of privacy, efficiency, and technology was expected to promote individual growth and create a clear separation between work and family leisure. Houses thus became a cornerstone of the TVA's grassroots efforts.

The TVA began its public persuasion by publishing the drawing of Norris houses, together with meticulous data about their construction.[65] The TVA's statecraft often highlighted in comparison mountain cabins in Appalachia, with their mud floors and without electricity or running water, which were materially inferior to the Norris houses. The message was also directed to farmers living in traditional farmhouses, which were composed of multi-purpose rooms connected to each other without corridors. Adopting the Norris House model, the TVA suggested, was a means to enter into the modern world.

The Norris houses conformed to the TVA's social ideals, but they did not meet its standards of efficiency. Some of the houses cost as much as a house designed by an architect for a specific client. If the agency was to support the social and economic welfare of the people of the region, it would have to develop houses that were both aspirational and affordable. This goal put the TVA in conflict with the regional building industry, which they assumed to be geared toward profit.

Campbell County, Tennessee

Deerfield Resort, Tennessee

The TVA first experimented with balancing their social and economic goals at Norris, Tennessee. The second group of Norris houses resembled the original models but utilized different construction methods and cost less per unit. The TVA then designed a series of houses that were more obviously low-cost. These houses were the agency's first attempt to create temporary houses that met their standards of layout and construction; though temporary, they were eventually refurbished and are still lived in today. The agency published the low-cost house designs as the "TVA's Yardstick for housing," as part of its effort to rein in industry.[66]

The TVA envisioned houses as a vehicle for social mobility, but in the context of the *river machine* it was the houses themselves that became mobile. Searching for efficient methods to supply thousands of employees and their families with houses, the TVA began moving houses from one construction site to another. This project began as an ad hoc solution: houses were cut from their foundations, loaded on barges, and transported down river to their new site. With complete administrative control of the river, however, the TVA was able to turn mobility—or "truckability"—into a new creative project. After experimenting with different prefabrication techniques, the TVA architects identified a sectional approach (a version of modularity) as the most cost-effective.

The TVA first deployed its "truckable" houses at its own construction camps. After the United States joined World War II, the agency also contributed housing to Muscle Shoals, Alabama, and Oak Ridge, Tennessee, where—unknown to the public—factories were enriching uranium as part of the Manhattan Project, and where the TVA worked as an agent (among several others) for the Department of Defense. The TVA continued building dams during the war; the need for hydroelectric power had increased dramatically.

In the early 1940s, the TVA's architects took "truckability" one step further and collaborated with commercial companies to design and produce ready-made trailer homes. These houses were deployed in the Fontana Dam village, located high in the mountains of North Carolina.

The TVA in fact embarked on its most inventive housing experiments when it was already completing its major construction projects, and its need for houses had begun to diminish. Many of the more daring ideas were not deployed in the field. The knowledge produced in partnership with private construction companies was not lost, however; it fed into the local housing economy, with lasting repercussions. Most notably, experimentation and "research" into trailer houses is still used today by Clayton Homes, the largest producer of pre-manufactured homes in the region. Clayton's system is based on the TVA's sectional approach, but it uses current manufacturing techniques to customize its houses to each consumer.[67] The Clayton houses thus stand as physical manifestations of the TVA's infrastructural power.

Blaine, Tennessee

Clayton Built
Clayton Built
Clayton Built
Clayton Built
Clayton Built

6

The Land Machine

Demonstration orchard below Norris Dam

The *land machine*, as a concerted effort to conserve soil and contain erosion in the Tennessee Valley, was intimately tied to the social and economic welfare of the Valley's residents. As the TVA board of directors explained dramatically in 1939:

> If this topsoil is without vegetative cover ... the effect of 6,000 tons of water upon 1,000 tons of topsoil is a simple problem in displacement. The answer is obvious in the abandoned farms, disintegrating homesteads, and in the degrading hand of poverty apparent in an area that is potentially a land of plenty.[68]

The TVA itself had a direct interest in stemming erosion: it sought to minimize the concentration of silt in the newly created reservoirs, which would otherwise impair the operation of the *river* and *power machines*.

The *land machine* had two components: reforestation, and the promotion of modern farming. President Franklin D. Roosevelt was especially interested in reforestation and discussed its role in the TVA project at length.[69] Reforestation was a centralized project undertaken on publicly owned land, much of it purchased as part of New Deal efforts. The TVA foresters, using data prepared by TVA geographers, prepared a program for the entire region. They also trained would-be foresters, offering them the opportunity to learn about preventing and controlling fires, constructing trails, and planting trees and shrubs.

The labor required to execute the forestry plans was provided by Civilian Conservation Corps (CCC) camps stationed in the Tennessee Valley. The CCC, another New Deal agency, hired young, unmarried men who quickly injected their modest wages into the economy. Under the TVA's direction, the CCC operated two tree nurseries and planted millions of trees on public land across the Tennessee Valley.[70]

The nurseries were used as a laboratory for identifying trees with economic value: as timber for construction, for fruit and nut crops, and even as forage crops for wild fowl such as quail.[71] One goal was to offer an economic alternative to Tennessee Valley residents who did not own land suitable for agriculture or dairy farming. After evaluating a range of trees, including a variety of pines, persimmons, and locusts, the TVA foresters promoted the black walnut as the species that offered the best utility.[72]

With centralized reforestation in place, the TVA foresters determined that the project should extend to private land as well. Landowners who chose to participate in the program could enter into an agreement with the TVA: the Authority would provide trees, and the farmer would maintain and protect them for five years.

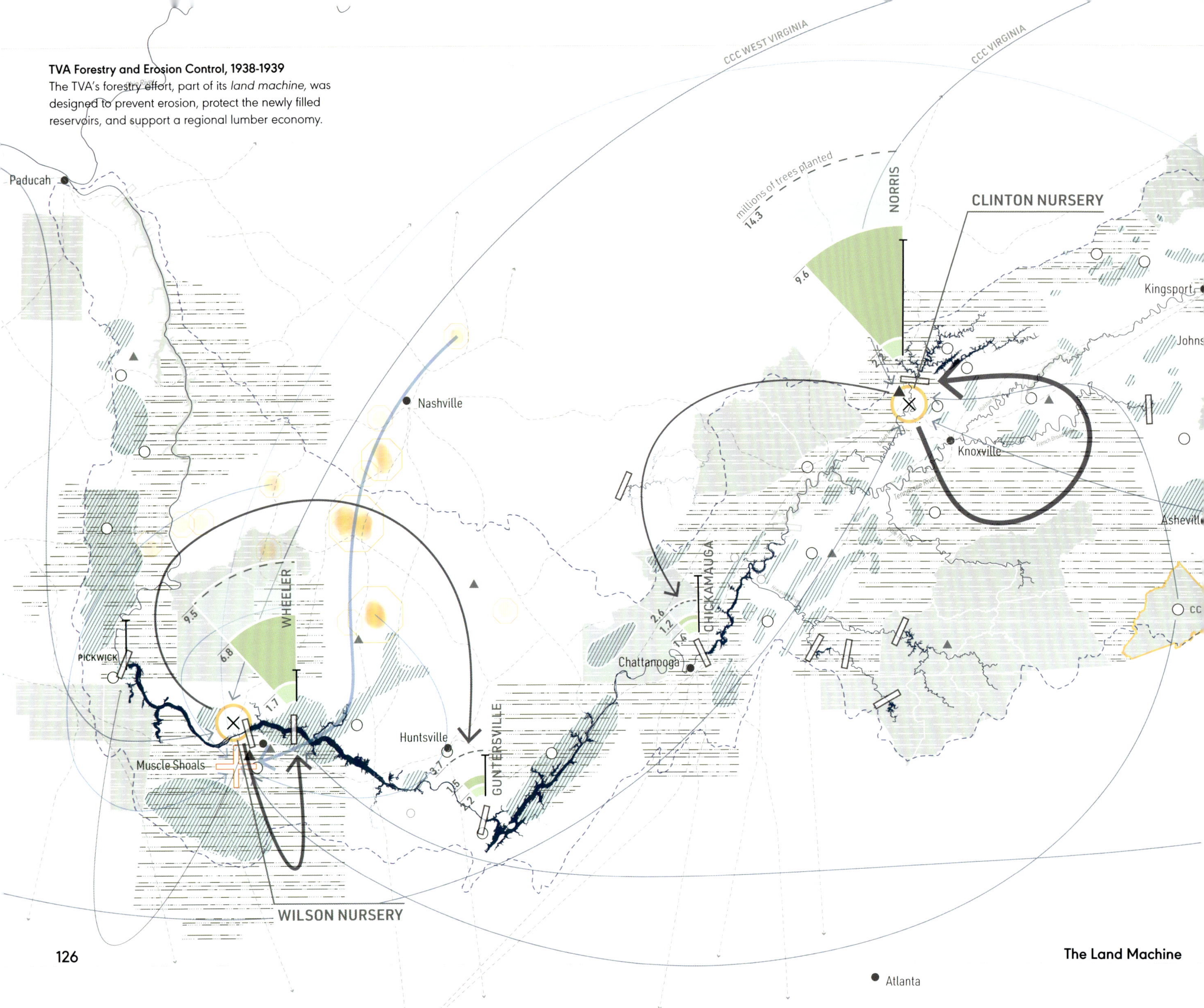

TVA Forestry and Erosion Control, 1938-1939
The TVA's forestry effort, part of its land machine, was
designed to prevent erosion, protect the newly filled
reservoirs, and support a regional lumber economy.

Paducah
CCC WEST VIRGINIA
CCC VIRGINIA
NORRIS
CLINTON NURSERY
millions of trees planted
14.3
9.6
Kingsport
Johns
Nashville
Knoxville
Asheville
WHEELER
9.5
6.8
1.7
PICKWICK
CHICKAMAUGA
2.6
1.2
Huntsville
GUNTERSVILLE
3.7
5
2
Chattanooga
CC
Muscle Shoals
WILSON NURSERY
Atlanta

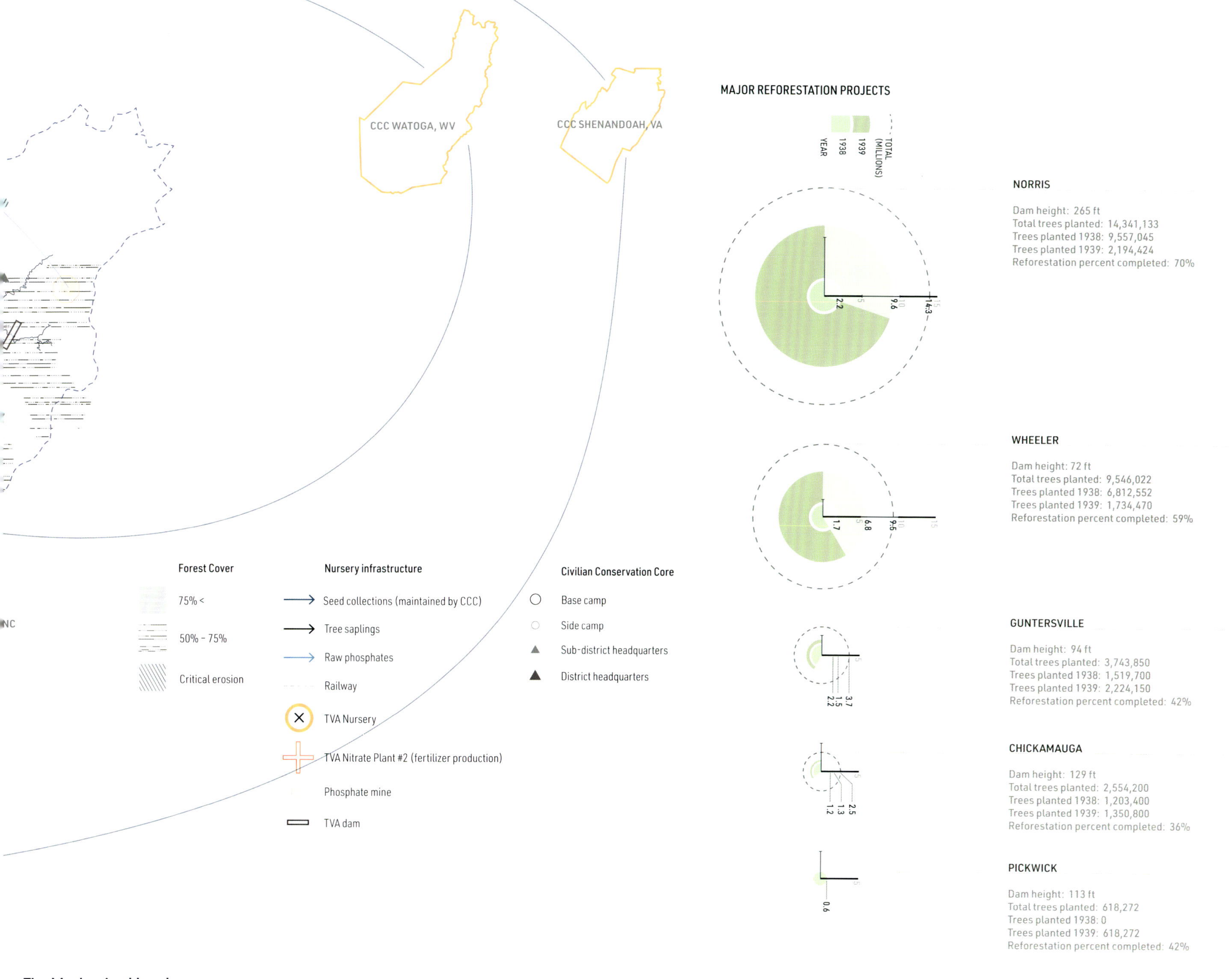

CCC WATOGA, WV
CCC SHENANDOAH, VA

MAJOR REFORESTATION PROJECTS

YEAR
1938
1939
TOTAL (MILLIONS)

NORRIS
Dam height: 265 ft
Total trees planted: 14,341,133
Trees planted 1938: 9,557,045
Trees planted 1939: 2,194,424
Reforestation percent completed: 70%

WHEELER
Dam height: 72 ft
Total trees planted: 9,546,022
Trees planted 1938: 6,812,552
Trees planted 1939: 1,734,470
Reforestation percent completed: 59%

GUNTERSVILLE
Dam height: 94 ft
Total trees planted: 3,743,850
Trees planted 1938: 1,519,700
Trees planted 1939: 2,224,150
Reforestation percent completed: 42%

CHICKAMAUGA
Dam height: 129 ft
Total trees planted: 2,554,200
Trees planted 1938: 1,203,400
Trees planted 1939: 1,350,800
Reforestation percent completed: 36%

PICKWICK
Dam height: 113 ft
Total trees planted: 618,272
Trees planted 1938: 0
Trees planted 1939: 618,272
Reforestation percent completed: 42%

Forest Cover
75% <
50% – 75%
Critical erosion

Nursery infrastructure
Seed collections (maintained by CCC)
Tree saplings
Raw phosphates
Railway
TVA Nursery
TVA Nitrate Plant #2 (fertilizer production)
Phosphate mine
TVA dam

Civilian Conservation Core
Base camp
Side camp
Sub-district headquarters
District headquarters

NC

Here, however, the TVA's regional authorization confronted its firmly held grassroots ethic.
Tennessee, like the other states that overlapped
the Tennessee Valley, had established agricultural experimental stations under the Hatch
Act of 1887. These stations brought knowledge
developed in academia into the field, instructing
farmers about new technologies and demonstrating their usefulness. Along with field agents, the
stations also used flyers, circulars, and displays.
Recognizing the importance of these institutions,
the TVA developed a circuitous process: requests
from landowners must be routed through and
approved by their state institutions, even if the
seedlings were furnished by the TVA.[73]

The second component of the *land machine*—
the promotion of modern farming—was similarly
a hybrid effort. Director Harcourt A. Morgan had
worked as an agronomer in the Tennessee Valley
for several decades before joining the TVA. He
worried that applying a centralized model to
the farming project would create unnecessary
tension and undermine its success. Harcourt
Morgan proceeded to develop a system of
knowledge-sharing between the TVA and valley
farmers. This model was also the basis for David
E. Lilienthal's argument for grassroots democracy. It allowed the TVA to claim that, though
Tennessee Valley farmers were not experts now—
the degradation wrought by the severe erosion
of the Appalachian section of the watershed
undermined that argument—they could become
experts, given government support.

Saving the soil and repurposing marginal
lands in the Tennessee Valley required changing farming practices: introducing cover crops
such as clover and lespedeza, and transition-
ing away from the focus on intensive row crops
such as cotton, corn, and tobacco. Most farmers
in the region, however, could not afford to make
this transition on their own. The key to making
the change possible, Harcourt Morgan argued,

The TVA oversaw the extraction, refinement, and distribution
of phosphate fertilizers to farmers participating in the TVA's
test farm program.

1. The TVA purchased or leased phosphate tracts from individual land
owners as well as mineral and mining corporations.

2. The TVA mined and shipped raw phosphates by train to Nitrate Plant #2 for
processing and refinement into usable fertilizer.

3. Phosphate fertilizers were then delivered to agriculture experiment
stations run by state land-grant universities.

4. The experiment stations managed the distribution of fertilizers to
individual farms via agricultural extension offices.

5. As part of the contract to receive fertilizers, farmers were required to
document and report yields back to the experiment stations, who in turn
reported to the TVA. Based on this data, the TVA tested and made
adjustments to the fertilizers for the next growing season.

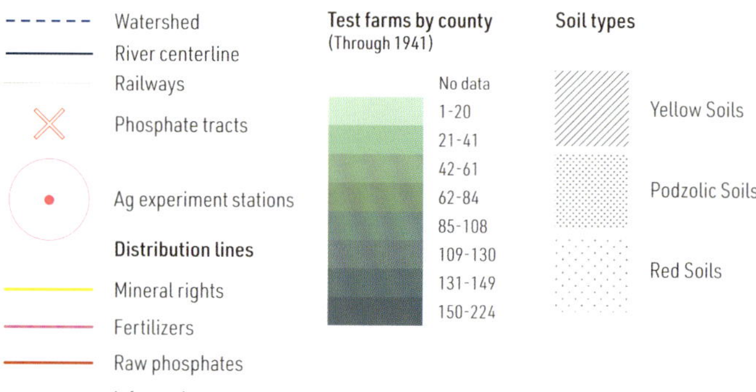

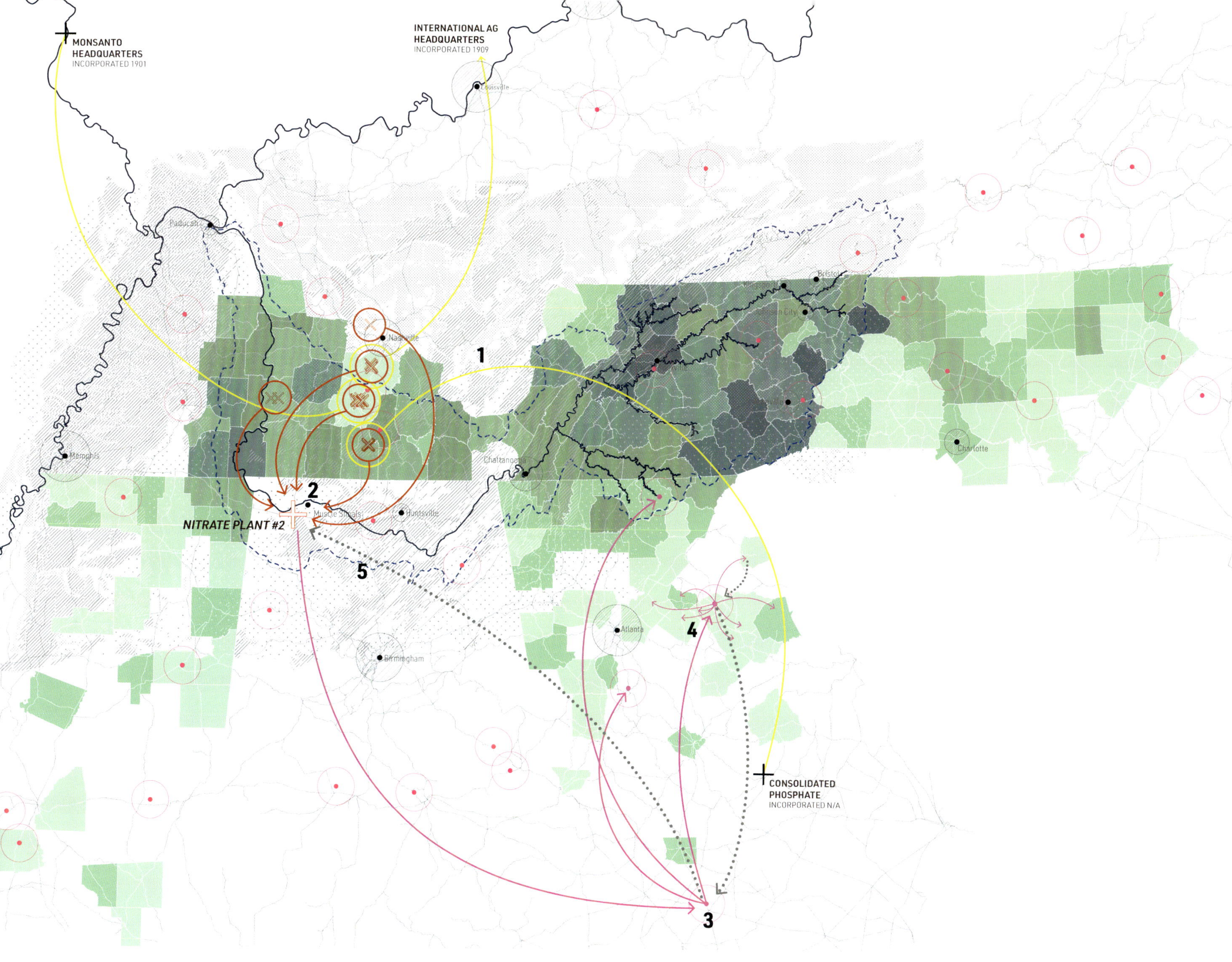
MONSANTO
HEADQUARTERS
INCORPORATED 1901
INTERNATIONAL AG
HEADQUARTERS
INCORPORATED 1909
Louisville
Paducah
Nashville
Memphis
Bristol
Johnson City
Chattanooga
Charlotte
Muscle Shoals
Huntsville
NITRATE PLANT #2
Atlanta
Birmingham
CONSOLIDATED
PHOSPHATE
INCORPORATED N/A
1
2
3
4
5

Calderwood Dam from the Calderwood Lake Lookout on Highway 129 (the Dragon Tail)

Farm in Washington County, Tennessee

Farm in McMinn County, Tennessee

was the use of fertilizers, which would replenish nitrogen in the ground and turn exploited land into fertile soil.

The fertilizer project was clearly stated in the TVA Act, which allowed the TVA to repurpose two WWI ammunition plants in Muscle Shoals, Alabama. The TVA was directed to keep these facilities in readiness for future conflict, but it could use them in the meantime to produce fertilizers. Conveniently, war production and agricultural production had overlapping manufacturing processes: the same equipment and processes used to create ammonium nitrate for high explosives could also be used to produce phosphorus-based agricultural fertilizers.

The region's landscape also played a role in shaping the land machine. One of the largest concentrations of phosphorous-bearing rock in the United States was located in Tennessee's Williamson, Maury, and Davidson Counties. In the early 1930s, these plots were owned by corporations such as Monsanto, International Ag, and Consolidated Phosphate. The TVA, following its ethic of regulating competitive business, purchased the mineral rights, thereby controlling the sites of extraction. By 1944, the TVA had secured 57 tracts comprising 1,703 acres of mineable land, containing an estimated 23,466,250 tons of brown phosphate matrix.[74] Once mined, the phosphorous-bearing rock was transferred by rail to Muscle Shoals, where the TVA used the Haber-Bosch process to produce advanced fertilizers. This process, developed in Germany, had been disseminated globally as part of the 1920 Versailles Treaty.

The centralization of the *land machine* began and ended at Muscle Shoals. The TVA did not deliver phosphates directly to Tennessee Valley farmers, nor were farmers compelled to utilize the TVA's products. Instead, the agency created a demonstration program. Enlisting the help of the agricultural experiment stations in each state, the TVA recruited landowners who were willing to use their private property as a test site. Unlike the forestry program, the TVA negotiated contracts directly with the participants. The TVA would provide fertilizers, and the farmers would agree to deploy them and then report crop yields back to the TVA.

The test demonstration program depended on the production and distribution of fertilizers, but the main currency in the system was knowledge. The TVA published technical papers on fertilizer manufacturing and secured numerous patents for the technologies it developed. Even more importantly, it used participating farms to test its products. As W. H. Droze comments, this system created a "three-way arrangement combining the farmer's lands, the knowledge of the agricultural scientists and extension workers of the land-grant universities, and the fertilizer and funds of the TVA."[75]

Broadly speaking, the demonstration farms worked: the TVA oversaw a sea change in farming practices in the Tennessee Valley. Paul K. Conkin notes that the fertilizer program was effective in his own village: as land was turned over to pasture, the landscape became greener.[76] The rural environment of the Tennessee Valley thus became a testament to the TVA project and a demonstration of how statecraft might be embedded in the environment. The TVA's robust fertilizer program also served as an example of putting infrastructural power into practice. The TVA created new environmental and material conditions and then encouraged the behaviors that would lead to their desired outcome. It gave farmers the opportunity to run their farm as they saw fit, while contributing to shared knowledge at the same. The *land machine*, though tailored to the specific conditions of the Tennessee Valley, was intended to serve as a model that could be scaled up and applied to other regions of the country.

Farm in Lauderdale County, Alabama

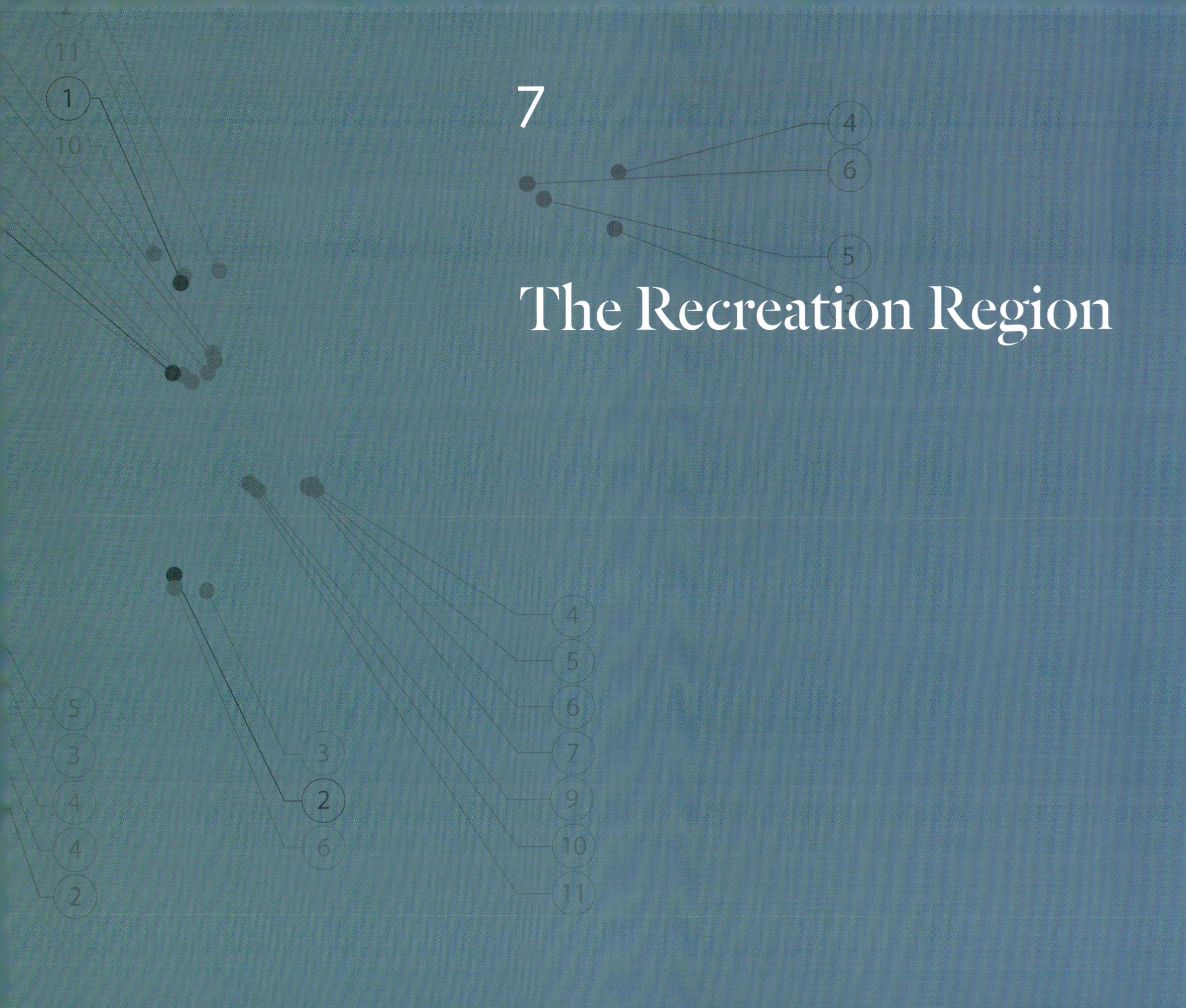

7

The Recreation Region

Public Forests and Parks in the Tennessee Valley, 1945-53

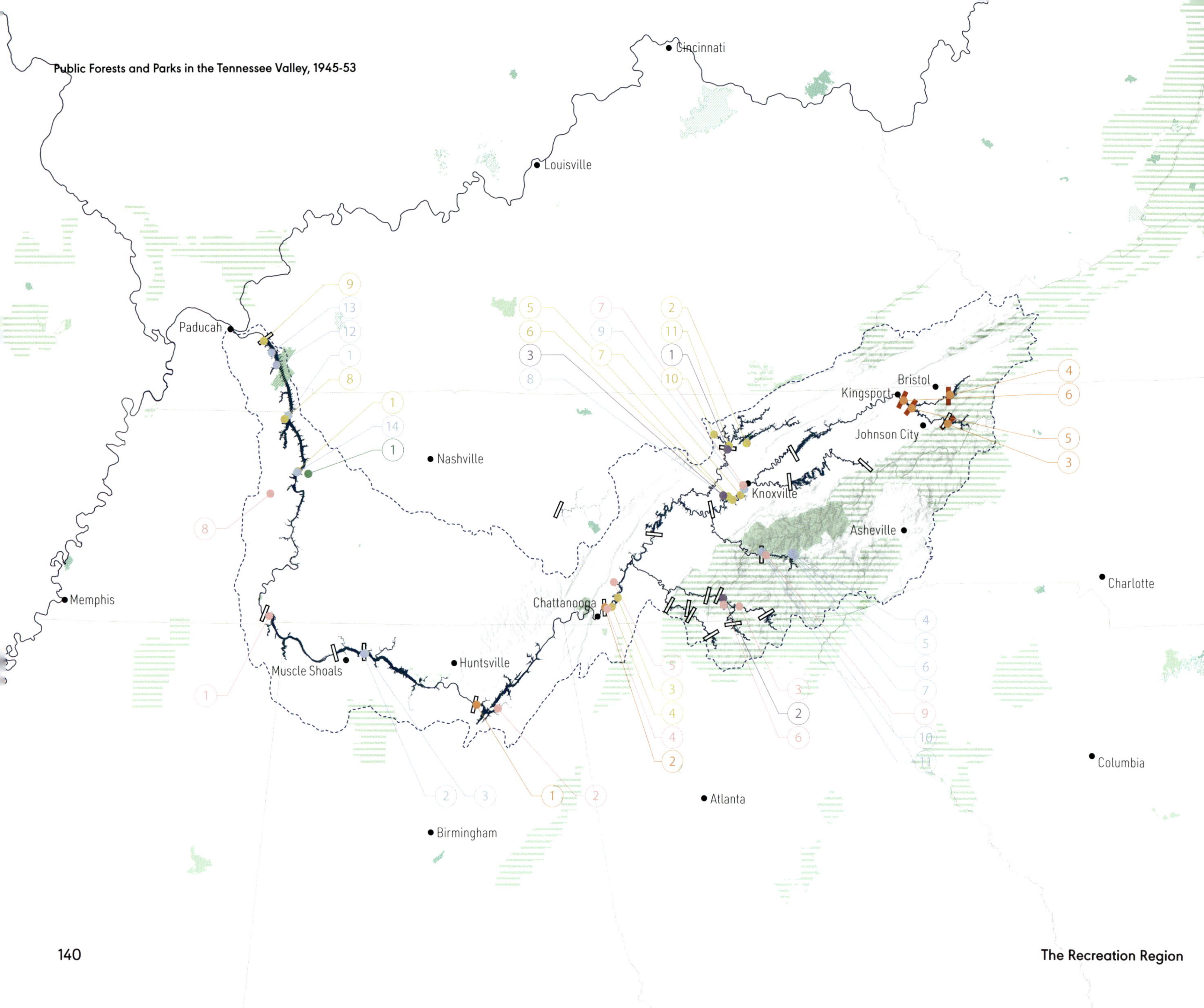

Cincinnati
Louisville
Paducah
Nashville
Memphis
Muscle Shoals
Huntsville
Chattanooga
Knoxville
Bristol
Kingsport
Johnson City
Asheville
Charlotte
Columbia
Atlanta
Birmingham

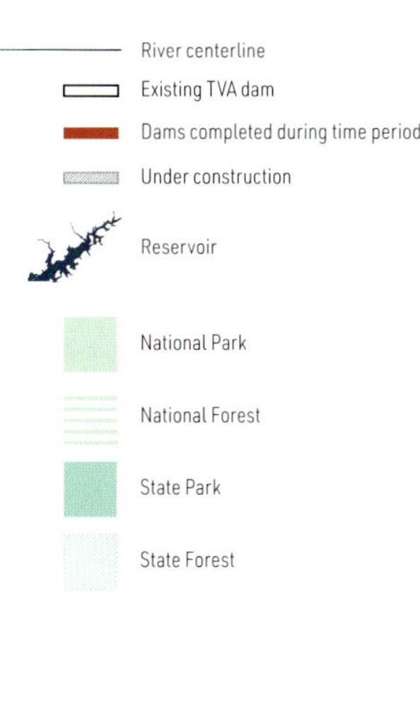

River centerline

Existing TVA dam

Dams completed during time period

Under construction

Reservoir

National Park

National Forest

State Park

State Forest

Park

1 Nathan Bedford Forrest Memorial Park
2 Big Ridge State Park
3 Harrison Bay State Park
4 Booker T. Washington State Park
5 Louisville Community Park
6 Lowes Ferry Park
7 Knoxville Waterfront Park
8 Paris Landing State Park
9 Kentucky Dam State Park
10 Cove Lake State Park
11 Norris Dam State Park

Marina

1 Pickwick Landing
2 Guntersville Marine Park
3 Murphy Marina (NC)
4 Chickamauga Marina
5 Soddy Marine Park
6 Persimmon Creek Dam
7 Knoxville Marine Park
8 Perryville Marine Area
9 Bee Cove/Fontana Village Marina

Recreation Area

1 Fort Heiman Recreation Area
2 Big Nance Creek Recreation Area
3 Wheeler Dam Recreation Area
4 Jenkins Branch Recreation Area
5 Indian Grave Recreation Area
6 Greasy Branch Recreation Area
7 Evans Gap Recreation Area
8 Fort Loudon Dam Recreation Area
9 Knob Creek Recreation Area
10 South Shore Recreation Area
11 North Shore Recreation Area
12 Jonathan Creek Recreation Area
13 Birmingham–Bear Creek Recreation Area
14 Trace Creek Recreation Area

Observation Gallery

1 Norris Dam Visitor Center
2 Hiwassee Dam Observation Gallery
3 Fort Loudoun Dam Observation Gallery

Overlook

1 Guntersville Dam Overlook
2 Chickamauga Dam Day Use Area
3 Watauga Dam Observation
4 South Holston Dam Observation
5 Boone Dam Observation
6 Fort Patrick Henry Dam Observation

Natural Feature

1 Paint Rock Bluff

The TVA forestry and agricultural projects transformed the environment of the Tennessee Valley, but they could not account for all the marginal land in the region, for which the agency had been directed to find a "proper" use. Moreover, much of the marginal land in the Valley would be of the TVA's making: building dams and creating reservoirs flooded the best farmland, and it created mile upon mile of shoreline that could not be used for agriculture, housing, or industry, as it had to be left clear for times when the TVA needed to store water and raise the level of the reservoir.

The TVA found that it could use the new shoreline to further its social aspirations and its environmental reform goals. Developing the shoreline as a landscape of leisure—devoting it to recreational facilities—would signal that leisure time was the reward for efficient farming and industry (with the support of the various TVA *machines*). It would also suggest that leisure was not to be squandered on drinking and gambling but should be devoted to outdoor recreation in a picturesque landscape.

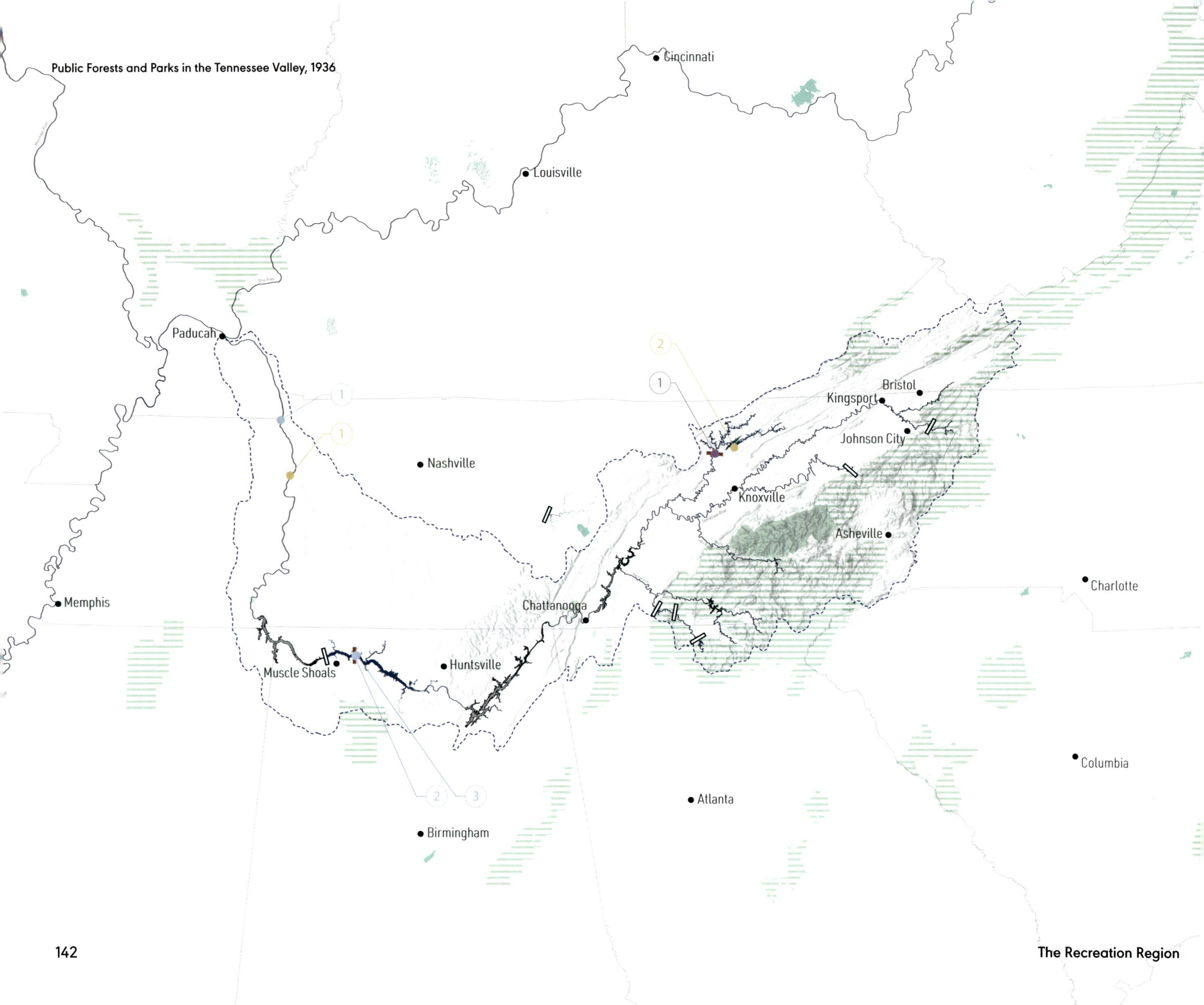

Public Forests and Parks in the Tennessee Valley, 1936
Cincinnati
Louisville
Paducah
Bristol
Kingsport
Johnson City
Nashville
Knoxville
Asheville
Memphis
Charlotte
Chattanooga
Muscle Shoals
Huntsville
Columbia
Atlanta
Birmingham

Boone Lake Beach at Boone Dam

Douglas Headwater Campground on Douglas Lake

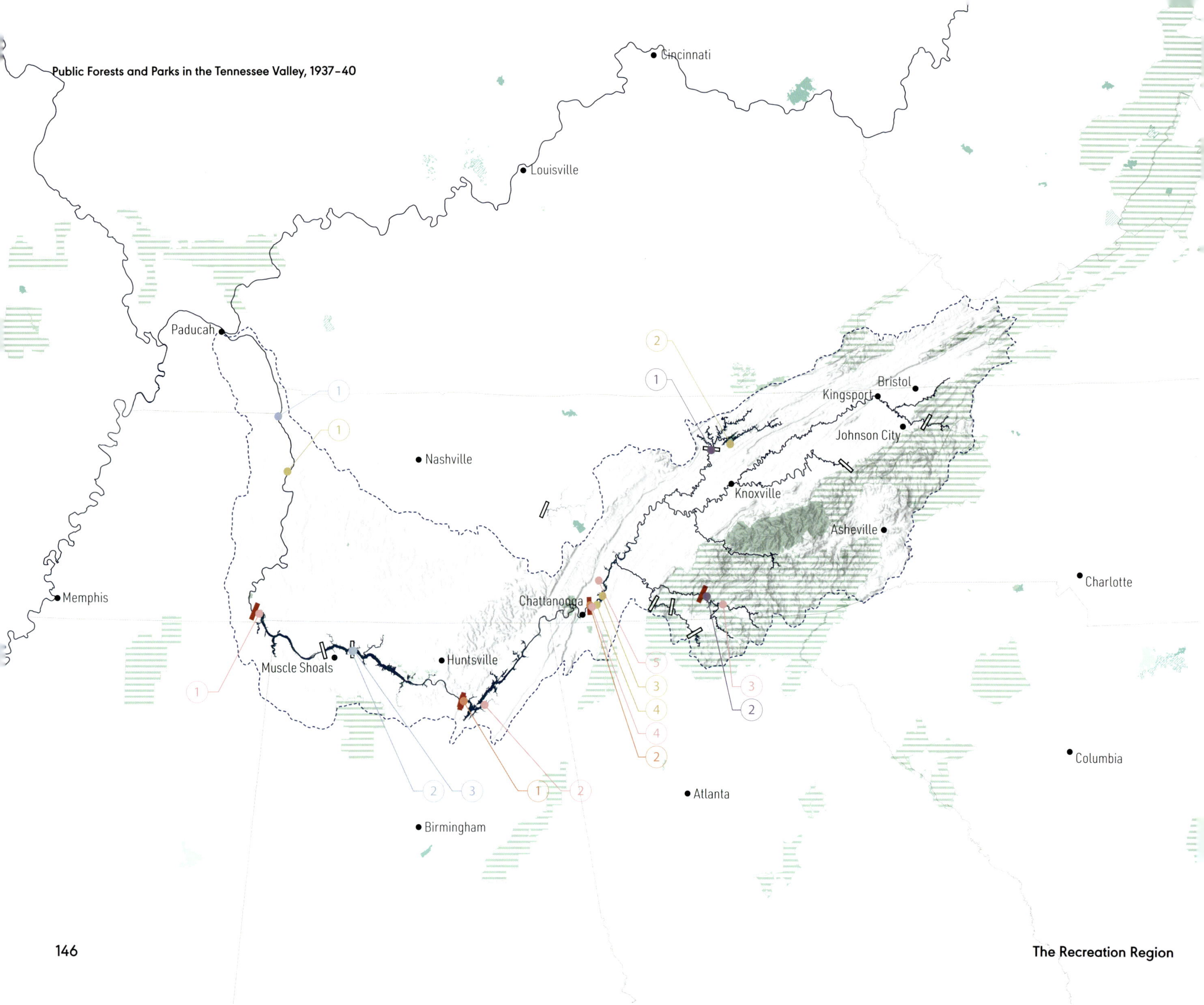

Public Forests and Parks in the Tennessee Valley, 1937–40
Cincinnati
Louisville
Bristol
Kingsport
Johnson City
Paducah
Nashville
Knoxville
Asheville
Memphis
Charlotte
Chattanooga
Muscle Shoals
Huntsville
Columbia
Atlanta
Birmingham

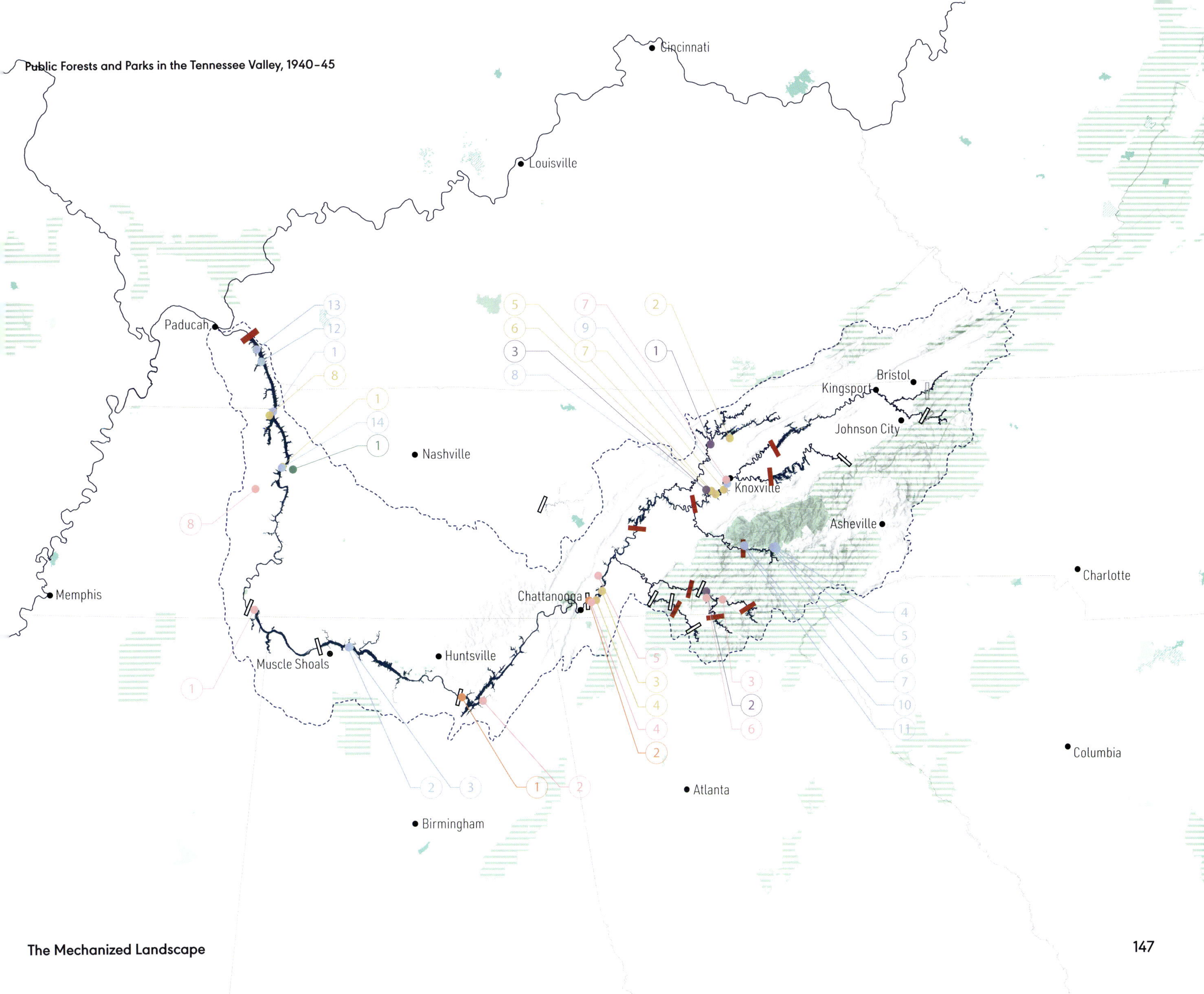

Public Forests and Parks in the Tennessee Valley, 1940–45
Cincinnati
Louisville
Paducah
Nashville
Memphis
Muscle Shoals
Huntsville
Chattanooga
Birmingham
Atlanta
Knoxville
Kingsport
Bristol
Johnson City
Asheville
Charlotte
Columbia
13
12
1
8
1
14
1
8
5
6
3
8
7
9
7
2
1
5
3
4
4
2
1
2
3
2
4
5
6
7
10
11
3
2
6

The TVA couched its promotion of recreation in the language of resource conservation, arguing that outdoor recreation was, simply, the best use of the Valley's resources. The agency also suggested that promoting a tourist industry would create new economic opportunities and would keep Tennessee Valley farmers in residence. TVA Director David E. Lilienthal explained: "The extensive recreational use of TVA's reservoirs provides a further illustration of how public interest in a natural resource—the use of these beautiful man-made lakes for recreation—and the private interest of businessmen in developing profitable enterprise can be harmonized."[77]

The TVA's comprehensive approach to the Tennessee Valley shaped its approach to the development of the tourist industry, creating a recreational region. Early TVA efforts focused on identifying naturally scenic locations, which were considered as "important a natural resource of the Tennessee Valley as are its soils, minerals, timber, or water power."[78] This approach, however, favored the eastern, mountainous portion of the region over the flat territory in the west, upsetting the regional emphasis. As the project developed, the TVA focused on human-made scenery; it promoted the entire region by reframing the *river machine* as a chain of lakes. The emerging mechanized landscape thus took precedence over the natural territory. This shift represented yet another interpretation of the term environment—as an experience to be purchased and enjoyed. Environment was not only a habitat, but also a commodity to be consumed.

The model region surrounding Norris Dam became a testing ground for several mechanisms through which to develop the landscape of leisure. The TVA could develop and manage facilities itself; it could transfer land to public entities to develop and maintain, as state,

Hiwassee Dam from the Hiwassee River
DANGEROUS WATERS
VIOLENT SURGES
OCCUR SUDDENLY
KEEP OUT

Caney Creek RV Resort from Roane County Park, Tennessee

county, or city parks; or it could lease or even sell land to private entities. Under Lilienthal's direction, the TVA engaged in all three approaches. In 1939, the TVA created the legal groundwork for this effort by recognizing recreation as an optimal, and therefore acceptable, use of land, in addition to agriculture, forestry, and industry.

The scenic routes at Norris and subsequent dams are examples of TVA-maintained recreation. These routes begin in the public spaces in and around the dams, but they extend beyond them into the landscape, itself a product of the TVA's statecraft. The TVA has furnished these routes with picnic tables and other facilities, allowing visitors to enjoy leisure time in the landscape transformed by its three *machines*. The TVA also developed swimming beaches, fishing spots, and boat launches, all open to the public. The land transferred to other public entities has been developed in a myriad of ways, from state parks (such as the one at Norris Dam) to camping facilities managed by local governments. The public identification of these locations as part of the TVA system is often reduced to a sign at the entrance.

The boat dock created in the quarry at Norris Dam was a model for the third type of development. With the dam complete and the reservoir filled, TVA invited private companies to bid for the license to manage the location. This system was deployed along the other lakes in the chain of lakes as well, creating a string of marinas and boat docks across the region.

The grassroots logic was applied to TVA construction camps as well, bringing the housing and recreation regions together in a "unified" manner. The Watts Bar camp and village is one example. In 1950, the TVA sold the site and its buildings to Pete Smith, his wife Sally, and his sister-in-law Katie Marshall, residents of Michigan. The new owners renovated the single-family homes on the site and opened a restaurant. They then installed a swimming pool, riding stables, and a boat dock to create the Watts Bar Resort. The resort drew visitors from across the nation, and it also functioned as a special destination for local residents. In 1970 the resort changed hands, but it continued to operate for another two decades.[79]

The TVA's entrance into the tourist industry has created an interesting situation. Locals in the mountainous eastern Tennessee Valley who fish, camp, and hike—as well as hospitality workers in the area—note the influence the TVA exerts over their seasonal and even daily routines. The Tennessee's tributary rivers are known for world-class whitewater, and the Ocoee River draws boaters from all over the world who want to take a stab at its Class IV rapids. In 1996 it famously served as the site for Olympic canoe and kayak events. Recreation is so important that the TVA publishes their water release schedules months in advance and provides continuous updates based on weather predictions. As one river guide put it: "The mechanics of the dam ruled your life. If they weren't letting the water flow you weren't working that day."[80]

Porch of a tourist cabin in Monte Sano State Park, Alabama

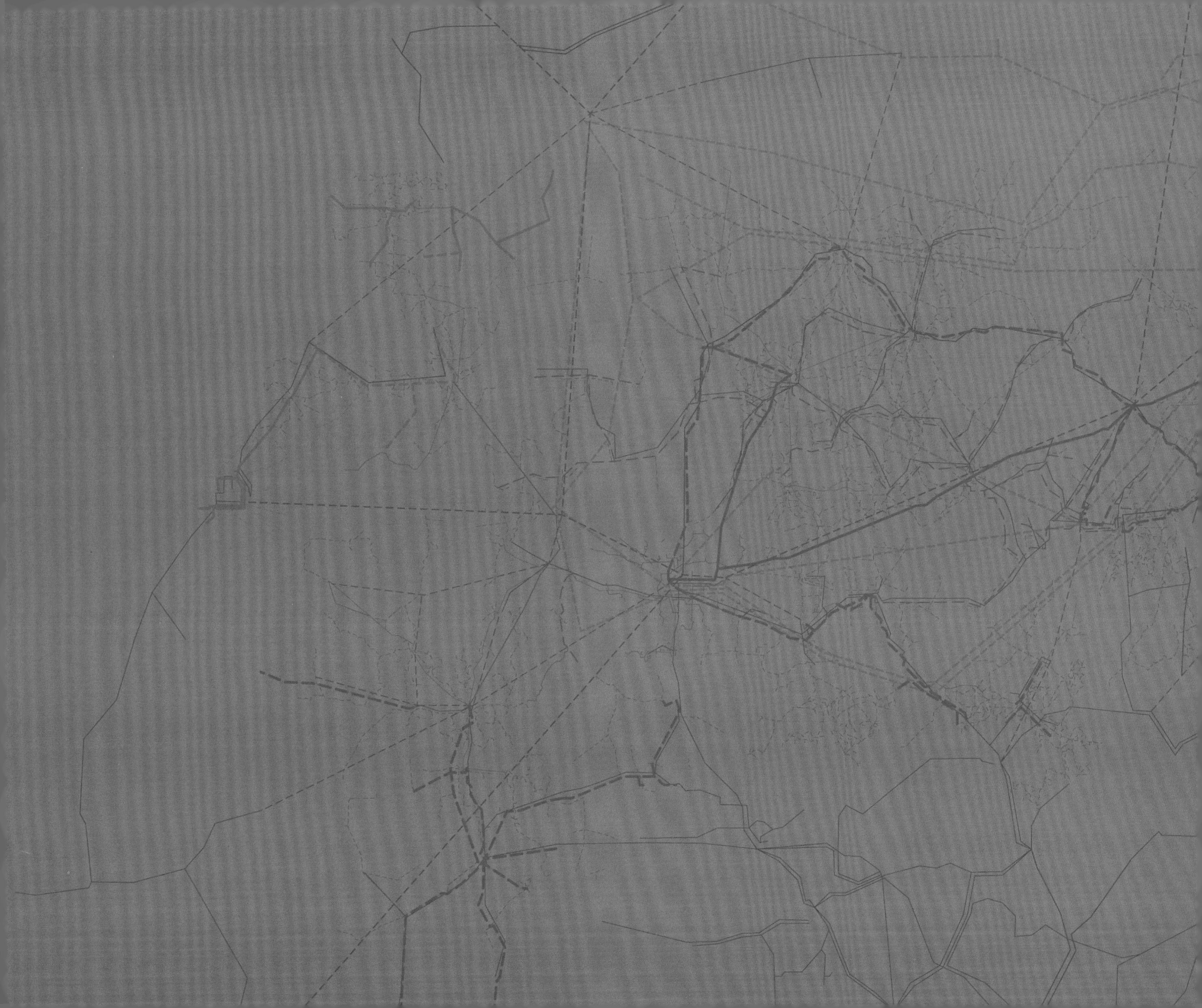

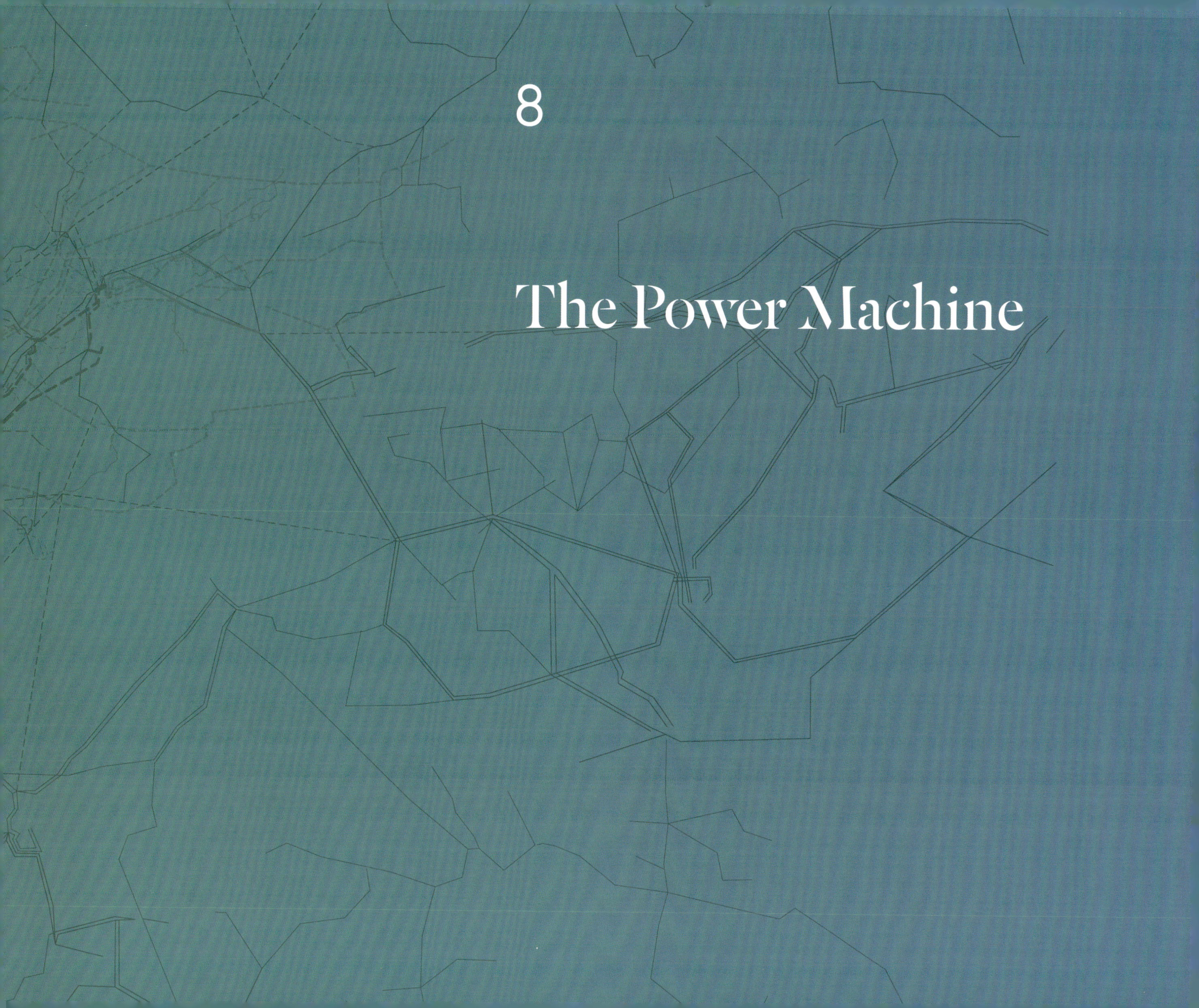

8

The Power Machine

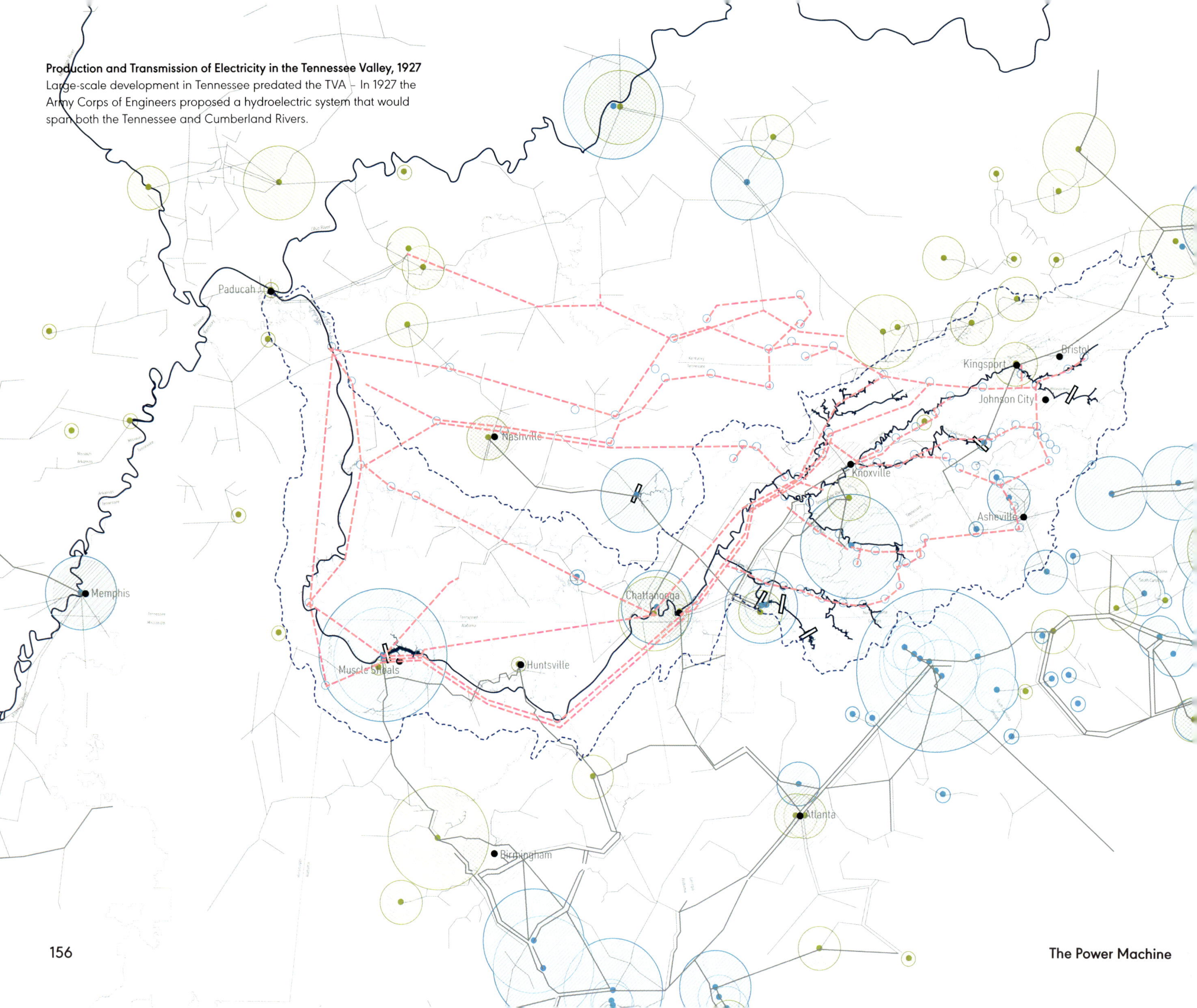

Production and Transmission of Electricity in the Tennessee Valley, 1927
Large-scale development in Tennessee predated the TVA — In 1927 the
Army Corps of Engineers proposed a hydroelectric system that would
span both the Tennessee and Cumberland Rivers.
Paducah
Bristol
Kingsport
Johnson City
Nashville
Knoxville
Asheville
Memphis
Chattanooga
Muscle Shoals
Huntsville
Atlanta
Birmingham

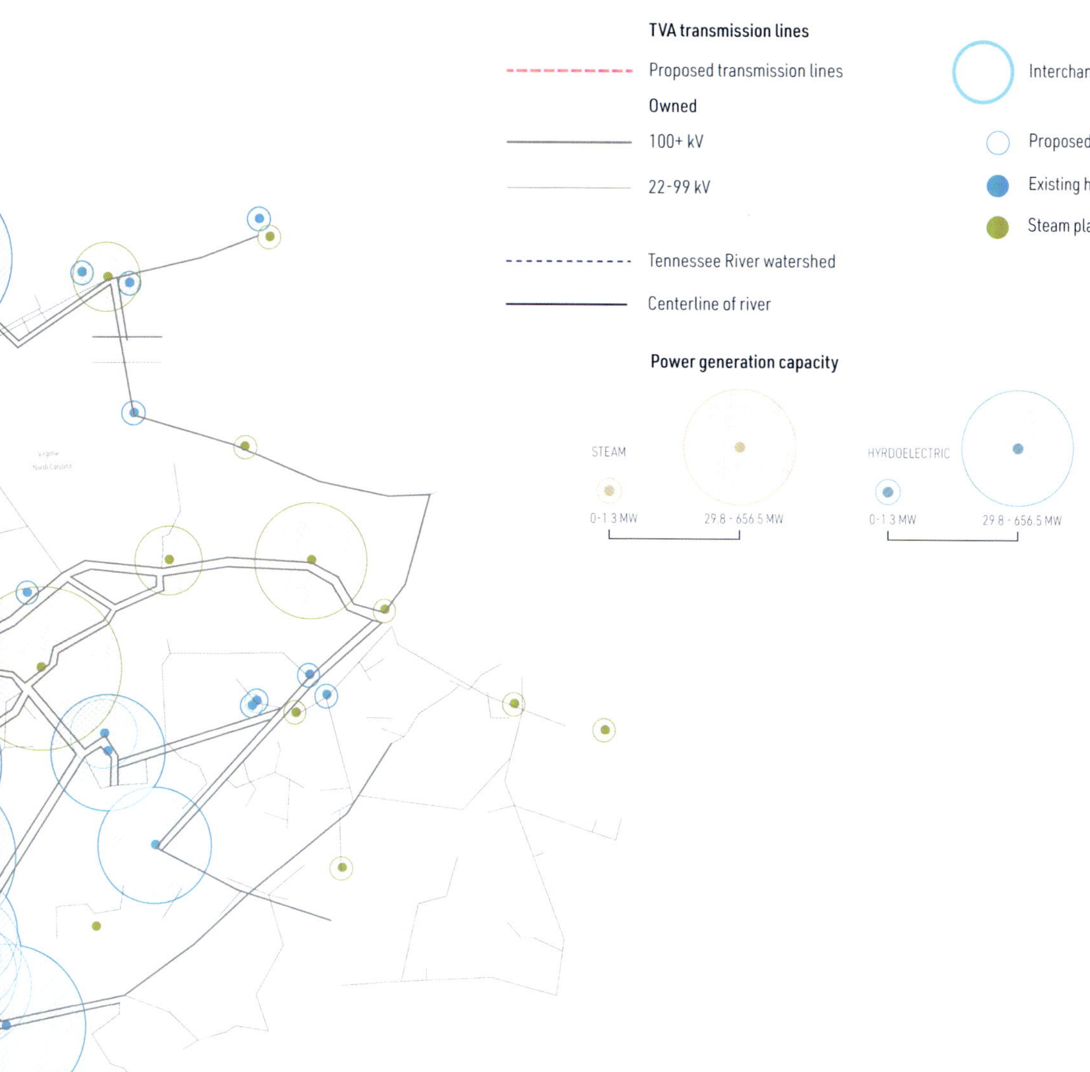

New Dealers beginning with President Franklin D. Roosevelt saw electricity as the key to keeping Americans on the land. Farmers, they assumed, would be less likely to seek work in urban industrial centers if electricity became available to simplify daily tasks. Refrigeration was especially important, as cooled produce could reach wider markets. Power, many TVA officials reasoned, would transform the "forgotten Americans" of the Tennessee Valley into willing, even eager, participants in regional development. At the same time, the call for electrifying farms created a rhetorical dilemma: why would farmers, the most independent and forward-thinking of Americans, need government help? The TVA resolved this tension by attributing the problem to the refusal of private electricity companies to invest in rural transmission, favoring the more lucrative urban markets.

The TVA prepared a comprehensive plan for rural electrification in the Tennessee Valley based, in part, on a 1927 proposal by the Army Corps of Engineers. The *power machine* was also designed to help integrate the region into the larger nation; the TVA imagined a system that would connect the Tennessee Valley to major urban areas as far north as Cincinnati and as far south as Atlanta and Southern Mississippi.

Production and Transmission of Electricity in the Tennessee Valley, 1934
Initially, the TVA proposed building power lines as far north as Cincinnati,
Ohio and as far south as Jackson, Mississippi.

TVA transmission lines

100+ kV
60-99 kV
22-99 kV
Proposed (1927)
Proposed by TVA (1934)
TVA dam
Proposed TVA dam

Tennessee River watershed
Centerline of river
Reservoir
Proposed reservoir
Population
City

Power generation capacity

STEAM
0-1.3 MW
29.8 - 656.5 MW

HYRDOELECTRIC
0-1.3 MW
29.8 - 656.5 MW

Memphis

Cincinnati
Louisville
Bristol
Kingsport
Johnson City
Nashville
Knoxville
Asheville
Charlotte
Chattanooga
Huntsville
Muscle Shoals
Atlanta
Birmingham

TVA Transmission lines

Proposed system, 1934

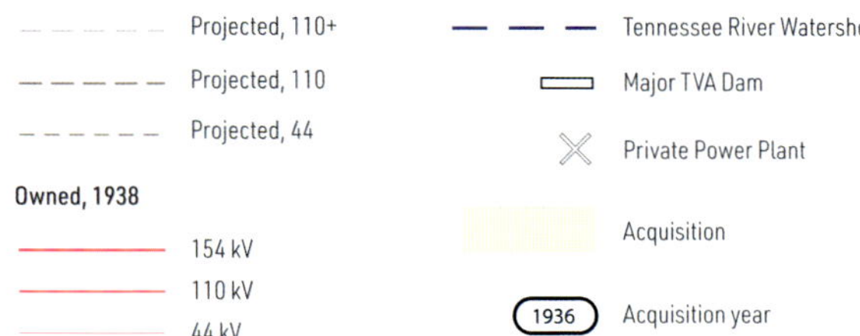

Owned, 1938

Private transmission lines

Power company, voltage (kV)

Power generation capacity

Expansion of the TVA *Power Machine,* 1934-1941

The TVA resolved to expand its power machine by purchasing private power companies and adding their transmission lines to its system. In 1934, the TVA acquired the Mississippi Power Company, but all other contracts were paused by litigation that challenged the TVA's authority to intervene in private enterprise. The process was resumed in 1936 following a ruling by the US Supreme Court in favor of the TVA.

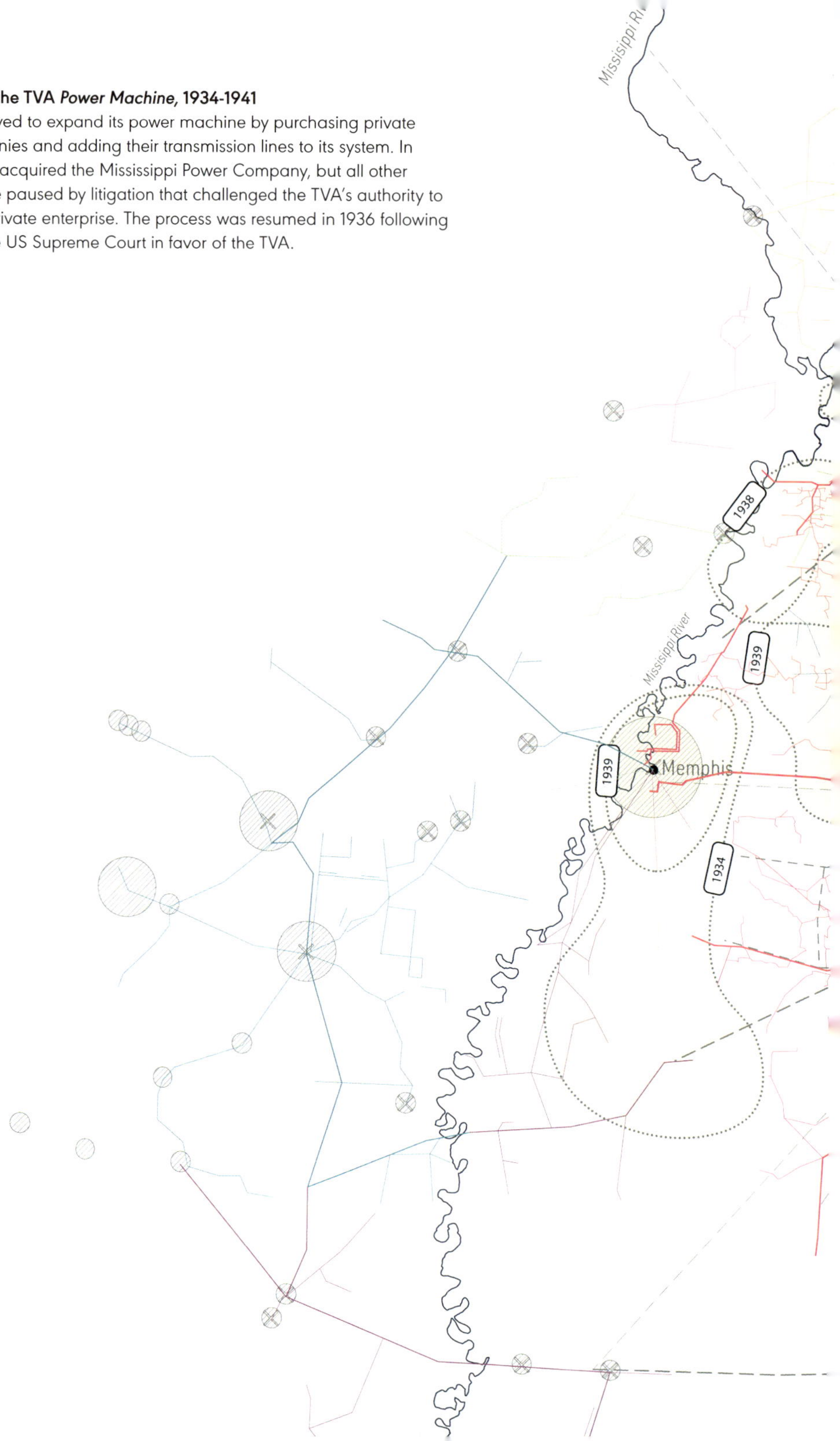

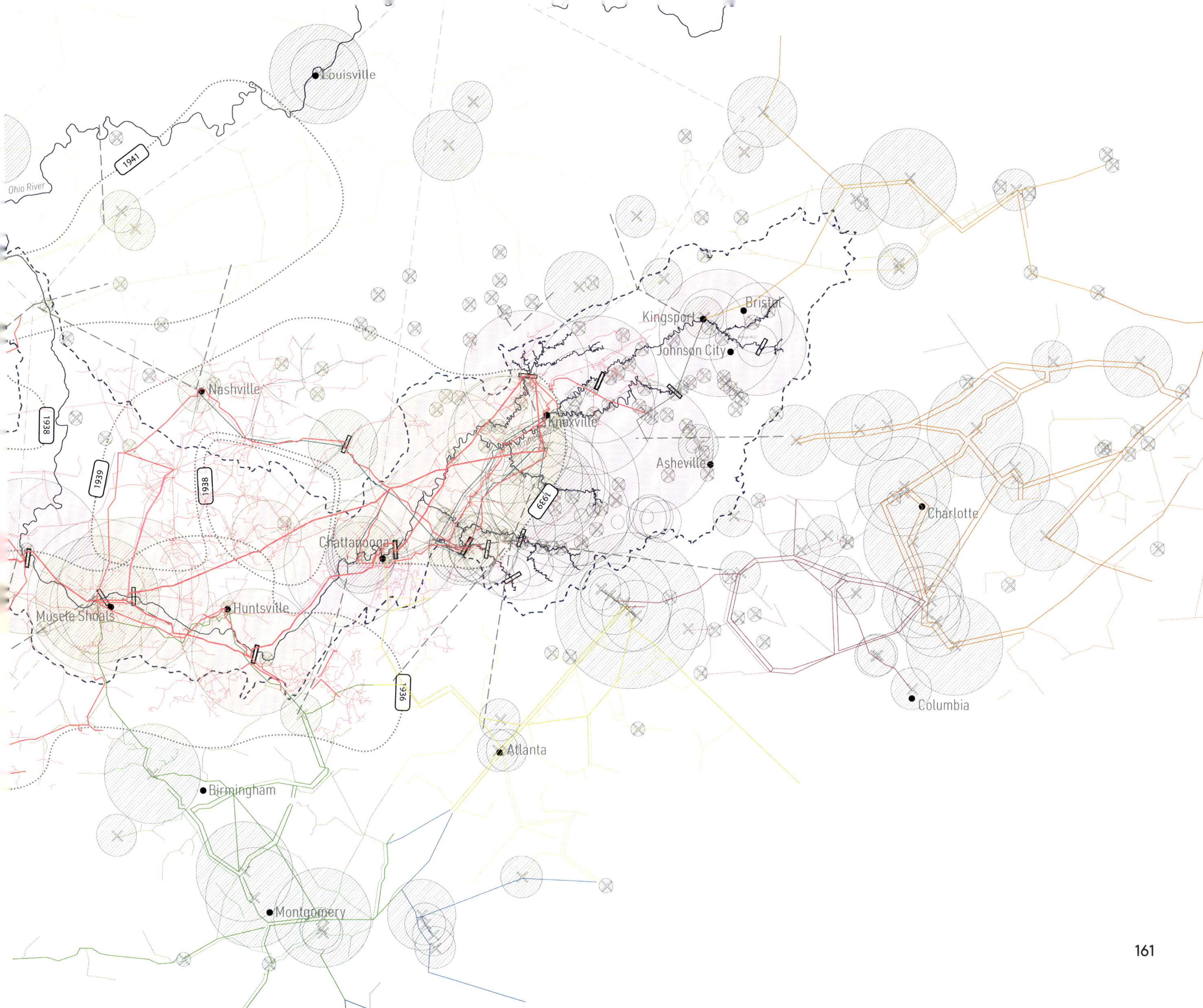

Ohio River
1941
1938
1939
1938
1936
1959
Louisville
Nashville
Kingsport
Bristol
Johnson City
Knoxville
Asheville
Charlotte
Chattanooga
Muscle Shoals
Huntsville
Columbia
Atlanta
Birmingham
Montgomery

Production and Transmission of Electricity in the Tennessee Valley, 1938
The TVA was prohibited from selling electricity directly to consumers. In 1938, it introduced Rural Distribution Areas and encouraged inhabitants to form local collectives that would enter into contracts with the TVA for the purchase of power.

Paducah

Memphis

TVA transmission lines

Owned
154 kV
110 kV
44 kV
<22 kV

Under construction
110 kV
44 kV

Proposed
100< kV
22-99 kV
<22 kV

Authorized
110 kV
44 kV

Acquired
100< kV
<100 kV

Pending
100< kV
<22 kV

Proposed TVA lines (1934)
100+ kV
22-99 kV

Private utilities (1934)
100+ kV
22-99 kV

Other infrastructure

Rural Distribution Area
TVA dam
Dam under construction
Interchange point

Reservoir
Proposed reservoir
Tennessee River watershed
River centerline
City

Power generation capacity

STEAM
0-1.3 MW   29.8 - 656.5 MW

HYRDOELECTRIC
0-1.3 MW   29.8 - 656.5 MW

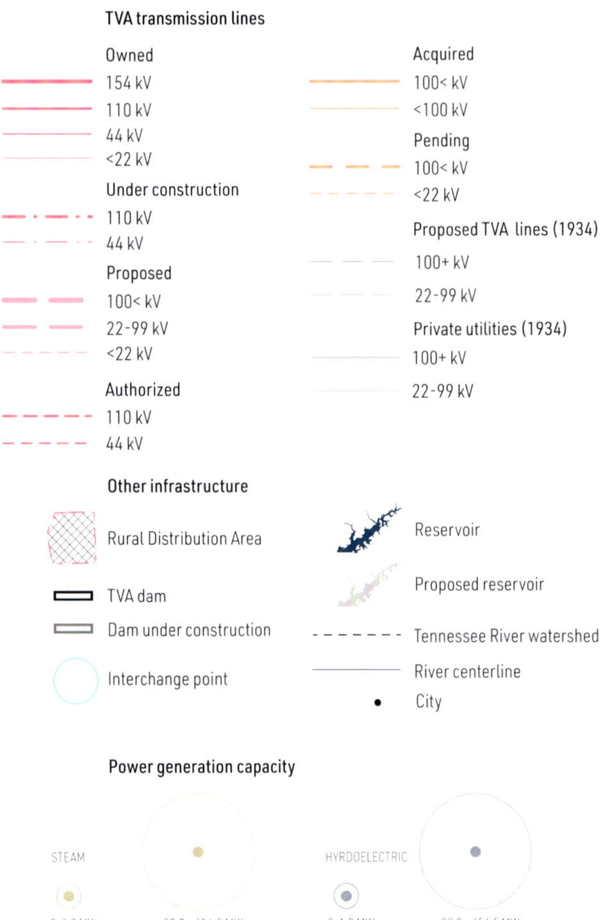

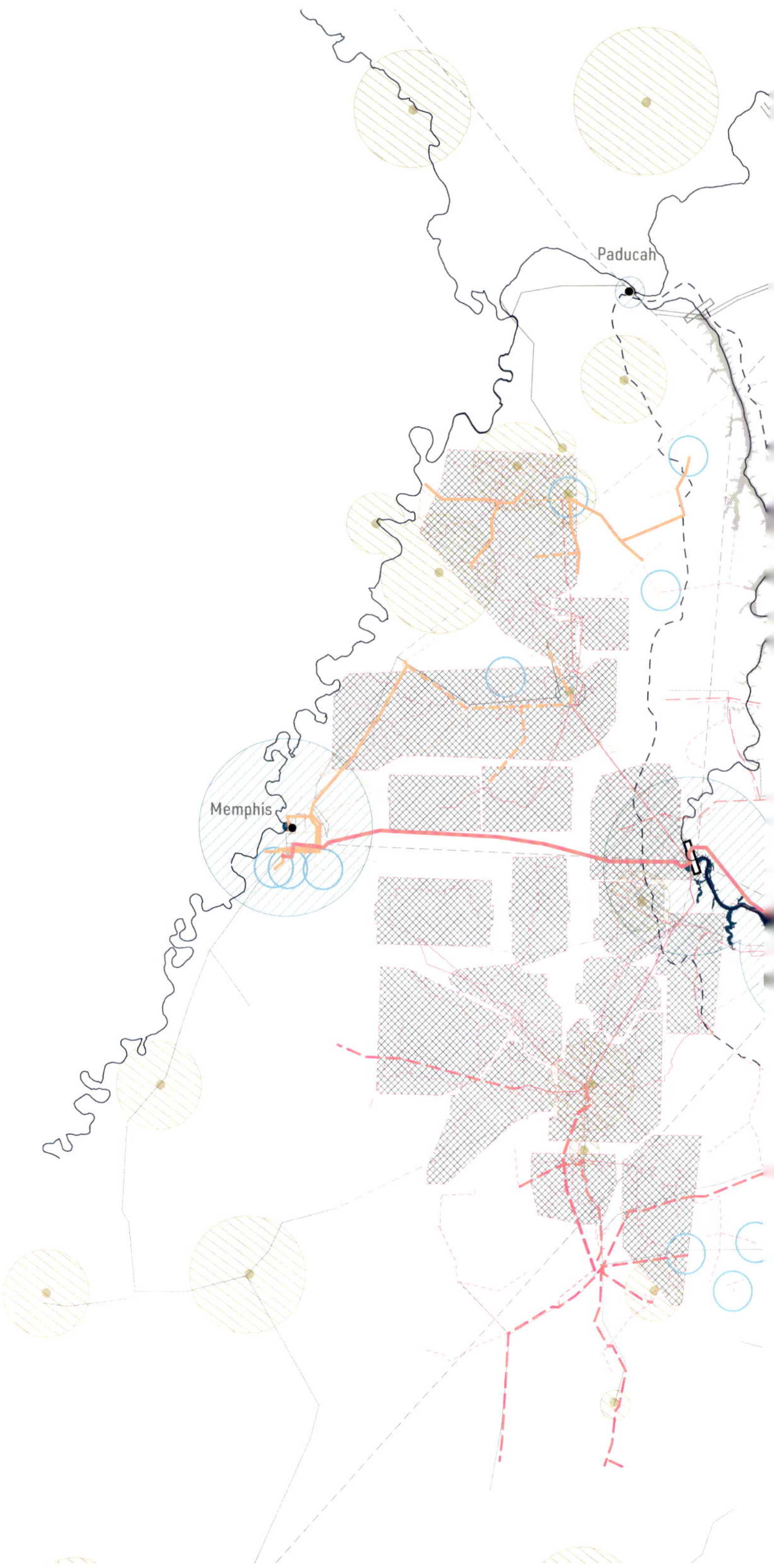

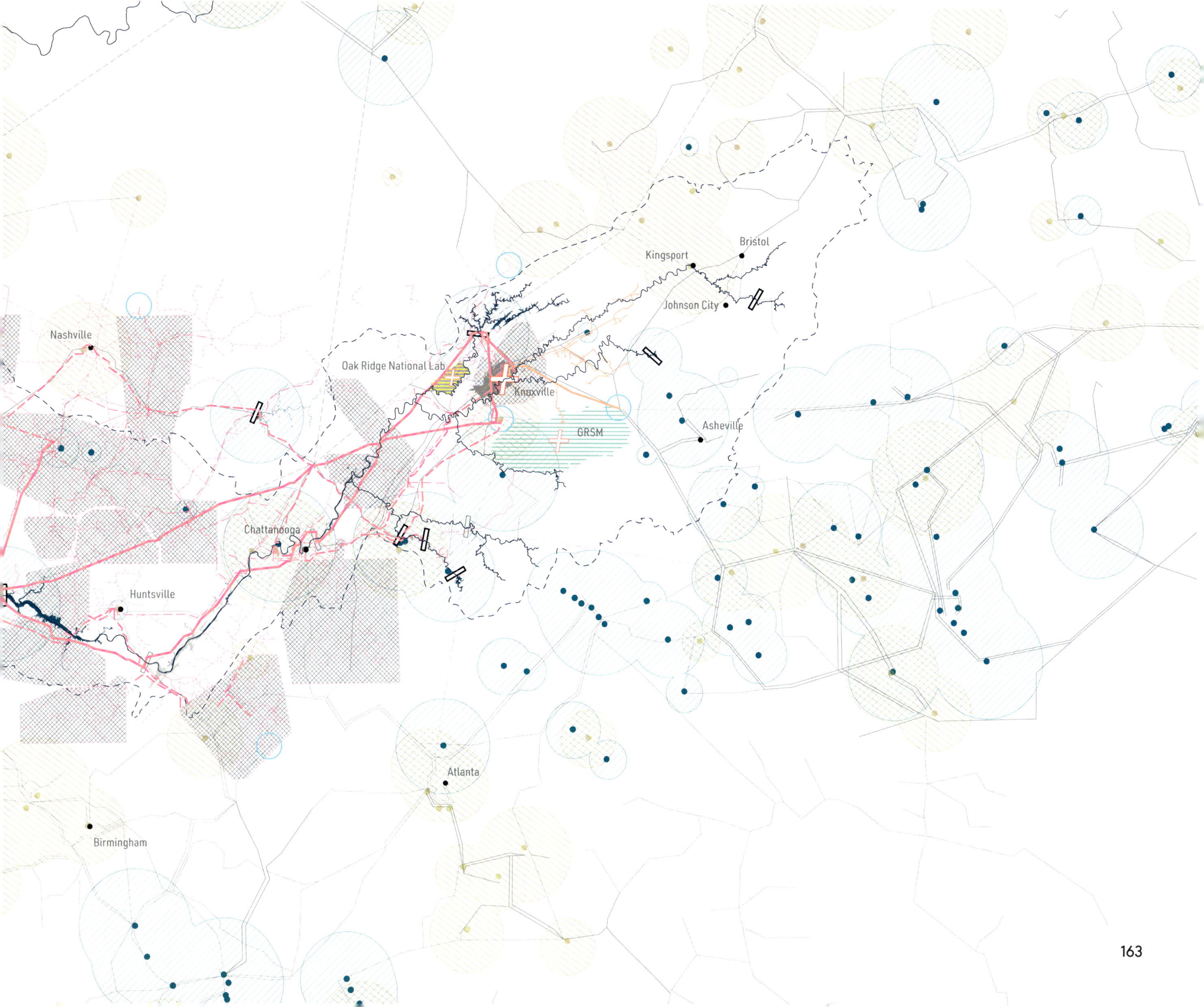

Kingsport
Bristol
Johnson City
Nashville
Oak Ridge National Lab
Knoxville
Asheville
GRSM
Chattanooga
Huntsville
Atlanta
Birmingham

Consolidation of the TVA Power Machine, 1947

By 1947 the TVA *power machine* had matured; the transmission system
was spatially coherent and the Rural Distribution Areas were replaced by
cooperatives in rural areas and municipal districts in urban areas.

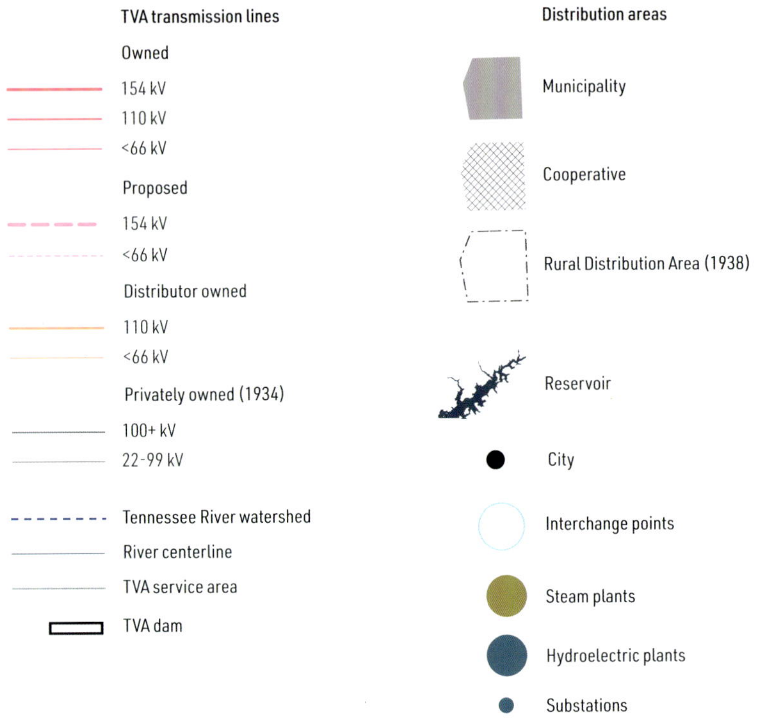

TVA transmission lines

Owned

154 kV

110 kV

<66 kV

Proposed

154 kV

<66 kV

Distributor owned

110 kV

<66 kV

Privately owned (1934)

100+ kV

22-99 kV

Tennessee River watershed

River centerline

TVA service area

TVA dam

Distribution areas

Municipality

Cooperative

Rural Distribution Area (1938)

Reservoir

City

Interchange points

Steam plants

Hydroelectric plants

Substations

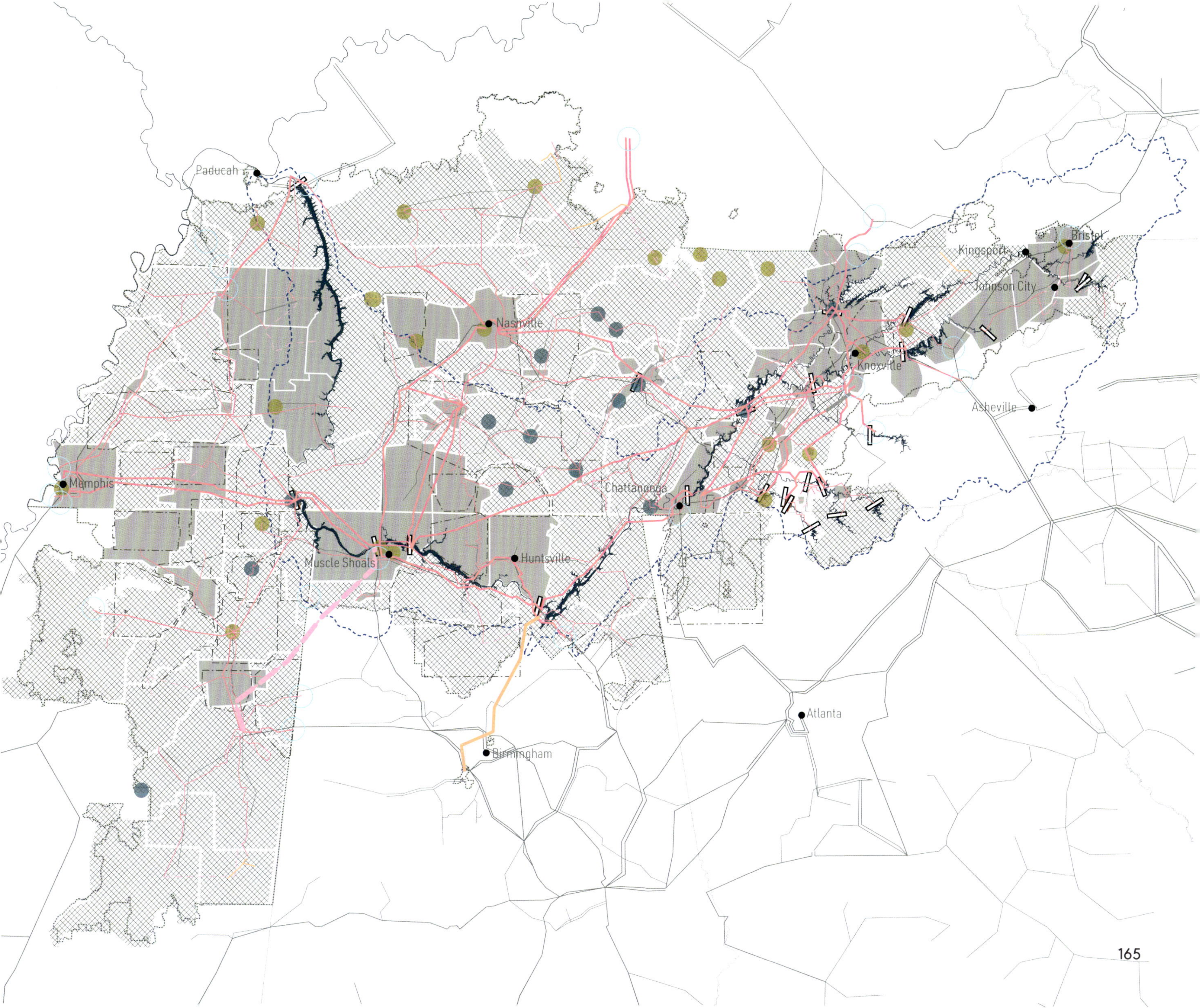

Paducah
Bristol
Kingsport
Johnson City
Nashville
Knoxville
Asheville
Memphis
Chattanooga
Muscle Shoals
Huntsville
Atlanta
Birmingham

Although the TVA Act of 1933 directed the agency to engage in rural electrification, the legality of this authorization was challenged in court almost immediately. The plaintiffs, representing private electric companies in the region, argued that the TVA's comprehensive plan was an existential threat to their business and evidence of government socialist tendencies, an overreach into the private energy market and an example of market manipulation. The electric companies, David E. Nye reports, "expended more effort to kill [the TVA plan] than to expand rural service."[81] Their argument resonated with local inhabitants and politicians whose skepticism of the federal government was grounded in the persistent conflict between states' rights and centralized federal power.

In 1938, however, the United States Supreme Court found in favor of the TVA, and David E. Lilienthal, the TVA director responsible for the *power machine*, opened the floodgates. By 1939, the TVA had increased its hydroelectric capacity to 420,000 kW and raised household consumption to nearly double the national average while halving energy prices. This process continued through World War II, as the TVA built new electrical lines and upgraded others to higher voltages across the region. The TVA also entered into negotiations with some of the private companies, incorporating their grids into its system. The outcome of this process became clear by 1947, as nothing less than a redefinition of the region. The TVA service area certainly overlaps with the watershed of the Tennessee River, but it extends well beyond it.

The business of rural electrification really began, however, with the construction of the actual transmission lines that connected, both visually and physically, the renewed farm with the TVA infrastructure. As Lilienthal declared: "And marching towards every point in the horizon you can see the steel crisscross of electric

Interior of the turbine hall in the Chicakmauga Dam Powerhouse

The substation at Guntersville Dam

Interior of the turbine hall in the Fontana Dam Powerhouse

transmission towers, a twentieth-century tower standing in a cove beside an eighteenth-century mountain cabin, a symbol and a summary of the change."[82] The TVA continues to maintain many of the transmission lines; it occasionally replaces the towers, but for the most part their spatial presence has not changed since the 1930s.

By producing and transmitting power, the TVA was in a position to augment the supply of power with cheaper electricity (i.e., below market price). As a government agency, however, it could not sell electricity directly to individual households. Instead, the agency invited the people of the Tennessee Valley to form electric cooperatives or municipalities, depending on their location in rural or urban parts of the Valley. The rural cooperatives introduced new spatial organizations into the region. Volunteer Electric Cooperative, for example, began as the Meigs County Power Association, until in 1939 it purchased the distribution facilities in neighboring counties from the TVA and changed its name.

The TVA supported many of the new cooperatives with loans, as did another New Deal agency, the Rural Electrification Administration (REA).[83] These loans were to be repaid from the proceeds of selling electricity, and this meant that producing and transmitting power was not enough: unless electricity was used by people in the region, the entire system fell apart. The TVA *power machine* was thus designed as a two-pronged attack. On the one hand, the Authority would influence the power market by supplying cheaper (below market price) electricity. At the same time, it would create new demand for power in rural regions. This dual approach, Lilienthal argued, would create a new "yardstick"—"a standard of performance for evaluating the efficiency of privately owned companies" that would encourage the expansion of rural electrification through competition.

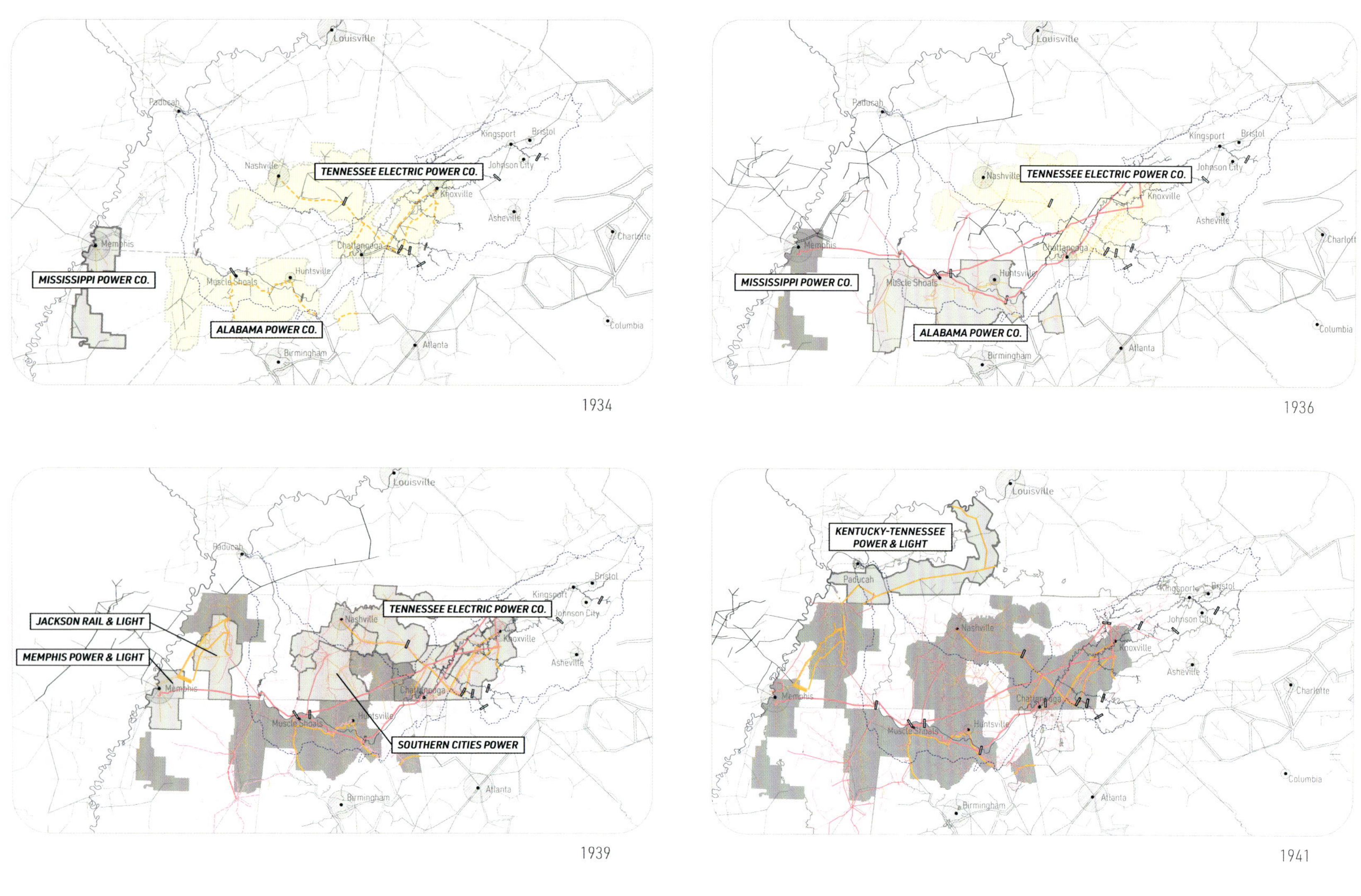
MISSISSIPPI POWER CO.
TENNESSEE ELECTRIC POWER CO.
ALABAMA POWER CO.
Louisville
Paducah
Kingsport
Bristol
Nashville
Johnson City
Knoxville
Asheville
Charlotte
Memphis
Muscle Shoals
Huntsville
Chattanooga
Columbia
Birmingham
Atlanta
1934
MISSISSIPPI POWER CO.
TENNESSEE ELECTRIC POWER CO.
ALABAMA POWER CO.
1936
JACKSON RAIL & LIGHT
MEMPHIS POWER & LIGHT
TENNESSEE ELECTRIC POWER CO.
SOUTHERN CITIES POWER
1939
KENTUCKY-TENNESSEE POWER & LIGHT
1941
Purchase contracts
Previous Acquisition
Executed
Disputed
Transmission lines
TVA Owned
154 kV
110 kV
44 kV
<22 kV
Under construction
110 kV
44 kV
Proposed
100< kV
22-99 kV
<22 kV
Authorized
110 kV
44 kV
Acquisition
Proposed acquisition
Acquisition
Privately owned
100+ kV
22-99 kV

The system would thus be a closed loop, a veritable machine.

Creating an electric market in the Tennessee Valley depended on the purchases of electric appliances, preferably large ones, such as threshers, corn huskers, and pumps on the farm as well as refrigerators, ranges, and washing machines in the home. In the early 1930s, however, such appliances were prohibitively expensive for the typical farmer in the region. To overcome this barrier the TVA created a second entity, the Electric Home and Farm Authority (EHFA), which furnished additional low-cost loans, allowing farmers to invest in "electrifying" their domains. The EHFA also worked directly with manufacturers to create an affordable line of appliances, which was identified with an official stamp. The TVA disseminated information on "electrifying" houses, including how-to guides for homeowners, and in 1936 it even proposed a program of test-farm demonstrations similar to that at the core of the *land machine*.[84] These efforts had a cultural as well as technological dimension. Relying on appliances allowed farmers to reorganize their daily schedule, and it brought residents one step closer to embracing middle-class values. The *power machine*, building on the agency's housing efforts, thus instilled the TVA social biases even more firmly in the region.

The TVA also made the *power machine* both salient and legible to residents and visitors. It opened the dams and powerhouses to the public, allowing guests to tour the turbine rooms and inspect the control rooms. Roland A. Wank, chief TVA architect, led his team to employ their professional expertise to enhance the visitors' experience. The unusual scale of the turbine halls (made even more impressive under their architectural guidance) allowed the team to experiment with roofing systems and finishes— from colorful tiles to raw concrete. The architects also repeated the logic of the scenic tours and provided visitors with multiple viewpoints—i.e., interior overlooks—into the internal functioning of the dam.[85]

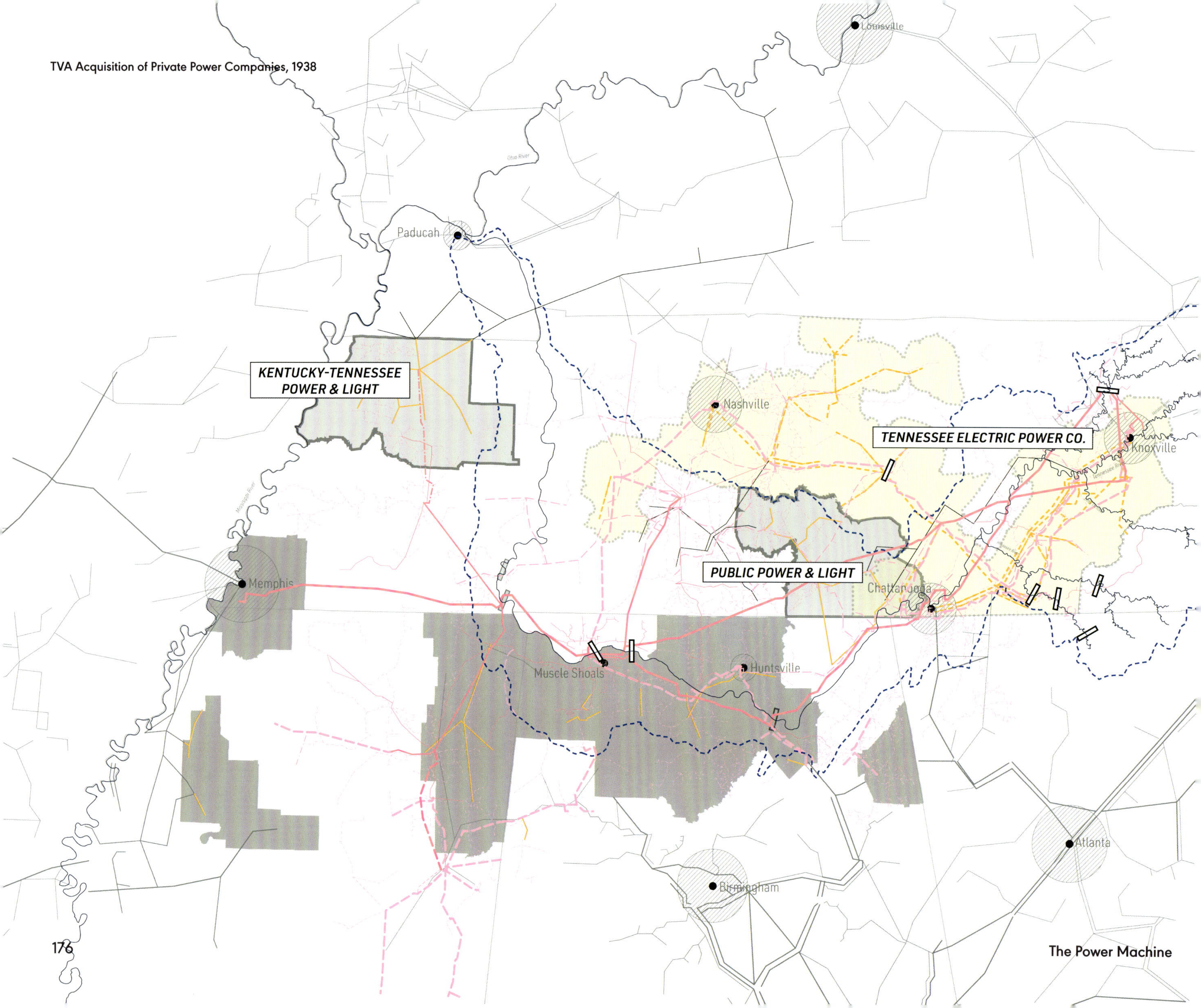
Louisville
Paducah
Ohio River
Mississippi River
KENTUCKY-TENNESSEE POWER & LIGHT
Nashville
Memphis
TENNESSEE ELECTRIC POWER CO.
Knoxville
Tennessee River
PUBLIC POWER & LIGHT
Chattanooga
Muscle Shoals
Huntsville
Birmingham
Atlanta

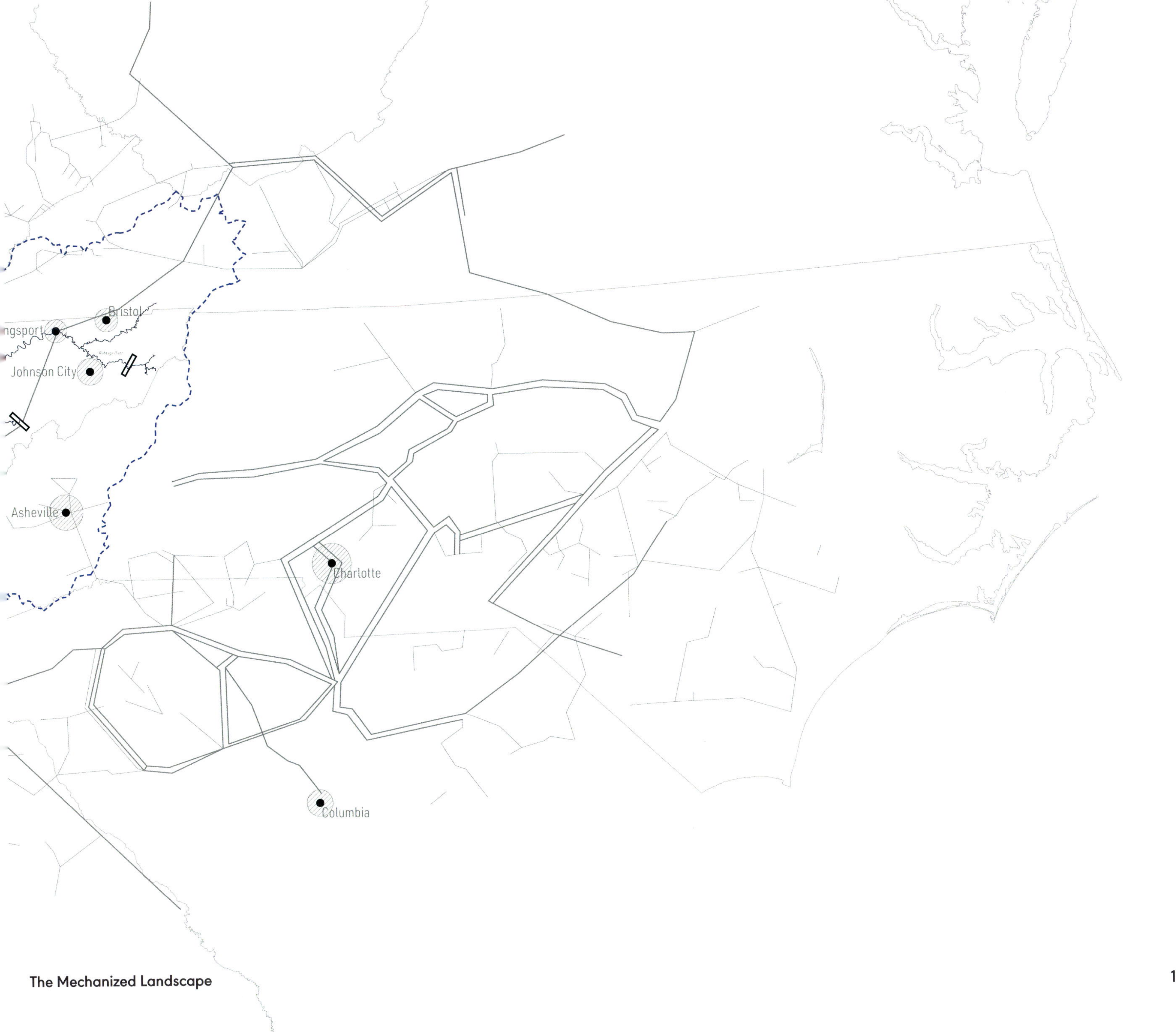

Bristol
ngsport
Johnson City
Asheville
Charlotte
Columbia

TVA Cherokee Dam

The substation at Fort Loudon Dam

9

The New Norris Model

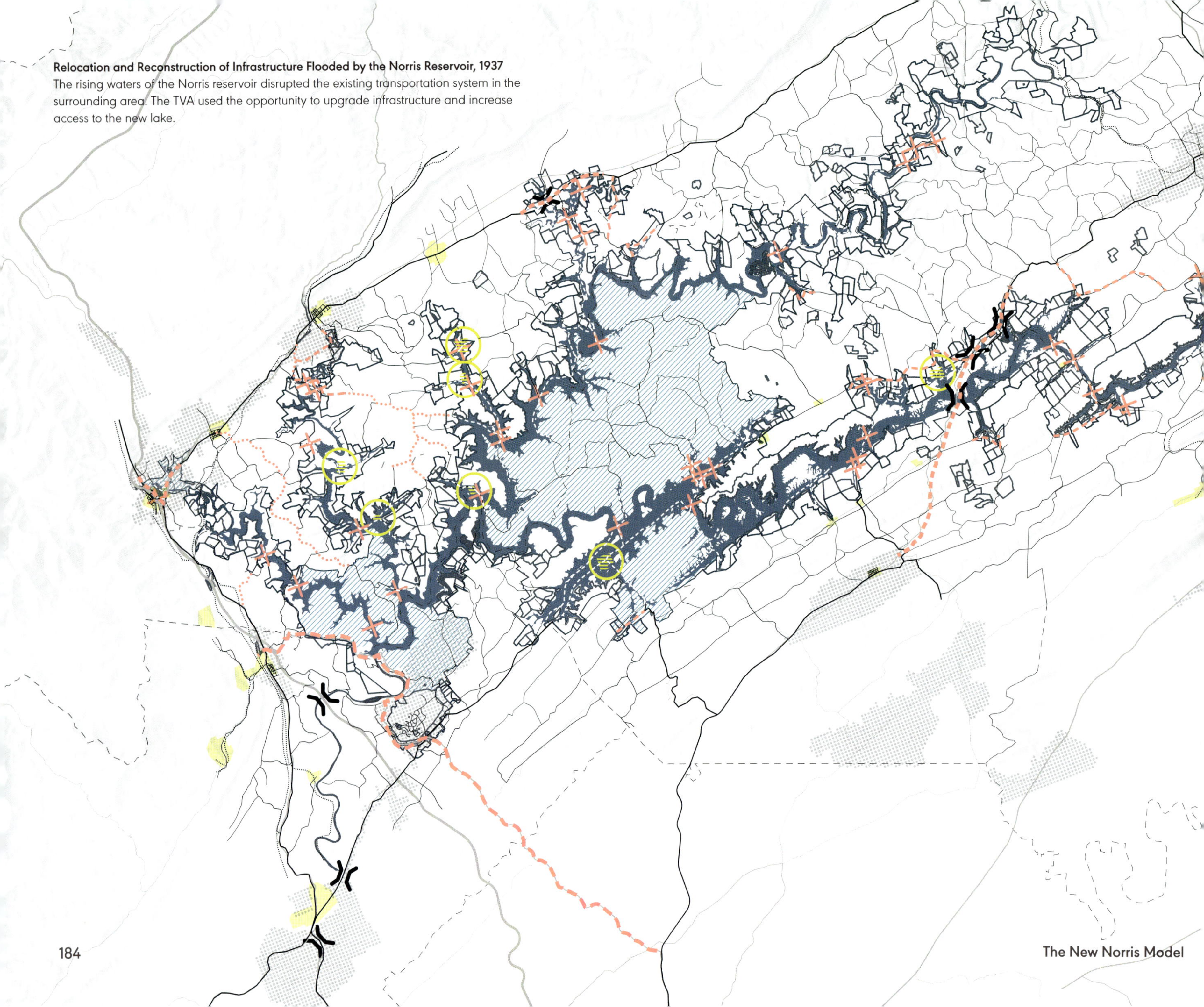

Relocation and Reconstruction of Infrastructure Flooded by the Norris Reservoir, 1937
The rising waters of the Norris reservoir disrupted the existing transportation system in the surrounding area. The TVA used the opportunity to upgrade infrastructure and increase access to the new lake.

The New Norris Model

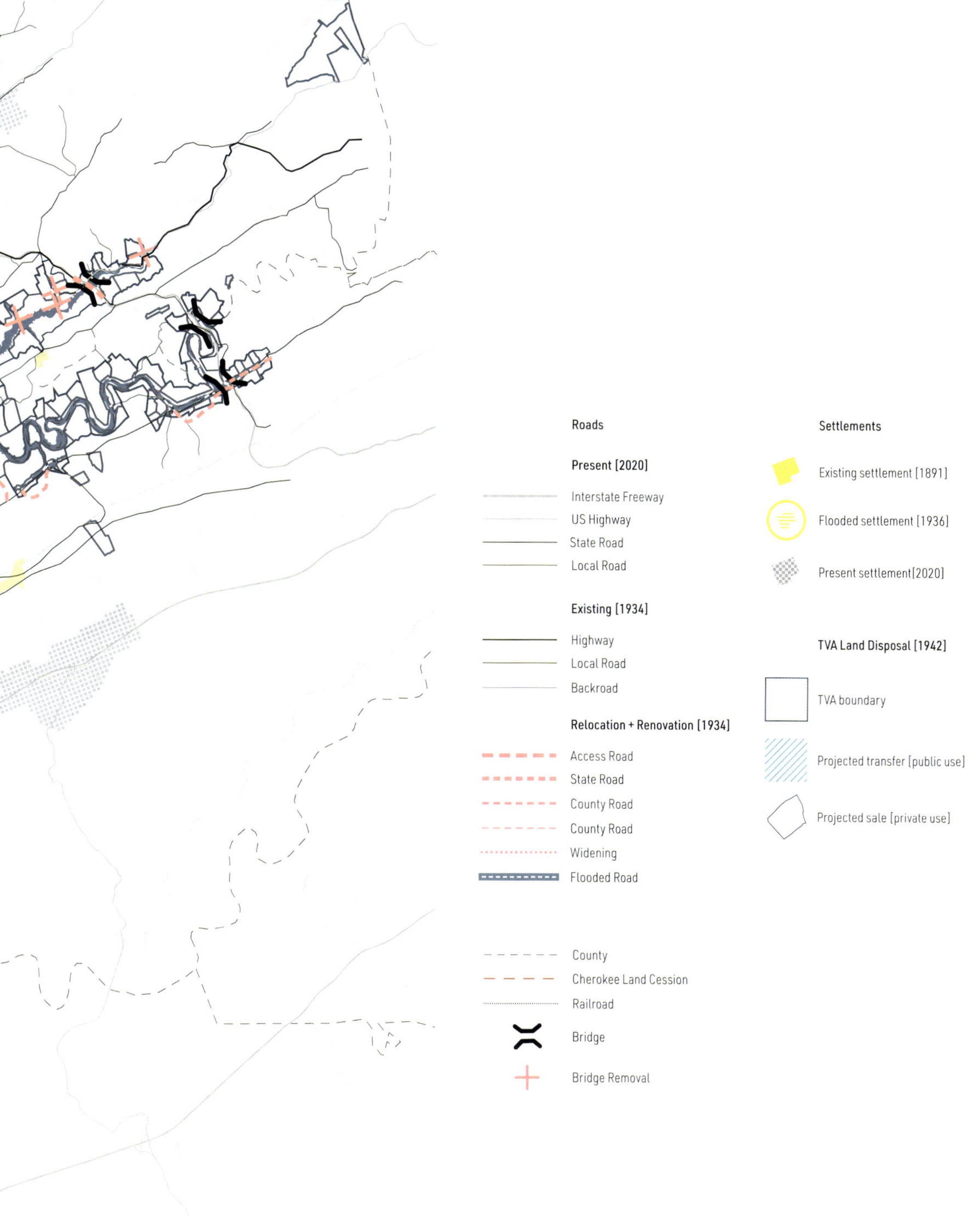

In 1933, the TVA began building Norris Dam, the first component in a system of multi-purpose dams along the Tennessee River and its tributaries. This project required purchasing large tracts of land, and Arthur E. Morgan, then Chairman of the Board of the TVA, decided to use the opportunity to demonstrate his vision for the entire Tennessee Valley. Under his direction, the vicinity of the dam was transformed into the most comprehensive display of regional planning and garden cities in the United States at the time. Morgan's demonstration was unique; it did not become a model for the TVA regional project. Under David E. Lilienthal's command, the agency moved away from centralized, utopian planning toward what he called the grassroots model. Still, the area known as Norris Lake—the reservoir and its surroundings—is, in many ways, a scaled and nested model of the mechanized landscape that resulted from the TVA's statecraft and its implementation. Several characteristics are worthy of mention.

Tazewell, Tennessee

Hickory Star Marina on Norris Lake.

Chuck Swan State Forest on Norris Lake.

There is a clear gap between the agency's statecraft and the environment it produced. The TVA spoke repeatedly about the "people" of the Tennessee Valley as the beneficiaries of its efforts, but most of the residents in the area today are not descendants of the people living there when the TVA began its operation. The agency played a role in this turnover. The territory that is now submerged below Norris Lake was not densely populated, but it was not empty. As part of building the *river machine*, the TVA cleared this land of its residents and their cemeteries. While the TVA recognized the hardships that accompanied such removal, it deemed it worthwhile for the greater public good. Michael J. McDonald and John Muldowney used the data about Norris Dam to reconstruct a comprehensive portrait of the people removed between 1933 and 1936 and to record the decisions they made following their "dispossession" by the TVA.[86]

The TVA emphasized the conservation and development of resources. Having controlled the floods on the Clinch and Powell Rivers (now submerged beneath the Norris Reservoir), the TVA actively engaged in forestry efforts and soil conservation on its banks. It also began producing electric power at the dam itself, transmitting it to residents around the new lake. The environment created by the TVA—the mechanized landscape—is far from a wilderness, but it did become a frontier, a place of opportunity. As such it attracted people from outside the region, who often arrive better prepared to take advantage of the new opportunities than the longtime residents. There is no Homestead Act for the Norris Lake region, but those who take advantage of its opportunities can, like the early pioneers on the historic frontier, rely on at least some government support for their efforts.

The most important resources the TVA developed around Norris Lake were associated with the tourist industry. It began by ensuring

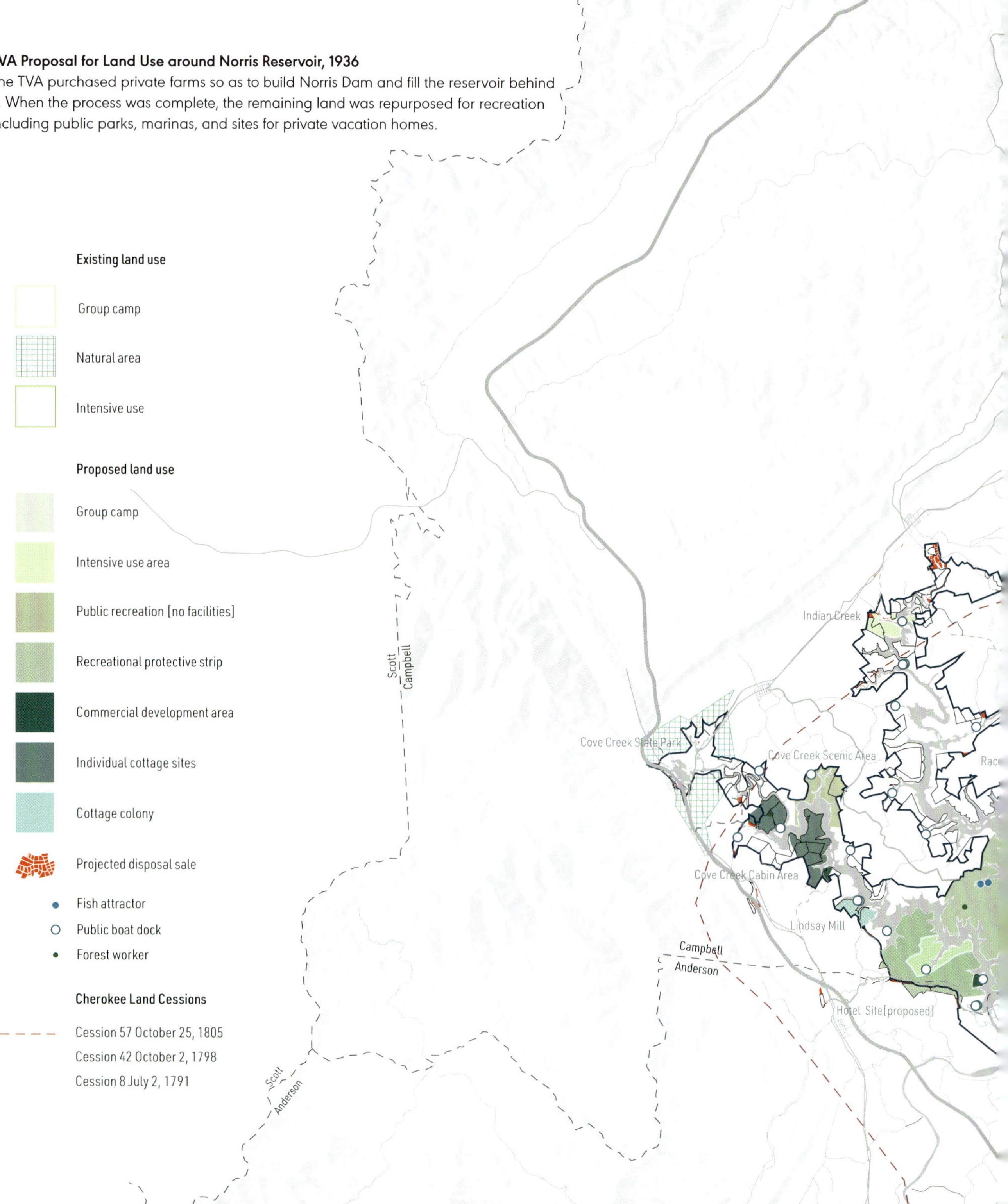

TVA Proposal for Land Use around Norris Reservoir, 1936
The TVA purchased private farms so as to build Norris Dam and fill the reservoir behind it. When the process was complete, the remaining land was repurposed for recreation including public parks, marinas, and sites for private vacation homes.

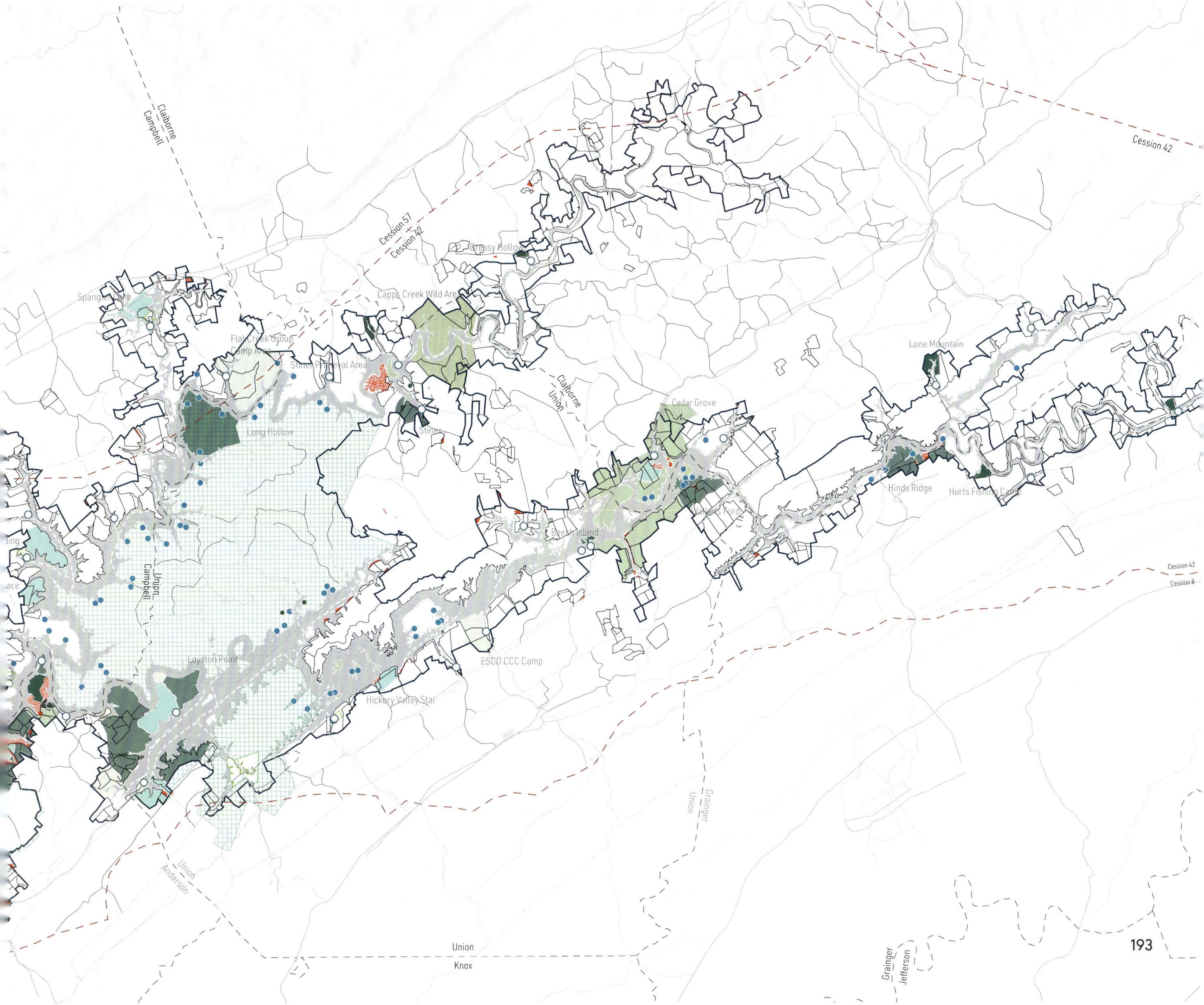

Cession 42
Cession 57
Cession 42
Cession 42
Cession 8
Claiborne
Campbell
Spangler Mine
Flat Creek Group Camp Area
Stiner Primeval Area
Capps Creek Wild Area
Greasy Hollow
Long Hollow
Stiner
Claiborne
Union
Cedar Grove
Lone Mountain
Hinds Ridge
Hurts Fishing Camp
Beech Island
Union
Campbell
Loyston Point
ESCO CCC Camp
Hickory Valley Star
Union
Anderson
Grainger
Union
Union
Knox
Grainger
Jefferson

Cedar Grove Marina and Campground on Norris Lake

The TVA's territorial administration of the Norris reservoir displaced several thousand inhabitants and upset a system of local jurisdictions. These people and entities, however, were themselves newcomers, heirs to the process of colonialization and the attendant expulsion of Indigenous People from the same land.

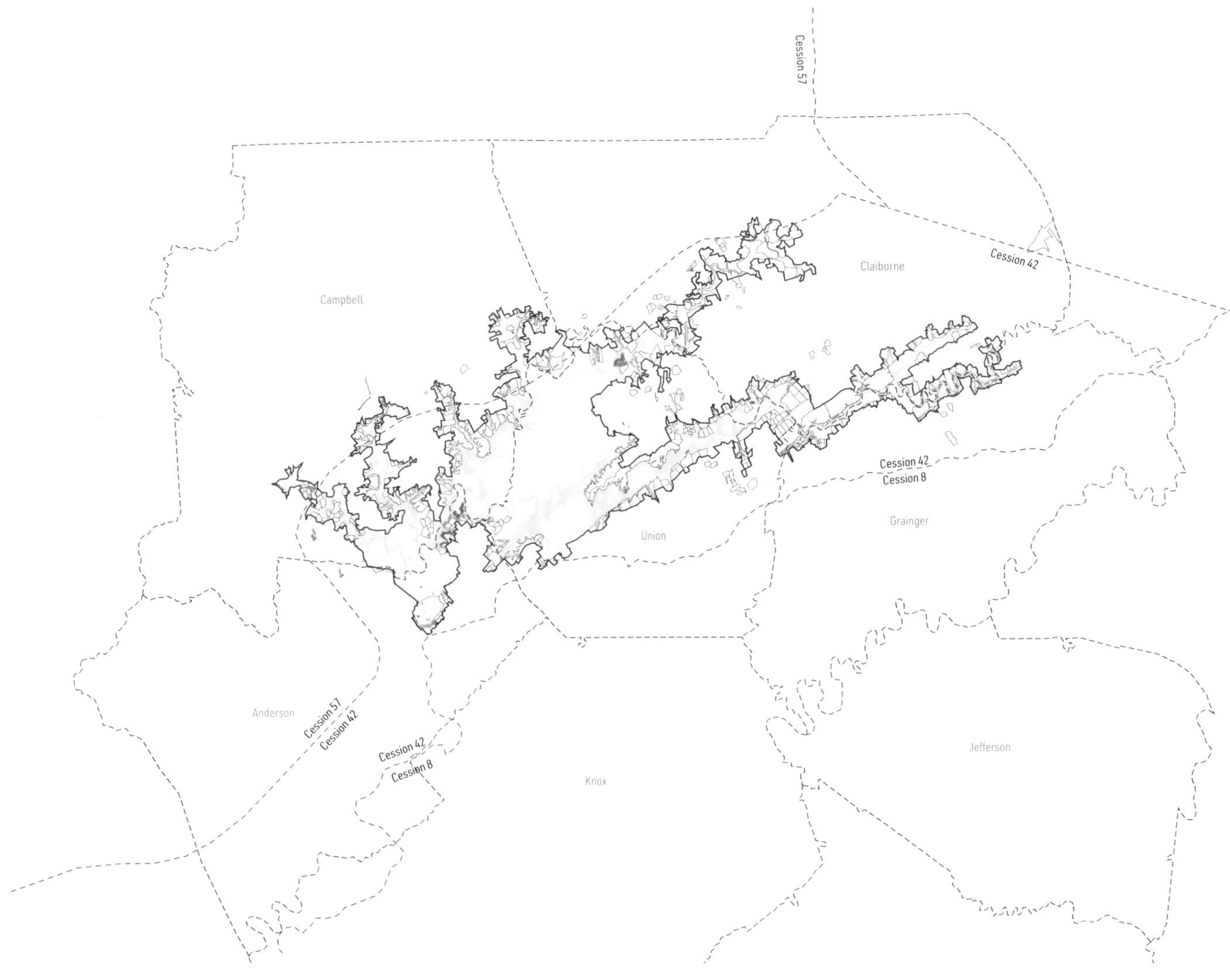

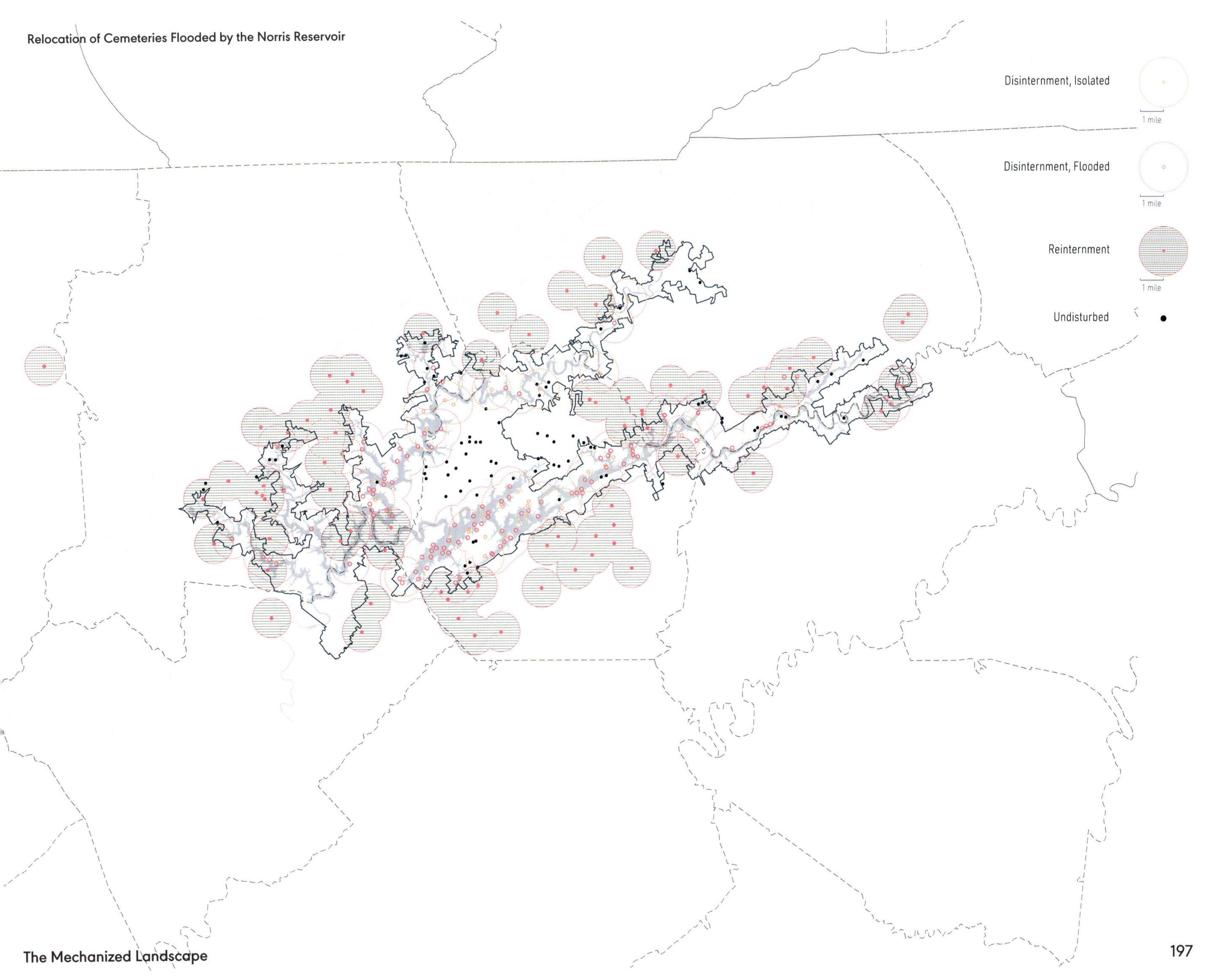
Disinternment, Isolated
1 mile
Disinternment, Flooded
1 mile
Reinternment
1 mile
Undisturbed

View of of Springs Dock and Resort on Norris Lake

access—rerouting key transportation routes that had been disrupted by the rising waters. Even more importantly, the TVA prepared a comprehensive plan for the shoreline of the lake, which it still controls. Following the original Norris model, this land-use plan includes public park and forests as well as boat docks and marinas operated by private companies. Cognizant of local boundaries, the TVA placed a marina in each of the existing counties, notwithstanding its overarching regional logic. These marinas continue to serve the local population, although developments of the past two decades show a marked tendency to cater to affluent clients visiting from Ohio, Indiana, and Florida.

Even more striking are the houses built around, and on, the TVA lakes. In 1939 the TVA, under pressure from Congress, began selling land for private development if it was not absolutely required for the operation of the dams and powerhouses. Would-be owners were, and still are, required to commit to comply with all TVA technical and engineering restrictions. The purchase allows them to invest in property for a first or second home. The TVA's promotion of middle-class values thus becomes conspicuous in the landscape, in what is distinctly a landscape of leisure. The TVA housing standards, prefabricated house models, and its symbolic borrowing of local motifs are all evident in the products of the construction industry.

A few miles from the shoreline of Norris Lake, the mechanized landscape returns to everyday purposes. The TVA statecraft emphasized farmers, especially those who adopted middle-class values. The reality of the TVA unified development, however, created a more complex society. The *land machine* and its many derivatives substantially benefited farmers in the Tennessee Valley and allowed them to broaden the scope and reach of their

enterprises. Rural electrification, on the other hand, enabled the development of rural industrialization. Free from the dictates of regional planners, industrialists located new plants in open areas rather than concentrating them in garden cities. These developments created unusual spikes in land values that disrupted existing agricultural patterns, leading many farmers to sell their farms for development. The navigation channel, created as part of the *river machine*, similarly engendered new commercial opportunities that have led to substantial growth in urban areas, but their overall footprint remains small.

The product of the TVA's competing projects— the mechanized landscape – is best described as "rurban."[87] Rather than demonstrating a clear distinction between rural and urban, the rurban landscape supports a single labor market.[88] Many farmers have found that full-time farming is no longer profitable and must supplement their income with industrial or service work. Others pursue multiple paths as a lifestyle choice, commuting regularly from the open countryside to cities or their sprawling edges.

In many ways, TVA statecraft and environmental intervention have brought regional land use full circle. When Indigenous territory was settled by Europeans, it was transformed into a system of private landholding. This land was then purchased by the government and made public, only to be offered once again for speculation and settlement. The frontier of accumulation created by the TVA may look dramatically different from the historic frontier, but as a process of supporting home ownership and the creation of wealth it functions in much the same way

Condominiums overlooking Norris Lake at Deerfield Resort in Tennessee

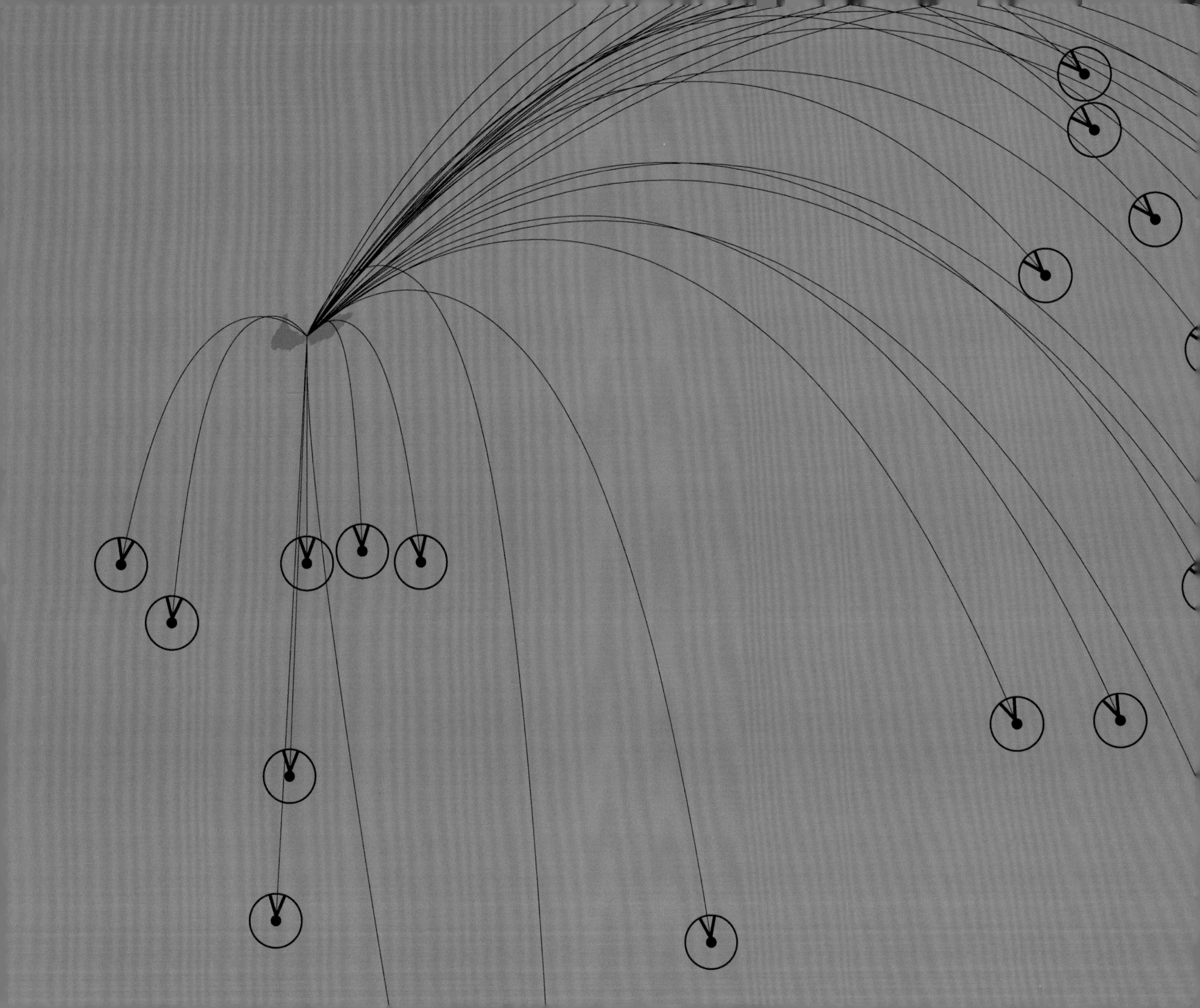

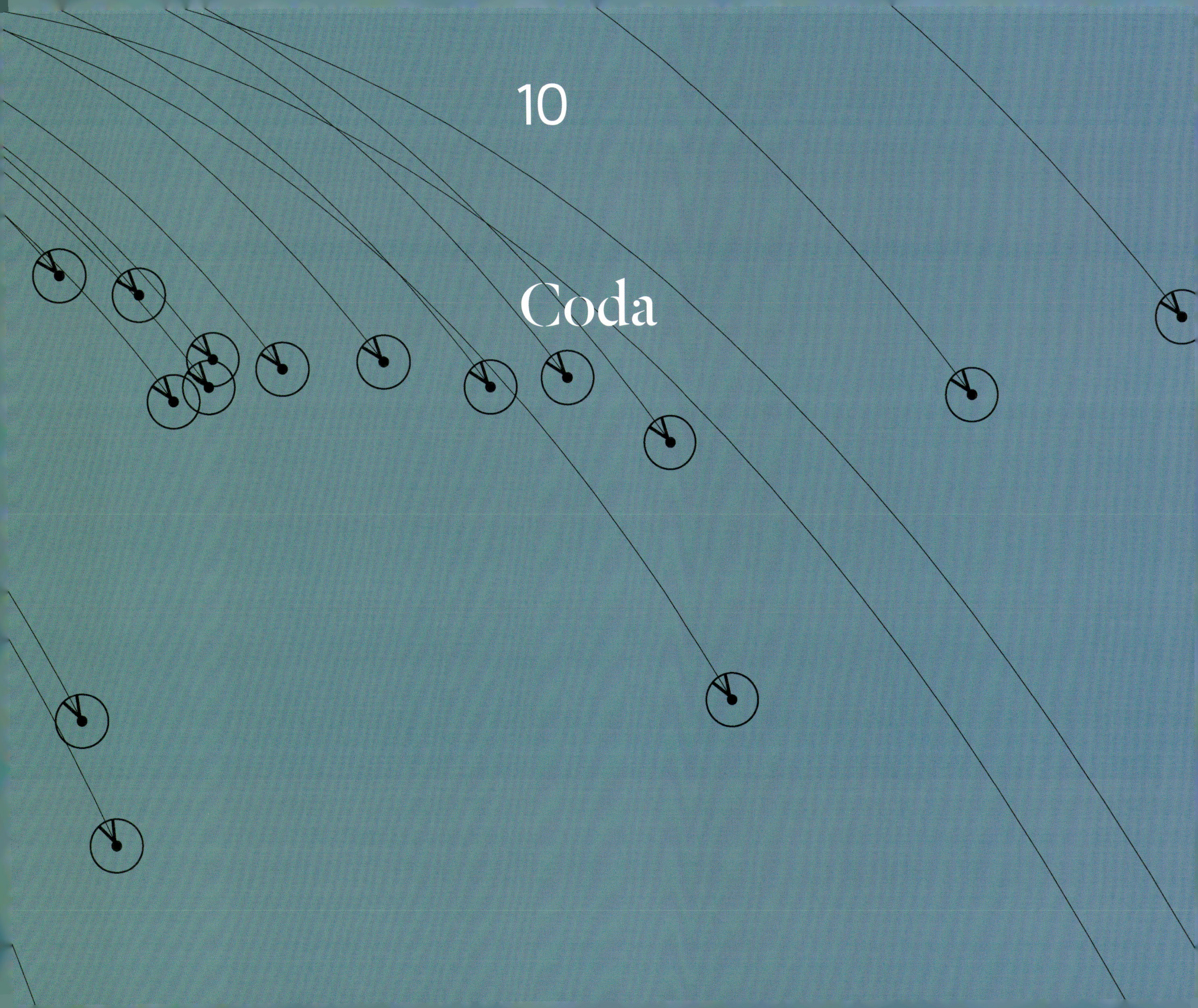

10

Coda

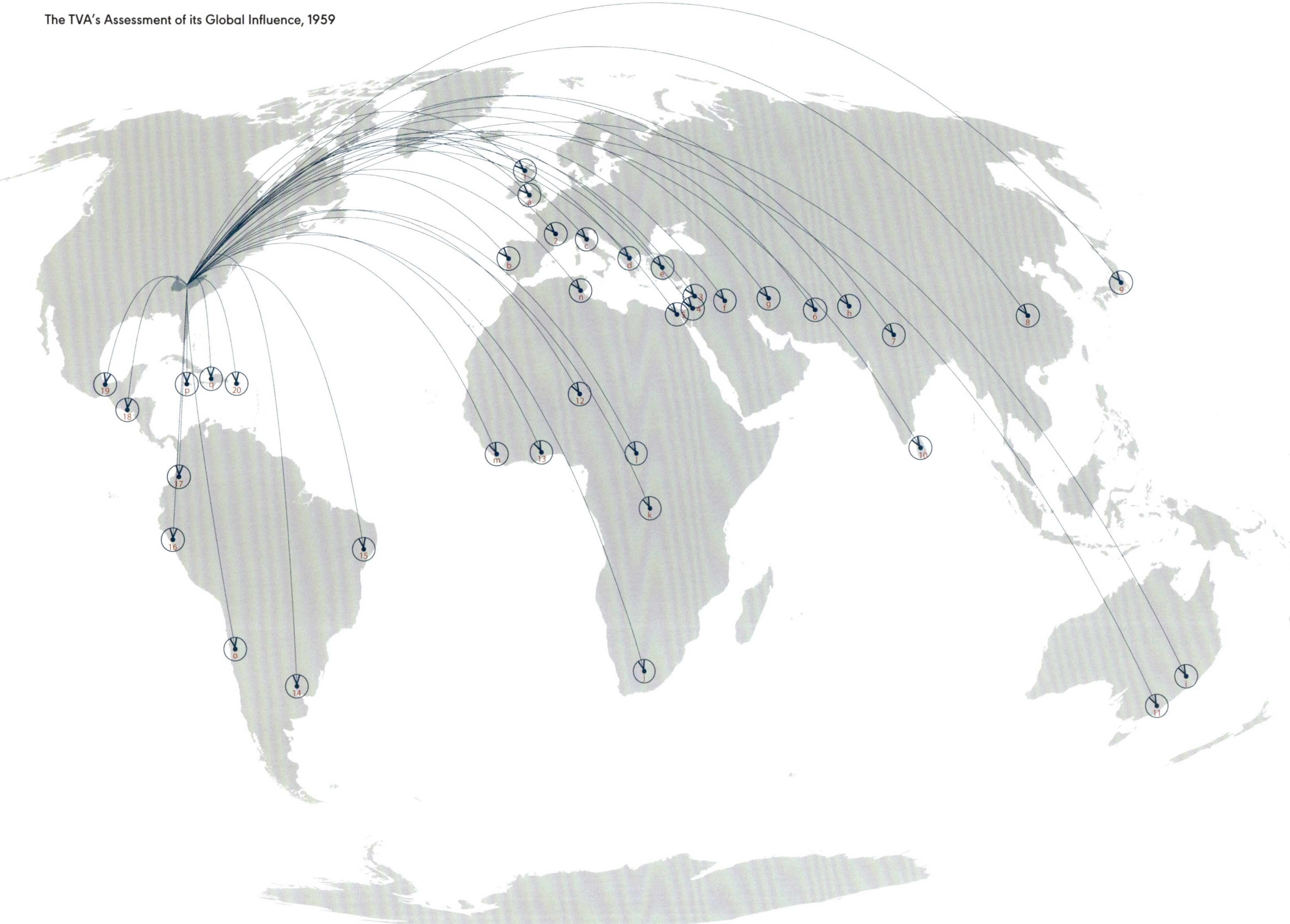

The TVA was established in 1933 to execute a vision of how environmental transformation would renew American democracy, region by region. As the agency developed its program in the following two decades, that vision was adjusted to the realities of the Tennessee Valley and to changing global conditions, creating what we have termed the mechanized landscape. By 1953, the three machines were, for the most part, complete. The river machine—a system of multi-purpose dams—controlled floods and opened navigation on the Tennessee River. The impact of the land machine, composed of both forestry and fertilizer programs, became visible in the landscape, even as the TVA transferred many of its responsibilities to regional institutions. Rural electrification, the goal of the power machine, had reached the corners of the Tennessee Valley and created a new reality for its residents. Two decades after its formation, as William C. Harvard commented, "TVA now [had] a history where it once simply had a vision."[89]

Visions, however, can persist without being attached to specific projects, and TVA statecraft is no exception. When the end of World War II was in sight, the TVA identified locations across the globe that might learn, or had learned, from its example.[90] In 1944, TVA director David E. Lilienthal published his seminal book, TVA: *Democracy on the March*, in which he heralded regional planning as a bulwark against totalitarianism and fascism.[91] The TVA also disseminated its expertise globally, sending its engineers abroad and hosting others at Norris Dam and other installations. In this version of the TVA project, statecraft and the environment were no longer engaged in mutual transformation. But the region—the watershed of the Tennessee Valley—continued to play a central role.

The road crossing Norris Dam

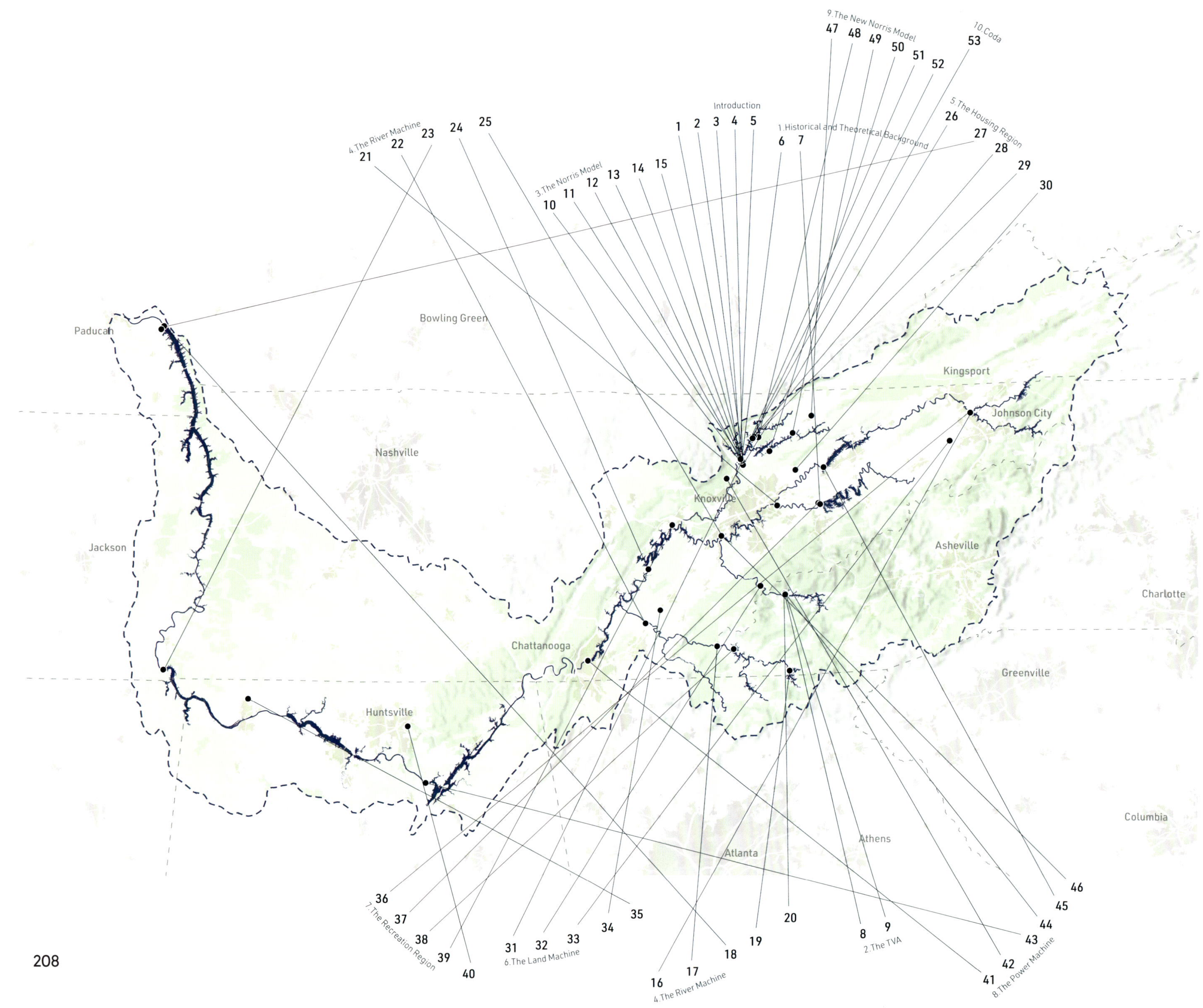

Introduction
1 2 3 4 5
6 7
1.Historical and Theoretical Background
9.The New Norris Model
47 48 49 50 51 52
10.Coda
53
5.The Housing Region
26 27 28 29 30
4.The River Machine
21 22 23 24 25
3.The Norris Model
10 11 12 13 14 15
Paducah
Bowling Green
Nashville
Kingsport
Johnson City
Knoxville
Asheville
Jackson
Charlotte
Chattanooga
Greenville
Huntsville
Columbia
Athens
Atlanta
7.The Recreation Region
36 37 38 39 40
6.The Land Machine
31 32 33 34 35
4.The River Machine
16 17 18 19
2.The TVA
20 8 9
8.The Power Machine
41 42 43 44 45 46

The Mechanized Landscape

Endnotes

1   Thomas Jefferson, *Notes on the State of Virginia* (Boston: Lilly and Wait, 1832).

2   Roderick Frazier Nash, *Wilderness and the American Mind* (New Haven: Yale University Press, 1967).

3   Leo Marx, *Machine in the Garden: Technology and the Pastoral Ideal in America* (New York: Oxford University Press, 1964).

4   Frederick Jackson Turner, *The Significance of the Frontier in American History* (Madison: State Historical Society of Wisconsin, 1894).

5   Benedict R. O'G. Anderson, *Imagined Communities: Reflections on the Origin and Spread of Nationalism* (London: Verso, 1983).

6   William Goodell Frost, "Our Contemporary Ancestors in the Southern Mountains," *Atlantic Monthly*, 1899.

7   James C. Klotter, "The Black South and White Appalachia," *The Journal of American History* 66, no. 4 (1980).

8   Leo Marx, "The Idea of Nature in America," *Daedalus* 137, no. 2, On Nature (Spring 2008).

9   Clayton R. Koppes, "Efficiency/Equity/Esthetics: Towards a Reinterpretation of American Conservation," *Environmental Review: ER* 11, no. 2 (Summer 1987).

10 Ashley Carse, *Beyond the Big Ditch: Politics, Ecology, and Infrastructure at the Panama Canal* (Cambridge, Massachusetts: The MIT Press, 2014).

11 Helen Matthews Lewis, Linda Johnson, and Donald Askins, eds., *Colonialism in Modern America: The Appalachian Case* (Boone, North Carolina: Appalachian State University, 1978).

12 George Perkins Marsh, *Man and Nature; or, Physical Geography as Modified by Human Action* (New York: Charles Scribner & Co., 1871).

13 Samuel P. Hays, *Conservation and the Gospel of Efficiency: The Progressive Conservation Movement, 1890-1920* (Pittsburgh Penn.: University of Pittsburgh Press, 2015).

14 John Wesley Powell, *Report on the Lands of the Arid Region of the United States; with a More Detailed Account of the Lands of Utah; with Maps* (Washington, DC: Government Printing Office, 1879).

15 Linda Nash, "The Changing Experience of Nature: Historical Encounters with a Northwest River," *The Journal of American History* 86, no. 4 (2000).

16 Bernhard Eduard Fernow, *Economics of Forestry, a Reference Book for Students of Political Economy and Professional and Lay Students of Forestry* (New York: T. Y. Crowell & Company, 1902).

17 *Report of the Secretary of Agriculture in Relation to the Forests, Rivers, and Mountains of the Southern Appalachian Region, December 19, 1901* (Washington, DC: United States Government Printing Office).

18 Henry David Thoreau, *Walden, or, Life in the Woods* (United States: Houghton Mifflin, 1893).

19 Phoebe Cutler, *The Public Landscape of the New Deal* (New Haven: Yale University Press, 1985).

20 Donald J. Pisani, "Water Planning in the Progressive Era: The Inland Waterways Commission Reconsidered," *Journal of Policy History* 18, no. 4 (2006).

21 William J. Novak, *New Democracy: The Creation of the Modern American State* (Cambridge: Harvard University Press, 2022), 1.

22 Michael Mann, "The Autonomous Power of the State: Its Origins, Mechanisms and Results," *European Journal of Sociology / Archives Européennes de Sociologie / Europäisches Archiv für Soziologie* 25, no. 2, Tending the Roots: Nationalism and Populism (1984).

23 David Hackett Fischer, *Liberty and Freedom: A Visual History of America's Founding Ideas* (Cary: Oxford University Press, Incorporated, 2004), 480.

24 Richard Plunz, *A History of Housing in New York City, Dwelling Type and Social Change in the American Metropolis* (New York: Columbia University Press, 1990).

25 Andrew M. Shanken, *194X Architecture, Planning, and Consumer Culture on the American Home Front*, (Minneapolis, London: University of Minnesota Press, 2009), 10.

26 Ebenezer Howard, *Garden Cities of to-Morrow (Being the Second Edition of "to-Morrow: A Peaceful Path to Real Reform")* (London: S. Sonnenschein & co., ltd., 1902).

27 Benton MacKaye, "An Appalachian Trail: A Project in Regional Planning," *Journal of the American Institute of Architects* 9, no. 9 (September 1921).

28 Ronald A. Foresta, "Transformation of the Appalachian Trail," *Geographical Review* 77, no. 1 (January 1987).

29 Benjamin Higgins, "The American Frontier and the TVA," *Society* 32, no. 3 (1995).

30 *Tennessee Valley Authority Act of 1933*.

31 Paul K. Conkin, "Intellectual and Political Roots," in *TVA Fifty Years of Grass-Roots Bureaucracy*, ed. Erwin C. Hargrove and Paul K. Conkin (Urbana and Chicago: University of Illinois Press, 1983).

32 *Tennessee Valley Authority Act of 1933*.

33 Conkin, in *TVA Fifty Years of Grass-Roots Bureaucracy*, 24.

34 Origin of the Regional Planning and Development Concept in TVA Legislation (Memo from Howard K. Menhinick to L. L. Durisch and Tracy B. Augur, February 6, 1943), Aelred J. Gray and David A. Johnson, *The TVA Regional Planning and Development Program: The Transformation of an Institution and its Mission* (Aldershot, England and Burlington, VT: Ashgate, 2005).

35 "Report to the Congress on the Unified Development of the Tennessee River System, Submitted by the Board of Directors of the Tennessee Valley Authority, March 1936" (Knoxville, Tenn.: Tennessee Valley Authority).

36 David E. Lilienthal, *TVA; Democracy on the March (10th Anniversary Edition)* (New York: Harper & Row, 1953).

37 Lilienthal, 149.

38 Lilienthal, 77.

39 Avigail Sachs, "Research and Democracy: The Architectural Research Division of the Tennessee Valley Authority," *Journal of Architecture* 24, no. 7 (2020).

40 Brian Black, "Organic Planning: Ecology and Design in the Landscape of the Tennessee Valley Authority, 1933-1945," in *Environmentalism in Landscape Architecture*, ed. Michel Conan (Washington, D.C.: Dumbarton Oaks Research Library and Collection, 2000), 79.

41 For a detailed account of these projects see: Avigail Sachs, *The Garden in the Machine: Planning and Democracy in the Tennessee Valley Authority* (Charlottesville: University of Virginia Press, 2023).

42 Lilienthal, 93.

43 Philip Selznick, *TVA and the Grass Roots; a Study in the Sociology of Formal Organization* (Berkeley: University of California Press, 1949).

44 Nancy L. Grant, *TVA and Black Americans, Planning for the Status Quo* (Philadelphia: Temple University Press, 1990).

45 W. H. Droze, "TVA and the Ordinary Farmer," *Agricultural History* 53, no. 1 Southern Agriculture Since the Civil War: A Symposium (January 1979).

46 Donald Davidson and Theresa Julienna (Sherrer) Davidson, *The Tennessee, Vol. 2 the New River, Civil War to TVA* (New York: Rinehart, 1946).

47 Mark G. Malvasi, *The Unregenerate South: The Agrarian Thought of John Crowe Ransom, Allen Tate, and Donald Davidson* (Baton Rouge: Louisiana State University Press, 1997).

48 Ebenezer Howard, *Garden Cities of to-Morrow (Being the Second Edition of "to-Morrow: A Peaceful Path to Real Reform")* (London: S. Sonnenschein & co., ltd., 1902).

49 Tracy B. Augur, "The Planning of the Town of Norris," *American Architect* 148 (1936): 19.

50 Marian Moffett and Lawrence Wodehouse, "Noble Structures Set in Handsome Parks: Public Architecture of the TVA," *Modulus* 17 (1984).

51	Thomas C. Hubka, *How the Working-Class Home Became Modern, 1900-1940* (Minneapolis: University of Minnesota Press, 2020).

52	Christine Macy, "The Architect's Office of the Tennessee Valley Authority," in *The Tennessee Valley Authority: Design and Persuasion*, ed. Tim Culvahouse (New York Princeton Architectural Press, 2007), 26.

53	Walter L. Creese, *TVA's Public Planning: The Vision, the Reality* (Knoxville: University of Tennessee Press, 1990), 247.

54	Tim Culvahouse, ed., *The Tennessee Valley Authority: Design and Persuasion* (New York: Princeton Architectural Press, 2007).

55	Tennessee Valley Authority, *Annual Report of the Tennessee Valley Authority for the Fiscal Year Ended June 30, 1939*, 2.

56	United States Army Corp of Engineers, *Index of Tennessee River and Tributaries, North Carolina, Tennessee, Alabama, and Kentucky* (Tennessee Valley Authority, 1933).

57	*Navigation and Economic Growth, Tennessee River Experience, a Report Prepared Pursuant to Section 22 of the TVA Act and Executive Order No. 6161 (June 8, 1933)* (Knoxville, Tennessee 37902 Tennessee Valley Authority, September 1966).

58	Thomas Jefferson, *Notes on the State of Virginia* (Boston: Lilly and Wait, 1832).

59	Donald J. Pisani, "Water Planning in the Progressive Era: The Inland Waterways Commission Reconsidered," *Journal of Policy History* 18, no. 4 (2006).

60	Paul K. Conkin, "Intellectual and Political Roots," in TVA Fifty Years of Grass-Roots Bureaucracy, ed. Erwin C. Hargrove and Paul K. Conkin (Urbana and Chicago: University of Illinois Press, 1983).

61	David E. Lilienthal, TVA; Democracy on the March (10th Anniversary Edition) (New York: Harper & Row, 1953), 4–5.

62	Lilienthal, xviii.

63	Brian Black, "Organic Planning: Ecology and Design in the Landscape of the Tennessee Valley Authority, 1933-1945," in Environmentalism in Landscape Architecture, ed. Michel Conan (Washington, D.C.: Dumbarton Oaks Research Library and Collection, 2000), 73.

64	For further details see: Avigail Sachs, *The Garden in the Machine: Planning and Democracy in the Tennessee Valley Authority* (Charlottesville: University of Virginia Press, 2023).

65	Avigail Sachs, "Research and Democracy: The Architectural Research Division of the Tennessee Valley Authority," *Journal of Architecture* 24, no. 7 (2020).

66	Earle S. Draper, "TVA's Yardstick for Housing," *Architectural Forum* 63, no. 3 (September 1935).

67	Avigail Sachs and Tricia A. Stuth, "Innovation and Tradition: Eighty Years of Housing Construction in Southern Appalachia," *Construction History* 28, no. 1 (2013).

68	Tennessee Valley Authority, *Annual Report of the Tennessee Valley Authority for the Fiscal Year Ended June 30, 1939*, 1.

69	Paul K. Conkin, "Intellectual and Political Roots," in *TVA Fifty Years of Grass-Roots Bureaucracy*, ed. Erwin C. Hargrove and Paul K. Conkin (Urbana and Chicago: University of Illinois Press, 1983).

70	*Annual Report of the Director of the Civilian Conservation Corps, Fiscal Year Ended June 30, 1941* (Washington, DC: United States Government Printing Office), 37.

71	Tennessee Valley Authority. Department of Forestry Relations Forestry Log. 1938/1941. SD11 T34 V.3, NO.5-V.6.COP.1.

72	Willis M. Baker and William M. Landess, "Education for Sustained Regional Productivity," *The Journal of Educational Sociology* 15, no. 3, The TVA Program – The Regional Approach to General Welfare (November 1941).

73	Kenneth J. Seigworth, "Reforestation in the Tennessee Valley," *Public Administration Review* 8, no. 4 (Autumn 1948).

74	Tennessee Valley Authority, Phosphate Reserves of the United States (Wilson Dam, Alabama: Tennessee Valley Authority, 1945).

75	W. H. Droze, "TVA and the Ordinary Farmer," Agricultural History 53, no. 1, Southern Agriculture Since the Civil War: A Symposium (January 1979): 194.

76	Paul K. Conkin, *A Revolution down on the Farm, Transformation of American Agriculture since 1929* (Lexington: The University of Kentucky Press, 2008).

77	David E. Lilienthal, *TVA; Democracy on the March (10th Anniversary Edition)* (New York: Harper & Row, 1953), 114.

78	Tennessee Valley Authority, *The Scenic Resources of the Tennessee Valley, a Descriptive and Pictorial Inventory* (Washington, DC: United States Government Printing Office, 1938), xi.

79	Tennessee Valley Authority, "Watts Bar Getaway."

80	Anja Cordell in private conversation with Micah Rutenberg.

81	David E. Nye, *Electrifying America: Social Meanings of a New Technology, 1880-1940* (Cambridge, Mass.: MIT Press, 1990).

82	David E. Lilienthal, *TVA; Democracy on the March (10th Anniversary Edition)* (New York: Harper & Row, 1953), 8.

83	Sarah Rovang, "Envisioning the Future of Modern Farming: The Electrified Farm at the 1939 New York World's Fair," *Journal of the Society of Architectural Historians* 74, no. 2, June (2015), Sarah Rovang, "The Grid Comes Home: Wiring and Lighting the American Farmhouse," *Buildings & Landscapes: Journal of the Vernacular Architecture Forum* 23, no. 2, Fall (2016).

84	Proposals for Electric Demonstration Farms (Attached to Letter from George W. Kable to F. W. Hunter, September 26, 1936), Board of Directors Papers, Box 223, Folder 926.9–36 Rural Electrification.

85	For further details see: Avigail Sachs, *The Garden in the Machine: Planning and Democracy in the Tennessee Valley Authority* (Charlottesville: University of Virginia Press, 2023).

86	Michael J. McDonald and John Muldowny, *TVA and the Dispossessed, the Resettlement of Population in the Norris Dam Area* (Knoxville: The University of Tennessee Press, 1982).

87	Leo Marx, "The American Ideology of Space," in *Denatured Visions: Landscape and Culture in the Twentieth Century*, ed. Stuart Wrede and William Howard Adams (New York: Museum of Modern Art, 1994), 76.

88	Paul K. Conkin, *A Revolution down on the Farm, Transformation of American Agriculture since 1929* (Lexington: The University of Kentucky Press, 2008), 90.

89	William C. Harvard Jr., "The Images of TVA: The Clash over Values," in *TVA Fifty Years of Grass-Roots Bureaucracy*, ed. Erwin C. Hargrove and Paul K. Conkin (Urbana and Chicago: University of Illinois Press, 1983), 309.

90	Tennessee Valley Authority, TVA as a Symbol of Resource Development in Many Countries (a Digest and Selected Bibliography of Information (TVA Technical Library, Knoxville, Tennessee, January 1952).

91	David E. Lilienthal, TVA: Democracy on the March (New York: Harper, 1944).

Map Sources

ARCHIVES
[If unpublished, item location is in brackets.]

Marshall Wilson Collection, Calvin M. McClung Historical Collection, Knox County Public Library, Knoxville, TN.
RG 142, TVA Records, The National Archives at Atlanta.
RG 142 Regional Maps, 1942 - 1956 Land Planning and Housing, The National Archives at College Park, Maryland.
RG 187, NRPB Central Office United States Planning, The National Archives at College Park, Maryland.

GENERAL DATA
David, Paul Theodore, and Tennessee Valley Authority. *Tennessee River and Tributaries, North Carolina, Tennessee, Alabama, and Kentucky.* (Washington, DC: United States Government Printing Office, 1930).
For specific maps from this book, see The River Machine and The Power Machine.
National Hydrography Dataset, United States Geological Survey, 2018, ESRI ArcGIS Online Portal.
Tennessee Valley Authority Dams and Driving Directions, TVA GIS & Mapping, 2020, ESRI ArcGIS Online Portal.
Tennessee Valley Authority, *Annual Report of the Tennessee Valley Authority,* Fiscal Years: 1934-1949 (Washington, DC: United States Government Printing Office).
Tennessee Valley Authority, *A Technical Review of the Hiwassee Project* (Washington, DC: United States Government Printing Office, 1940).
Tennessee Valley Authority. Construction Dept. *Plans and Specifications for the Norris Dam.* 2d ed. (Knoxville: N.P., 1946).
Tennessee Valley Authority, *The Chickamauga Project: A Comprehensive Report on the Planning, Design, Construction and Initial Operations of the Chickamauga Project* (Knoxville, TN: Tennessee Valley Authority, 1942).
Tennessee Valley Authority, *The Douglas Project: A Comprehensive Report on the Planning, Design, Construction and Initial Operations of the Douglas Project* (Washington, DC: United States Government Printing Office, 1949).
Tennessee Valley Authority, *The Fort Loudon Project: A Comprehensive Report on the Planning, Design, Construction and Initial Operations of the Fort Loudon Project* (Washington, DC: United States Government Printing Office, 1949).
Tennessee Valley Authority, *The Guntersville Project: A Comprehensive Report on the Planning, Design, Construction and Initial Operations of the Guntersville Project* (Knoxville, TN: Tennessee Valley Authority, 1941).
Tennessee Valley Authority, *The Kentucky Project: A Comprehensive Report on the Planning, Design, Construction and Initial Operations of the Kentucky Project* (Washington, DC: United States Government Printing Office, 1951).
Tennessee Valley Authority, *The Norris Project: A Comprehensive Report on the Planning, Design, Construction and Initial Operations of the Tennessee Valley Authority's First Water Control Project* (Washington, DC: United States Government Printing Office, 1940).
Tennessee Valley Authority, *The Watts Bar Project: A Comprehensive Report on the Planning, Design, Construction and Initial Operations of the Watts Bar Project* (Washington, DC: United States Government Printing Office, 1949).
Tennessee Valley Authority, *The Wheeler Project: A Comprehensive Report on the Planning, Design, Construction and Initial Operations of the Wheeler Project* (Washington, DC: United States Government Printing Office, 1940).
U.S. Topographic Map, United States Geological Survey, 1935, 1936, 1941.
Watershed Boundary Dataset, United States Geological Survey, 2018, ESRI ArcGIS Online Portal.

SOURCES BY CHAPTER

INTRODUCTION
Norris, Tennessee, United States Geological Survey, 1941.
Town of Norris, Tennessee, TVA Division of Land Planning and Housing, 1935. [Regional Maps.]

HISTORICAL AND THEORETICAL BACKGROUND
USA Federal Lands, ESRI, 2013, ESRI ArcGIS Online Portal.

THE TVA
Areas Proposed for Improvement Authorities, National Resources Planning Board, 1935. [NRPB Central Office.]

THE NORRIS MODEL
Chart of Concrete Progress by Location, Tennessee Valley Authority, 1935. [TVA Records.]

Developed Portion Town of Norris, Tennessee, Tennessee Valley Authority, Regional Studies Department, 1942. [TVA Records.]

General Plan of Construction Plant, Tennessee Valley Authority, Norris Dam Project Field Office, 1934. [TVA Records.]

Norris Dam General Layout, Tennessee Valley Authority, Norris Project, 1937. Included in *Plans and Specifications for the Norris Dam.*

Norris Project General Plan, Misc. Lighting and Services, Tennessee Valley Authority, Engineering Design Department, 1937. Included in *Plans and Specifications for the Norris Dam.*

Suggested Development of Norris Dam, Tennessee, Valley Authority, 1935. [TVA Records.]

THE RIVER MACHINE

Airways, Airports, and Landing Fields, Tennessee Valley Authority, Division of Land Planning and Housing, 1936. [Regional Maps.]

Extent of Navigation, U.S. Army Corps of Engineers, 1927. Included in *Tennessee River and Tributaries.*

Freight Tonnage, U.S. Army Corps of Engineers, 1928. Included in *Tennessee River and Tributaries.*

Freight Tonnage Carried by Rail Across Area, U.S. Army Corp of Engineers, 1928. Included in *Tennessee River and Tributaries.*

Freight Tonnage Carried by Rail Between North and West and Area, U.S. Army Corp of Engineers, 1928. Included in *Tennessee River and Tributaries.*

Freight Tonnage Carried by Rail Between South and East and Area, U.S. Army Corp of Engineers, 1928. Included in *Tennessee River and Tributaries.*

Mineral Resources Map, Tennessee River Survey, U.S. Army Corps of Engineers, 1927. [Regional Maps.]

Navigation and Economic Growth: Tennessee River Experience, Tennessee Valley Authority, 1966.

Principal Highways and Railroads: Cumberland and Tennessee River Basins, Tennessee Valley Authority, 1945.

Tennessee River and Interconnected Inland Waterway System, Tennessee Valley Authority, Commerce Department, 1942.

The Tennessee River Navigation System: History Development, and Operation, Tennessee Valley Authority, 1964.

Tentative Plan, Through Highways System, Tennessee Valley Region, Tennessee Valley Authority, Division of Land Planning and Housing, 1937. [TVA Records.]

Terminals, Tennessee River Survey, U.S. Army Corps of Engineers, 1927. Included in *Tennessee River and Tributaries.*

Terminals on the Tennessee River, Tennessee Valley Authority, Construction Department, 1939. [TVA Records.]

THE HOUSING REGION

See list of TVA Annual and Project Reports under general data.

THE LAND MACHINE

Atlas of American Agriculture Soils of the United States, Tennessee Valley Authority, Division of Land Planning and Housing, 1936. [Regional Maps.]

Critical Erosion Areas in the Tennessee Valley Region, Tennessee Valley Authority, Department of Forest Relations, 1938. [TVA Records.]

Graphic Appraisal of The Tennessee Valley, Tennessee Valley Authority, Department of Forest Relations, 1937. [TVA Records.]

Phosphate Reserves of the United States, Tennessee Valley Authority, Department of Chemical Engineering, 1945. [TVA Records.]

Results of Cooperative Tests of TVA Plant-food Materials by the Valley-States Land-Grant Colleges, U.S. Department of Agriculture and the Tennessee Valley Authority, 1941. [Special collections, University of Tennessee, Knoxville.]

Watershed Protection Division Headquarters and Location of TVA-CCC Camps, Tennessee Valley Authority, Department of Forestry Relations Watershed Protection Division, 1940. [TVA Records.]

THE RECREATION REGION

Scenic Recreational Areas of the Tennessee Valley Region, Tennessee Valley Authority, Division of Land Planning and Housing, 1937. [TVA Records.]

Tennessee Valley Authority Recreation Inventory, Tennessee Valley Authority, 2021, ESRI ArcGIS Online Portal.

THE POWER MACHINE

Present and Projected Transmission Lines in the Tennessee Valley Region, Tennessee Valley Authority, Power Division, 1934. [TVA Records.]

Map of Tennessee Valley Authority Service Area, Tennessee Valley Authority, 1940. Included in *Annual Report of the Tennessee Valley Authority for the Fiscal Year Ended June 30, 1940.*

Tennessee and Cumberland River Watersheds Power Transmission System, Tennessee River Survey, U.S. Army Corps of Engineers, 1928. Included in *Tennessee River and Tributaries.*

Tennessee River Survey of Electric Transmission Systems and their Generating Plants, U.S. Army Corps of Engineers, 1927. Included in *Tennessee River and Tributaries.*

Tennessee Valley Authority Power System, Tennessee Valley Authority, Maps and Surveys Division, 1947. [TVA Records.]

Transmission and Distribution Systems of TVA and its Municipal and Co-Operative Power Contractors Showing Recent, Pending, and Proposed Acquisitions, Tennessee Valley Authority, Department of Operations, 1938. [TVA Records.]

THE NEW NORRIS MODEL

Cemetery Index Map Norris Reservoir, Tennessee Valley Authority, 1937. [TVA Records.]

Highway Relocations and Construction, Norris Reservoir, Tennessee Valley Authority, Engineering Design Department, Highway and Railroad Division, 1937. [TVA Records.]

Indian Land Cessions in the United States, U.S. Environmental Protection Agency Office of Mission Support, 2021, ESRI ArcGIS Online Portal.

Map of Norris Reservoir and Surrounding Region, Tennessee Valley Authority, Engineering Service Division, 1935. [TVA Records.]

Norris Reservoir Existing and Proposed Land Use, Tennessee Valley Authority, 1935. [Marshall Wilson Collection, Calvin M. McClung Historical Collection, Knox County Public Library, Knoxville, TN.]

Road Study Areas, Norris Reservoir, Tennessee Valley Authority, Engineering Design Department, Highway and Railroad Division, 1937. [TVA Records.]

CODA

"The TVA Idea," *The Milwaukee Journal*, March 22, 1959.

Acknowledgments

Research and Publication were supported
by the Lawrence B. Anderson Award,
School of Architecture + Planning, MIT
and the James Musgraves Research Award,
College of Architecture and Design,
University of Tennessee, Knoxville.

A special thanks to the University of Tennessee
School of Architecture and School of Landscape
Architecture for their generous support.

Numerous student research assistants worked
with us over the years to make this project
possible: Keith Coffindaffer, Mark Colen,
Anja Cordell, Matt Cowan, Emily Craig,
Blake Dreier, Teig Dryden, Logan Guidera,
James Halliwell, Sarah Kenney, Phillip Minton,
Jakeb Moore, Wyatt Pless, Chris Rubio,
Lydia Russell, Caley Shoemaker, Michael Swartz,
Dustin Toothman, Fernando Turpin, Kyra Wu.